SINGLE-CASE EXPERIMENTAL DESIGNS FOR CLINICAL RESEARCH AND NEUROREHABILITATION SETTINGS

This book is a practical resource designed for clinicians, researchers, and advanced students who wish to learn about single-case research designs. It covers the theoretical and methodological underpinnings of single-case designs, as well as their practical application in the clinical and research neurorehabilitation setting. The book briefly traces the history of single-case experimental designs (SCEDs); outlines important considerations in understanding and planning a scientifically rigorous single-case study, including internal and external validity; describes prototypical single-case designs (withdrawal-reversal designs and the medical N-of-1 trial, multiple-baseline designs, alternating-treatments designs, and changing-criterion designs) and required features to meet evidence standards, threats to internal validity, and strategies to address them; addresses data evaluation, covering visual analysis of graphed data, statistical techniques, and clinical significance; and provides a practical ten-step procedure for implementing single-case methods. Each chapter includes detailed illustrative examples from the neurorehabilitation literature.

Novel features include:

- A focus on the neurorehabilitation setting, which is particularly suitable for single-case designs because of the complex and often unique presentation of many patients/clients.
- A practical approach to the planning, implementation, data analysis, and reporting of single-case designs.
- An appendix providing a detailed summary of many recently published SCEDs in representative domains in the neurorehabilitation field, covering basic and instrumental activities of daily living, challenging behaviours, disorders of communication and cognition, mood and emotional functions, and motor-sensory disabilities.

It is valuable reading for clinicians and researchers in several disciplines working in rehabilitation, including clinical and neuropsychology, education, language and speech pathology, occupational therapy, and physical therapy. It is also an essential resource for advanced students in these fields who need a textbook for specialised courses on research methodology and use of single-case design in applied clinical and research settings.

Robyn L. Tate, a clinical and neuropsychologist, is Research Professor at the John Walsh Centre for Rehabilitation Research, Sydney Medical School, University of Sydney, Australia. She has extensive clinical and research experience in the fields of single-case methodology, evidence-based practice in acquired brain injury, and health outcome instrument development.

Michael Perdices is a neuropsychologist with 30 years' clinical and research experience. His clinical work primarily involves assessment and diagnosis of acquired brain injury in a broad spectrum of neurological conditions. Over the past 15 years, single-case methodology and evidence-based practice have been his main foci of research interest. He is currently Senior Clinical Neuropsychologist at the Royal North Shore Hospital, Sydney, Australia.

NEUROPSYCHOLOGICAL REHABILITATION: A MODULAR HANDBOOK

Neuropsychological rehabilitation is influenced by a number of fields both from within and outside psychology. Neuropsychology, behavioural psychology and cognitive psychology have each played important roles in the development of current rehabilitation practice, along with findings from studies of neuroplasticity, linguistics, geriatric medicine, neurology and other fields. Neuropsychological Rehabilitation: A Modular Handbook series reflects the broad theoretical base of the discipline, and is not confined to one conceptual framework. Although each volume is based on a strong theoretical foundation relevant to the topic in question, the main thrust of the majority of the books is the development of practical, clinical methods of rehabilitation arising out of this research enterprise.

The series is aimed at neuropsychologists, clinical psychologists and other rehabilitation specialists such as occupational therapists, speech and language pathologists, rehabilitation physicians and other disciplines involved in the rehabilitation of people with brain injury.

Series Editors: Barbara A. Wilson and Ian Robertson

Titles in the series:

Rehabilitation of Visual Disorders After Brain Injury, Second Edition
Josef Zihl

Self-Identity after Brain Injury
Tamara Ownsworth

Assessing Pain and Communication in Disorders of Consciousness
Edited by Camille Chatelle and Steven Laureys

Single-Case Experimental Designs for Clinical Research and Neurorehabilitation Settings
Planning, Conduct, Analysis and Reporting
Robyn L. Tate and Michael Perdices

For more information about this series, please visit: https://www.routledge.com/ Neuropsychological-Rehabilitation-A-Modular-Handbook/book-series/SE0515

SINGLE-CASE EXPERIMENTAL DESIGNS FOR CLINICAL RESEARCH AND NEUROREHABILITATION SETTINGS

Planning, Conduct, Analysis and Reporting

Robyn L. Tate and Michael Perdices

Routledge
Taylor & Francis Group

LONDON AND NEW YORK

First published 2019
by Routledge
2 Park Square, Milton Park, Abingdon, Oxon OX14 4RN

and by Routledge
52 Vanderbilt Avenue, New York, NY 10017

Routledge is an imprint of the Taylor & Francis Group, an informa business

British Library Cataloguing in Publication Data
A catalogue record for this book is available from the British Library

Library of Congress Cataloging in Publication Data
Names: Tate, Robyn L., author. | Perdices, Michael, 1950- author.
Title: Single-case experimental designs for clinical research and neurorehabilitation settings : planning, conduct, analysis and reporting / Robyn L. Tate, Michael Perdices.
Other titles: Neuropsychological rehabilitation. 1466-6340
Description: Abingdon, Oxon ; New York, NY : Routledge, 2018. |
Series: Neuropsychological rehabilitation: a modular handbook | Includes bibliographical references and index.
Identifiers: LCCN 2018007607| ISBN 9781138595620 (hb : alk. paper) | ISBN 9781138595637 (pb : alk. paper) | ISBN 9780429488184 (ebk)
Subjects: | MESH: Research Design | Neurological Rehabilitation--methods | Case-Control Studies
Classification: LCC RC337 | NLM WL 140 | DDC 616.80072--dc23
LC record available at https://lccn.loc.gov/2018007607

ISBN: 978-1-138-59562-0 (hbk)
ISBN: 978-1-138-59563-7 (pbk)
ISBN: 978-0-429-48818-4 (ebk)

Typeset in Sabon
by Taylor & Francis Books

For our parents, Kevin and Dr Audrey Tate, Miguel Perdices and Paulina Rodriguez, and for our dearest friend Dr Brett Tindall.

CONTENTS

ILLUSTRATIONS

Figures

Tables

SERIES EDITORS' PREFACE

Rehabilitation in general is a process whereby people are enabled to return to as normal a life as possible following injury or disease. They work together with professional staff, relatives, and members of the wider community to achieve their optimum physical, psychological, social, and vocational well-being. Neuropsychological rehabilitation (NR) is concerned with the amelioration of cognitive, emotional, psychosocial, and behavioural deficits caused by an insult to the brain. It includes all measures aimed at reducing the impact of handicapping and disabling conditions, and at enabling disabled people to return to their most appropriate environment. It is concerned with the assessment, treatment, and natural recovery of people who have sustained damage to the brain.

NR is not only offered to patients who are expected to recover, partially or completely, but to all patients with long-term problems (Donaghy 2011). There are increasing numbers of people requiring NR due to medical advances in recent decades (Noggle, Dean, and Barisa 2013). NR is not synonymous with recovery (if by recovery we mean getting back to what one was like before the injury or illness). Nor is it the same as treatment (this is something we *do* to people or *give* to people when, for instance we prescribe drugs or administer surgery). Instead, it is a two-way interactive process. Ylvisaker and Feeney (2000) remind us that rehabilitation involves personally meaningful themes, activities, settings, and interactions.

NR is influenced by a number of fields both from within and without psychology. Neuropsychology, behavioural psychology, and cognitive psychology have each played important roles in the development of current rehabilitation practice. So too have findings from studies of neuroplasticity, linguistics, geriatric medicine, neurology, and other fields. Our discipline, therefore, is not confined to one conceptual framework; rather, it has a broad theoretical base (Wilson, Winegardner, van Heugten, and Ownsworth 2017).

We hope that this broad base is reflected in the modular handbook. The first book was by Roger Barker and Stephen Dunnett, *Neural Repair, Transplantation and Rehabilitation*. The second title, by Josef Zihl, was entitled *Visual Disorders After Brain Injury*. Other titles in the series include *Behavioural Approaches to Rehabilitation* by Barbara Wilson, Camilla Herbert, and Agnes Shiel; *Neuropsychological Rehabilitation and People with Dementia* by Linda Clare, and a second edition of Josef Zihl's *Rehabilitation of Visual Disorders After Brain Injury*. The next book was Tamara Ownsworth's *Self-Identity After Brain Injury*, a popular topic in current NR. This was followed by Camille Chatelle and Steven Laurey's volume *Assessing Pain and Communication in Disorders of Consciousness*. This latest book is by Robyn Tate and Michael Perdices entitled *Single-case Experimental Designs for Clinical Research and Neurorehabilitation Settings*.

Future titles will include volumes on specific cognitive functions such as language, memory, and motor skills, together with social and personality aspects of NR.

Although each volume will be based on a strong theoretical foundation relevant to the topic in question, the main thrust of the majority of the books will be the development of practical, clinical methods of rehabilitation.

The series is for neuropsychologists, clinical psychologists, and other rehabilitation specialists such as occupational therapists, speech and language pathologists, rehabilitation physicians, and other disciplines involved in the rehabilitation of people with brain injury.

NR is at an exciting stage in its development. On the one hand, we have a huge growth of interest in functional imaging techniques to tell us about the basic processes going on in the brain. On the other hand, the past few years have seen the introduction of a number of theoretically driven approaches to cognitive rehabilitation from the fields of language, memory, attention, and perception.

In addition to both the above, there is a growing recognition from health services that rehabilitation is an integral part of a healthcare system. Of course, alongside the recognition of the need for rehabilitation is the view that any rehabilitative practice has to be evaluated. To those of us working with brain-injured people, including those with dementia, there is a feeling that progress is being made, and we hope this volume reflects this in its efforts to integrate theory and practice.

Barbara A. Wilson
Ian Robertson

FOREWORD

Single-case experimental design (SCED) methodology has a long tradition in clinical and educational settings as a means of evaluating the efficacy of interventions with single individuals or with a small number of individuals. But the emergence of the evidence-based medicine movement with an emphasis on randomized double-bind placebo controlled trials as the gold standard perhaps diminished the focus on SCED methods for a period of time. However, in recent years there has been a resurgence of interest in SCED methods, driven in no small part by the work of Robyn Tate and Michael Perdices.

Some clinical conditions or problems are relatively uncommon, at least in a single clinic or even area, and so numbers would never be sufficient for a large scale randomized controlled trial (RCT). When devising new interventions, it is useful to test out the intervention on a small number of people. With some interventions that are time or resource intensive it may be prohibitively expensive to run large-scale RCTs. We need therefore scientifically strong designs that allow us to draw clear conclusions about the efficacy of interventions in these situations. In 2011 the University of Oxford Centre for Evidence-Based Medicine recognized in its *Levels of Evidence* document that systematic reviews of RCTs and N-of-1 trials *both* provide Level 1 (the highest quality) evidence in relation to whether an intervention helps. While this development was important recognition for the potential contribution that can be made by SCED studies, Tate, Perdices, and their colleagues took another important step when they developed their methodological quality tool for SCEDs, which in its revised form is known as the Risk-of-Bias-in-N-of-1-Trials (RoBiNT). This provides researchers with a tool to rate the quality of published studies, but even more importantly perhaps, it supports researchers when planning SCED studies. I always use this tool, and insist students and trainees use it, when planning a SCED study.

Using a methodologically strong design is important but it is also important that the details of the study are reported comprehensively so that the quality of the study is clear. Here again Tate, Perdices, and their colleagues have played a key role by developing the Single-Case Reporting guideline In BEhavioural interventions (SCRIBE), which will hopefully ensure more consistent reporting of SCED studies, and in turn make it easier to synthesise studies.

In summary then, in recent years Robyn Tate and Michael Perdices have been a driving force in attempting to raise the quality of SCED studies. Now, in this book they bring all of that knowledge together to provide a comprehensive account of how to run SCED studies. It is very much a practical 'how to' manual, taking the reader through all of the key decisions that must be made when designing, running, analysing, and reporting a SCED study. A particularly helpful aspect of this book is the number of clinical examples from the literature that Tate and Perdices use to illustrate aspects of design and analysis, which takes things from the hypothetical (and potentially difficult to see how to implement) to the clinically realistic. On the issue of analysis, this has been another area in which there has been substantial development in the last few years. From a situation where there were very few options available to researchers a few years ago, we have moved to a position where there is now a plethora of different methods all with various strengths and weaknesses, which can be confusing for even more experienced SCED researchers. Hence a particularly helpful chapter in this book is the one dedicated to describing the most useful methods of analysis, which I'm sure will be a huge help to novice and experienced researchers alike.

SCED methodology has the potential to make a much bigger contribution to the development of our evidence base relating to interventions with many clinical populations. But for that to happen we need research studies to be of the highest possible calibre so that those writing clinical guidelines have confidence to make strong recommendations. This book will enable clinical researchers to design, analyse, and report those high-quality SCED studies and for that we should be very grateful to Tate and Perdices for all of the hard work that has clearly gone into this excellent book.

Professor Jonathan Evans
University of Glasgow
January 2018

PREFACE

In 2001, we launched our own space odyssey (apologies to Arthur C Clarke and Stanley Kubrick), which eventually led to this book. We, together with our colleagues, Professor Skye McDonald and Professor Leanne Togher, were charged with the task of developing a database containing evidence for behavioural interventions to treat the psychological consequences of acquired brain impairment. After a few years spent in refining procedures and trawling through thousands of articles, in 2004 we launched PsycBITE (Psychological database of Brain Impairment Treatment Efficacy, www.psycbite.com). And it has kept us busy ever since.

One of our early challenges was the problem of assessing the scientific quality of single-case studies. This was necessary because we evaluated and ranked the primary between-groups studies (i.e. randomised and other controlled trials) on the database in order of their methodological strength. For this purpose, we applied the PEDro Scale, which uses ten items to evaluate internal validity and whether there is sufficient statistical information to make the trial interpretable. When we attempted to apply the PEDro Scale to single-case designs, it quickly became clear to us that it did not capture the cardinal features that distinguished a scientifically robust single-case study from a poor one; nor was it developed for that purpose, in any case.

Accordingly, in 2003 we embarked upon the task of designing a critical appraisal scale specifically for single-case designs, there being no other tool available at that time. The past 15 years have been given over to developing the Single-Case Experimental Design Scale (Tate et al., 2008), revising and refining it (now called the Risk of Bias in N-of-1 Trials (RoBiNT) Scale, Tate et al., 2013a; 2015), and coordinating an international effort to develop a reporting guideline In the CONSORT tradition (Single-Case Reporting guideline In BEhavioural interventions, SCRIBE; Tate et al., 2016a, 2016b). We believe that the RoBiNT Scale and the SCRIBE are useful tools to help produce high-quality single-case studies.

In our ongoing training and supervision of students and research staff, together with teaching clinicians and researchers in critical appraisal and use of single-case methods, we saw a gap in the literature. We could not find the precise textbook that we thought would assist in these endeavours and that was also specifically aimed at the neurorehabilitation clinician/researcher. So, we decided that such a book on single-case methods would be the next step in our odyssey.

We wrote this book with a number of aims in mind. One of the goals was not only to cover the prototypical designs, but also to go beyond these and visit the basics of what is actually involved in the dependent variable (target behaviour) and independent variable (interventions) and considerations that need to be made in their implementation. Moreover, we have grounded the book in the neurorehabilitation field with illustration of approximately 90 studies from the literature, including an appendix that provides a detailed summary of a large number of recently published studies to demonstrate the use of single-case methodology in evaluating interventions for persons with acquired brain impairment. The book is intended for a multidisciplinary readership who work in the neurorehabilitation setting, including clinical and neuropsychologists, speech and language pathologists, physical and occupational therapists.

It was also our aim to grapple with what can often appear to be the esoteric aspects of validity and pin this down to exactly how to proceed to conduct a study with careful attention to scientific standards. Nonetheless, we have endeavoured to strike a balance between optimising scientific rigour in the context of the practical limitations that are encountered in applied settings. It is not always possible to conduct a textbook-perfect, single-case study. Furthermore, we give detailed consideration to issues related to the dependent and independent variables in their own right.

The structure of the book reflects our goal of spanning both theoretical and practical aspects of single-case methodology. The introductory chapter provides a brief historical context of single-case research, particularly in neurorehabilitation, and introduces basic concepts. The following three chapters aim to give the reader an understanding of the building blocks underpinning single-case methods. Chapters 2 to 4 on validity, the dependent variable and independent variable, cover important considerations in planning and conducting a methodologically robust single-case study. Chapters 5 to 8 describe prototypical single-case designs (withdrawal-reversal designs and the medical N-of-1 trial, multiple-baseline designs, alternating-treatments designs, and changing-criterion designs) in terms of their framework, required features to meet design and evidence standards, threats to address internal validity, and strategies to address them. Chapter 9 is concerned with data evaluation, covering visual analysis of graphed data, statistical techniques, and clinical significance. The final chapter brings together information from previous chapters to show how single-case methods can be implemented in a scientifically rigorous way, using a practical 10-step procedure. Each chapter of the book includes detailed illustrative examples from the neurorehabilitation literature.

Much of our work over the years, and particularly in writing this book, has been informed by classic texts and seminal publications by leaders in the field, notably David Barlow, David Gast, Michel Hersen, Robert Horner, Alan Kazdin, Thomas Kratochwill, Rumen Manolov, Matthew Nock, Patrick Onghena, Richard Parker, William Shadish, Kimberly Vannest, and many others. Both the content and structure of this book owe much to these clinicians and researchers and their landmark works. Ours has been a learning odyssey on many levels. The experience has been enriched by discussions with our research team members and trainees over many years, as well as the innovative and elegant work reported by authors of primary studies, a selection of which we have included in the Appendix.

Finally, we acknowledge with gratitude Professor Jonathan Evans, Institute of Health and Wellbeing, University of Glasgow, and Ulrike Rosenkoetter, John Walsh Centre for Rehabilitation

Research, University of Sydney, for their detailed appraisal of the final drafts of this book. Their critical and thoughtful commentary on all of the chapters was immensely helpful.

Robyn Tate and Michael Perdices
Sydney, Australia
May 2018

1

INTRODUCTION TO SINGLE-CASE EXPERIMENTAL DESIGNS

Historical overview and basic concepts

Historical overview

Nomothetic and ideographic approaches

In 1894, Windelband (1894/1980) coined the terms nomothetic and ideographic to describe contrasting approaches in science for gathering evidence-based knowledge. According to him "The nomological sciences are concerned with what is invariably the case. The sciences of process [which he called ideographic] are concerned with what was once the case" (p. 175). In other words, the nomothetic (from the Greek word nomos, meaning law) approach focuses on establishing general laws (and generalisations) applicable to a class of phenomena; the ideographic approach focuses on describing and explaining single events or what Windelband describes as a "coherent sequence of acts or occurrences" (p. 174). Five years later, the terminology was introduced to psychology by Münsterberg (Hurlburt & Knapp, 2010); the nomothetic *versus* ideographic distinction in psychology was subsequently popularised by Allport (Robinson, 2011).

The nomothetic approach eventually became equated with the group-based methodology and statistical techniques being developed in the first quarter of the twentieth century to study individual differences (Robinson, 2011). For instance, in the context of neurorehabilitation, the nomothetic approach to investigating the effectiveness of an intervention (independent variable) on a cognitive/behavioural/motor impairment (dependent variable) consists of treating one group, while another group that is comparable in terms of relevant clinical characteristics is left untreated but is otherwise exposed to the same conditions as the treated group. Group differences on the variable of interest are then analysed using inferential statistics. Results can then (theoretically) be generalised to the population from which the study samples were drawn. This is, in essence, the between-groups methodology that has been firmly established in psychological research for the last century and with which most (if not all) rehabilitation clinicians are familiar.

The ideographic approach eventually became equated with the case-study method, although, strictly speaking, the ideographic approach does not refer to a particular method but to an objective, which is to explain an individual thing or phenomenon (Robinson, 2011). Traditionally, the case-study method has been used in a variety of disciplines throughout the nineteenth and twentieth centuries. Case studies in the medical (e.g. Broca, 1861; Wernicke, 1874) and psychoanalytic (e.g. Freud & Breuer, 1895/2004) literature were primarily qualitative and descriptive, and contained little, if any, quantitative data, and there was certainly no attempt to exercise experimental control. Pioneers in experimental psychology such as Fechner, Wundt, Ebbinghaus, and Pavlov focused on the intensive study of individual organisms, but also collected and recorded quantitative data (Barlow & Nock, 2009; Barlow, Nock, & Hersen, 2009). Developments in behavioural theory (particularly, operant conditioning techniques) during the first half of the twentieth century and the advent of behaviourism and subsequent focus on applied behaviour analysis, further popularised the use of single-case methodology in psychological research. Systematic collection of empirical data along with experimental control of variables was incorporated in single-case research, giving rise to what we now call single-case experimental designs (Barlow, Hersen, & Miss, 1973; Barlow & Nock, 2009).

The early years of single-case methods in neurorehabilitation

The 1960s saw studies using single-case methodology in neurorehabilitation gaining a presence in the literature. An early report is that of Goodkin (1966) who described four cases in a rehabilitation setting. Goodkin conducted a series of A-B designs (see Chapter 5) to evaluate the effect of the intervention (comprising feedback, contingent reinforcement and extinction) on a variety of presenting problems: speed of handwriting and operating a machine with the nondominant hand in a woman with left hemisphere stroke, speed and distance of propelling a wheelchair in a woman with Parkinson's disease, increasing intelligible speech in a man whose left hemisphere stroke resulted in moderate to severe receptive and expressive aphasia, and decreasing irrelevant responses to questions and perseverative responses in a woman with (non-specified) speech disorder after left hemisphere stroke. Around the time of Goodkin's article, single-case experiments already had a firm basis in the clinical psychology and education fields, focusing on the use of operant procedures, and frequently addressing challenging behaviours. Specialist journals, such as the *Journal of Applied Behavior Analysis* first published in 1968 and *Behavior Therapy* in 1970, provided an avenue to publish the single-case experimental design (SCED), and, along with early textbooks (e.g. Hersen & Barlow, 1976; Kratochwill, 1978), saw SCEDs obtain standing as an established and accepted methodology.

By the 1970s, the field of neurorehabilitation saw SCEDs being increasingly applied in two domains in particular: challenging behaviours and neurogenic communication disorders. It was a logical step to adapt procedures used in clinical psychology for the treatment of challenging behaviours and apply them to neurological patients. Examples include use of A-B designs to reduce self-injurious behaviour in a 14-year-old girl with epilepsy (Adams, Klinge, & Keiser, 1973) and involuntary crying in an adult with multiple sclerosis (Brookshire, 1970).

From the outset, the field of speech and language pathology has embraced SCEDs and journals such as *Aphasiology* and the *American Journal of Speech-Language Pathology* among others regularly publish studies using SCED methodology. McReynolds and Kearns's (1983) textbook, specifically aimed at using SCEDs in communication disorders, has exerted major influence in that field. The widespread use of the SCED has resulted in a rich evidence base, with SCED studies addressing different interventions for speech/language disorder. Early studies focused on aphasia after stroke, evaluating use of a range of interventions, such as stimulus repetition (Helmick & Wipplinger, 1975). The Helmick and Wipplinger study is probably one of the first studies in neurorehabilitation to use an alternating-treatments design (ATD) (see Chapter 7). The investigators examined the efficacy of two therapeutic procedures regarding dosage comparing amount of practice (6 vs 24 stimulus repetitions).

By contrast, during the 1970s there was only a smattering of SCED studies in other cognitive domains, such as memory, where Gianutsos and Gianutsos (1979) were among the first to use the multiple-baseline design (MBD) (see Chapter 6) in neurorehabilitation. They evaluated mnemonic training to improve verbal recall in four patients, three of whom had stroke. But it was not until the 1980s that studies using single-case methods were applied in a broader range of cognitive areas, such as attention (Sohlberg & Mateer, 1987; Wood, 1986), executive function (Cicerone & Wood, 1987; Jenning & Lubinski, 1981), memory (Glisky & Schacter, 1987; Wilson, 1981, 1982), neglect (Robertson, Gray, & McKenzie, 1988; Webster, Jones, Blanton, Gross, Beissel, & Wofford, 1984), and social communication skills (Brotherton, Thomas, Wisotzek, & Milan, 1988; Sohlberg, Sprunk, & Metzelaar, 1988). The 1980s also saw reports addressing everyday function in neurological patients, such as urinary continence (Cohen, 1986; O'Neil, 1982), washing and dressing (Giles & Morgan, 1988; Giles & Shore, 1989) and other functional activities involving arm and hand function (Kerley, 1982; Tate, 1987), wheelchair navigation (Gouvier, Cottam, Webster, Beissel, & Woffard, 1984), supported employment (Wehman et al., 1989) and consumer advocacy skills (Seekins, Fawcett, & Mathews, 1987). The O'Neill study is one of the earliest neurorehabilitation investigations to use a changing-criterion design (CCD) (see Chapter 8). The investigator treated urinary frequency in a 32-year-old woman with multiple sclerosis by increasing the duration between voiding in four incremental steps.

A number of reports from this early period used sophisticated designs with strong internal validity. Schloss, Thompson, Gajar, and Schloss (1985), for example, described a self-monitoring intervention to improve conversational skills of two males, aged in their twenties, with traumatic brain injury. The investigators used an MBD across behaviours within which was embedded an ATD to evaluate the effects of the self-monitoring training. The strong internal validity (described in more detail later in this chapter and in Chapter 2) was demonstrated by the investigators implementing the following procedures: (i) the study design contained experimental control in that the independent variable was experimentally manipulated, (ii) use of randomisation in the alternating-treatments component, (iii) measurement of the target behaviours continuously in each phase, (iv) use of observers to measure the target behaviours who were independent of the therapist delivering the intervention, (v) evaluation of inter-rater agreement of the observations which was found to be high (around 90%), and (vi) assessment of treatment adherence, which was also found to be high (100%).

From these beginnings, the SCED literature has grown. The NeuroRehab Evidence database (www.neurorehab-evidence.com),[1] for example, contains more than 800 single-case experiments addressing the cognitive, communication, behavioural, emotional, and functional consequences of acquired brain impairment. The Appendix to this book summarises a set of 66 SCEDs in neurorehabilitation, mostly published during the past 15 years. The aim of the Appendix is to illustrate the variety of neurological conditions and functional domains treated, the types of target behaviours addressed and different ways in which they are measured, along with a range of interventions and design options.

Surveys of SCEDs in the literature

Table 1.1 summarises the findings of seven surveys that, inter alia, document the type of single-case designs published in various fields of research.[2]

1   PsycBITE (www.psycbite.com) contains NeuroRehab Evidence (www.neu rorehab-evidence.com), within the PsycBITE project (www.psycbite.com), which is a database specific to neurorehabilitation. The database is multi-disciplinary and comprises all of the published empirical studies on non-pharmacological interventions to treat the psychological consequences of acquired brain impairment. As at September 2017, it contained more than 5,200 records that are ranked on the database in terms of methodological strength. Clinical trials and single-case experiments are individually rated for scientific quality.

2   An explanatory note: in each survey, the taxonomy used to classify SCEDs differed slightly. For example, Shadish and Sullivan (2011) based their classification on the typology used in the What Works Clearinghouse Evidence Standards for SCEDs (Kratochwill et al., 2010). They classified withdrawal/reversal designs (WRD) as having either a phase change with reversal in which there was a reversion to a previous phase (e.g. A-B-A-B) or a phase change without reversal in which there was no reversion to a previous phase (e.g. A-B or A-B-C-D). They did not, however, specify or quantify the various different designs subsumed in these rather broad categories. By contrast, others, such as Hammond and Gast (2010), did not use this classification, but instead classified A-B, A-B-A and A-B-A-B designs as separate categories. Consequently, some degree of interpretation has been necessary to compare all surveys with a 'common classification denominator'.

TABLE 1.1 Summary of surveys of types of SCEDs in the published literature

Authors	Didden, Korzilius, van Oorsouw, and Sturmey (2006)	Perdices and Tate (2009)	Hammond and Gast (2010)	Shadish and Sullivan (2011)	Smith (2012)	Barker, Mellalieu, McCarthy, Jones, and Moran (2013)	Tate et al. (2016c)
Publication years	1980–2006	1991–2008	1983–2007	2008	2000–2010	1997–2012	2004–2013
Journals	7	1	8	21	134	16[11]	70
Journal field	behaviour research, developmental disability	neuropsychological rehabilitation	special education, behaviour research, disability / developmental disability	special education, behaviour research, psychology, developmental disability	primarily behaviour research, special education and psychology, but also neuropsychological rehabilitation, speech pathology, occupational therapy, and medicine	behaviour research, psychology, sport psychology	primarily speech pathology, neuropsychology, rehabilitation, neurology, and gerontology
Type of intervention/ target behaviour	challenging behaviours in persons with mild mental retardation	not specified	not specified	not specified	not specified	psychological skills and behaviour modification / performance-related target behaviours	communication, cognition, behaviour, mood, motor-sensory, activities of daily living
Source articles	80	478	1,936	113	490	not specified	198

	132		47		545[4]		809		433		66		96	
Total SCEDs [1]	n	%	n	%	n	%	n	%	n	%	n	%	n	%
DESIGN TYPE														
A-B	82	62.1	9[2]	19.1	16[5]	2.9	7[7]	0.9	not included		8	12.1	27	28.1
A-B-A	—		33[3]	70.2	6	1.1	66[8]	8.2	not included		2	3.0	30[13]	31.3
A-B-A-B	32	24.2	—	—	91	16.7	—	—	70[9]	16.2	4	6.0	—	—
B-A-B	—	—	—	—	2	0.4	—	—	not included		—	—	—	—
Multi-treatment	—	—	—	—	44	8.1	—	—	—	—	3	4.5	—	—
MBD	18	13.6	5	10.6	240	44.0	439	54.3	283	65.4	47	71.2	28	29.2
participants	—	—	—	—	155	28.4	—	—	—	—	43[12]	65.2	—	—
settings	—	—	—	—	59	10.8	—	—	—	—	3	4.5	—	—
behaviours	—	—	—	—	26	4.8	—	—	—	—	1	1.5	—	—

(Continued)

TABLE 1.1 (*Continued*)

Authors	Didden, Korzilius, van Oorsouw, and Sturmey (2006)		Perdices and Tate (2009)		Hammond and Gast (2010)		Shadish and Sullivan (2011)		Smith (2012)		Barker, Mellalieu, McCarthy, Jones, and Moran (2013)		Tate et al. (2016c)	
ATD	—	—	—	—	108[6]	19.8	65	8.0	28[10]	6.5	1	1.5	4	4.2
PTD	—	—	—	—	2	0.4	—	—	—	—	—	—	0	0
CCD	—	—	—	—	not included		21	2.6	18	4.2	1	1.5	0	0
Combination	—	—	—	—	36	6.6	211	26.1	24	5.5	—	—	7	7.3
Time series	—	—	—	—	—	—	—	—	10	2.3	—	—	—	—

Notes: — = no information provided; multi-treatment designs=withdrawal designs with more than one treatment, e.g., A-B-A-B-A-C-A-D; MBD=multiple-baseline design; ATD=alternating-treatments design; PTD=parallel treatments designs consisting of two simultaneous multiple-probe designs replicated across functionally equivalent behaviours; CCD=changing-criterion design; combination=combine two or more designs, e.g., A-B-A-B nested in the tiers of an MBD. (1) Some articles report data for more than one SCED; (2) includes variants, e.g., B-A; (3) includes variants of the standard design; (4) non-concurrent MBD/multiple probe designs, and simultaneous treatment designs (cf. ATD) not included in survey; (5) includes A-B-C designs; (6) includes adapted ATDs, which used two interventions focused on two similar but independent target behaviours; (7) includes A-B and designs that do not revert to a condition from the previous phase, e.g., A-B-C-D; (8) might have included A-B-A-B but this is not specified in the survey; (9) may include designs with additional phases, e.g., A-B-A-B-A-B, but this is not specified; (10) includes simultaneous treatment designs (cf. ATD); (11) 16 journals are identified in the article, but there is indication that more journals might have been surveyed; (12) includes two across-groups designs.; (13) includes variants (e.g. A-B-A-B; B-A-B)

The most salient feature of Table 1.1 is that, except for the Didden, Korzilius, van Oorsouw, and Sturmey (2006), Perdices and Tate (2009), and Tate, Sigmundsdottir, Doubleday, Rosenkoetter, Wakim, and Perdices (2016c) surveys, MBDs are the most common type of design, both in the behaviour/psychology and the sport psychology literature. According to Barlow et al. (2009) MBDs have become "the most well-known and widely used of the three alternatives to withdrawal or reversal designs" (p. 202). In a brief search of PubMed on 6 June 2007, they found 1,036 articles listed under the term "multiple baseline" while only 123 and 30 were listed under the term "alternating treatment" and "changing criterion" respectively. It is possible that there is some degree of sampling bias in the Perdices and Tate (2009) study, given that only one journal with a specific focus on neuropsychological rehabilitation was surveyed. Even so, in a more recent review of the neurorehabilitation literature sampling from a broader range of journals (n=70), Tate et al. (2016c) found that in general the MBD was not more common than other designs. The frequency of other design types is variable: of the 24 "mixed designs"[3] identified by Smith (2012), 12 combined an MBD with a reversal design; of the 211 "combination designs" identified by Shadish and Sullivan (2011), 80 combined an MBD with an ATD. In addition to the four major designs discussed in this and the following chapters, there is a multitude of variations and combinations whose number would be "impossible to convey" (Kazdin, 2011, p. 227).

In a neurorehabilitation setting, the primary clinical focus is the treatment of one, or a small group of individuals. SCEDs interface seamlessly with this clinical focus (Hayes, 1981; Perdices & Tate, 2009; Tate, Taylor, & Aird, 2013b; Wilson, 1987). For neurorehabilitation practitioners, SCEDs provide not only a framework to systematically monitor and record clinical data, but also the means to analyse those data so that results can inform clinical practice, consistent with a practice-based evidence approach. Moreover, interventions can be delivered with scientific rigour and potentially more beneficial clinical outcomes achieved. In other words, they provide a scientifically sound tool that is accessible to the practitioner to help establish and foment evidence-based practice – that is, to be a scientist/practitioner within the setting of everyday clinical practice (see also Chapter 10).

---

3 The "mixed" and "combination" designs are sometimes referred to as nested designs.

Basic concepts

What is a SCED?

SCEDs are studies or clinical trials focusing on a single individual (or unit), rather than comparison of two or more groups of participants. According to Kazdin (1981), however, the term SCED is somewhat of a misnomer because: "Single-case research designs refer to a particular methodological approach and not necessarily to the number of subjects studied in any particular instance" (p. 134). That is, SCEDs can involve several individuals each of whom is studied as a single case. Alternatively, a group of individuals may be studied as a single *unit*. For example, in education research, the behaviour of interest might be the performance of an entire classroom of students where the intervention consists of a specific method of instruction; within a neuro-residential setting, it might be the performance of the entire ward of patients or residents. Throughout this book, when we refer to the singular 'case', 'individual', and so forth, it is implied that we also include the scenario of a unit (of individuals), as well as a series of single cases. Following Kazdin, our use of the term SCED refers to the method rather than the number of cases.

In essence, SCEDs compare the behaviour of an individual or participant before, during, and often after the implementation of an intervention to address that behaviour. But the SCED does more than simply compare in that:

1. the individual is prospectively and intensively studied and serves as his or her own control;
2. an a priori methodology is used;
3. the dependent variable (target behaviour) is continuously measured and recorded in a standardised fashion by trained observers throughout all phases of the study; and
4. the independent variable (intervention) is systematically manipulated in a controlled way.

These four features comprise the essential elements of single-case methodology, and a study needs to meet all of them for it to be classified as using single-case methodology. The reason is that without these fundamental building blocks it is not possible to achieve the objective of a SCED. What is that objective? The aim of SCEDs is to establish a functional (i.e. cause and effect) relationship between the target behaviour (dependent variable) and the intervention (independent variable). In other words, to determine whether or not an intervention exerts an effect on the target behaviour under investigation. At a broad level, SCEDs are scientifically rigorous and flexible tools for developing and evaluating hypotheses. Their flexibility is manifest in how at the planning stage, designs can be specifically tailored to the situation under investigation or combined to best address the clinical or research question. There is also flexibility in how designs can be modified ad hoc during the conduct of the study without losing experimental control (e.g. Connell and Thompson, 1986). In the behavioural sciences field, whether in the context of applied research or clinical practice, they can be used to: (i) evaluate new interventions; (ii) isolate effective intervention components and refine the effectiveness of interventions; and (iii) compare and evaluate interventions.

There is a variety of designs that can be used to study a single individual (see Figure 1.1). Some designs meet defining criteria for SCEDs, and others do not. The latter category includes (i) case descriptions, (ii) studies in which only pre- and post-intervention measures of treatment effectiveness are taken, and (iii) studies that consist of a single cycle of treatment (B phase training studies); these are shown below the solid line in Figure 1.1. Case descriptions are primarily narrative and may or may not include empirical data. In pre- and post-intervention studies the behaviour of interest is not continuously and repeatedly measured throughout all phases of the study, including the intervention phase. Studies that involve a single cycle of treatment or single training (B) phase do not include a control condition (i.e. baseline phase; see below). None of these three designs systematically manipulate variables or contain all four essential elements of the methodology of single-case designs as enumerated at the beginning of this section. Consequently, they cannot be used to establish a functional relationship between the intervention and the behaviour being treated – in essence, they are not SCEDs.

SCEDs themselves come in many shapes and sizes, and these are shown above the solid line in Figure 1.1. The biphasic A-B design does not incorporate sufficient opportunities to demonstrate the experimental effect (see section on standards of evidence below) in order to provide credible evidence for the effectiveness of an intervention (see Chapter 5). Hence, we separate them from the other SCEDs (see dotted horizontal line), even though they fulfil the four defining criteria of the SCED. Briefly, the four prototypical SCEDs are as follows:

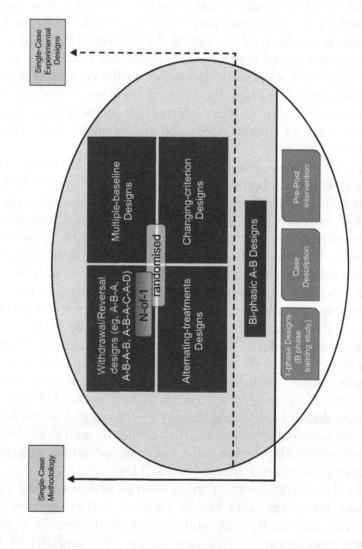

FIGURE 1.1 Classification of designs published in the literature that use a single participant
Source: Tate et al. (2015); reprinted with permission

- Withdrawal/reversal designs (WRDs): investigate the effect that systematically introducing and withdrawing the intervention has on the target behaviour. Mainly used for evaluating effectiveness of a single intervention, they can also be used to compare two or more interventions (see Chapter 5).
- MBDs: investigate the effect of an intervention when applied simultaneously, but in a staggered sequence, to different participants, or alternatively, different target behaviours or different settings for the same individual (see Chapter 6).
- ATDs: Compare the effectiveness of two or more interventions (one of which can be a 'no-treatment' condition) in the same participant (see Chapter 7).
- CCDs: investigate how effective an intervention is in gradually inducing therapeutic change in the target behaviour (see Chapter 8).

We also mention the medical N-of-1 trial which is, essentially, a variant of the WRD (see Chapter 5 for more detail). Figure 1.1 also shows that randomisation can be incorporated in the designs, and this is discussed further in Chapter 9.

The four prototypical designs alone account for more than half of the published SCED studies in the clinical psychology and special education fields (see Table 1.1), but many combinations, variations, and adaptations of these four are also used (Shadish & Sullivan, 2011). Some designs are better suited than others for answering different questions. Each design has particular strengths and weaknesses. Specific challenges to internal validity may be manifested differently and require different control strategies. The selection of the type of design that is to be used should be guided by all these considerations. But perhaps as importantly, selection of a specific design should be guided by considering how well the design can address the question being asked (Kearns, 1986).

Nomenclature and terminology

In the literature, SCEDs are variously referred to as single-system designs, single-subject designs, single-case research designs, single-participant designs, interrupted time-series designs, and N-of-1 trials. Throughout this book we refer to them as SCEDs. Several fundamental components and concepts that characterise SCEDs are defined and explained below:

- **participant:** the person taking part in the study and to whom the intervention is directed. This term is used throughout this book, rather than patient or client.
- **practitioner:** the person implementing the intervention. The person could be an interventionist, clinician, therapist, educator, instructor, investigator, experimenter, or other person.
- **phase:** discrete observation periods in which an individual's behaviour is repeatedly and continuously measured under the same conditions. Phases in the SCED are identified by capital letters where, by convention, 'A' denotes a baseline or no-intervention phase, and 'B', 'C', 'D' and so forth, denote phases in which different, active, interventions are implemented.
- **baseline:** the control condition during which no intervention occurs. According to Barlow et al. (2009) "Virtually all single-case experimental designs (the exception being the B-A-B design) begin with a baseline" (p. 65). Baselines have a crucial role in the rationale and logic of SCEDs. "Essentially, the projected level of baseline serves as a criterion to evaluate if treatment has led to change. Presumably, if treatment is effective, performance during the treatment phase will differ from the projected baseline" (Kazdin, 1983, p. 425). In other words, the baseline serves to predict what the target behaviour would be like if it were left untreated. This provides a comparison standard against which any changes in the target behaviour during the intervention phase can be evaluated. Most published reports use the letter A to denote the baseline phase, but there are some exceptions. When ATDs are discussed in the literature, one of the active interventions is sometimes identified as 'A', and the other one as 'B'. This is confusing because 'A' is also used to identify the baseline phase or no-intervention phase in ATDs. In our discussion of ATDs (see Chapter 7), and throughout the book, 'A' refers exclusively to a no-intervention or baseline phase, and all active interventions are identified by other letters.
- **target behaviour:** the behaviour that is being treated and measured throughout the study. It constitutes the dependent variable in the SCED, comparable to the primary outcome measure in a between-groups study. Target behaviours are operationally defined in precise terms that can be objectively measured, and accurately reflect the construct under investigation (see Chapter 3). In the context of neurorehabilitation, the target behaviour can be a cognitive, communicative, functional, behavioural,

emotional, or sensory-motor impairment that has occurred as a consequence of acquired brain impairment.

• **intervention**: the independent variable in SCEDs referring to the treatment under investigation (see Chapter 4). Throughout this book we generally use the term intervention, rather than treatment.

• **experimental effect**: the hypothesised effect that the intervention will have on the target behaviour. Consequently, we use the terms experimental effect and intervention effect interchangeably in this book.

• **experimental control**: is established through systematic manipulation of the independent variable (e.g. introducing/withdrawing the intervention). In order to have adequate experimental control, the design must provide sufficient opportunities to demonstrate the experimental effect (see section on standards of evidence below). The experimental effect can be repeatedly demonstrated either within a participant (direct *intra*-subject replication) or across participants (direct *inter*-subject replication).

• **level**: the magnitude or value (usually the mean or median) of the data within a given phase.

• **trend**: the slope of a straight line of best-fit for the data within a phase.

• **variability**: the range (maximum and minimum values) of data within a phase or dispersion of data (e.g. the standard deviation) about the line of best-fit.

• **time series**: an ordered sequence of repeated, successive measures (i.e. data points) of a variable taken at (usually) equally spaced time intervals.

Graphical representation of SCED data

SCED data are short time series of measures of the target behaviour. In a survey of 809 designs published in 2008, the median and mode number of data points per design was 20, and 90.6% had fewer than 49 data points (Shadish & Sullivan, 2011). Historically, SCED data have been plotted as line graphs, and they are the most commonly used format, although bar graphs and cumulative graphs are also used. Measures of the target behaviour (e.g. frequency, percent, mean) are plotted on the y-axis, and the time variable across phases is plotted on the x-axis. Often, sessions are the metric used in the x-axis. Because session numbers are evenly spaced along the x-axis, the implication is that the time interval between sessions is the same, yet this might not be the case at all. Carr (2005) recommends that the x-axis for MBDs (see Chapter 6) should be scaled as units of time (e.g. day, week) rather than sessions. He argues that a real-time metric enables more accurate visual evaluation of the design's experimental control. We suggest that a comparable rationale is applicable to other types of design. Plotting data points on a chronological metric (e.g. day) yields a more accurate depiction of data patterns and arguably more reliable visual evaluation of results. That is, plotting results on a real timeline gives a much more accurate picture of the intervention's impact over time. For instance, how quickly the target behaviour responds to treatment may be an important index of intervention effectiveness. If 'sessions' are used as a metric and if inter-session intervals are not equal, then response latency might be distorted so that it may appear to be either brisker or slower than it really is. Spriggs, Lane, and Gast (2014) do not make specific prescriptions about the metric that should be used on the x-axis, or under what conditions session or time (e.g. day) should be used, but they do recommend that graphs should "use appropriate proportions and scales that do not deceive readers" (p. 155). They argue that "The primary function of a graph is to communicate without assistance from the accompanying text" (p. 161), and they provide useful guidelines for selecting the most suitable graphical format (i.e. line, bar, cumulative) and constructing the graph. Their main recommendations can be summarised as follows:

- avoid clutter;
- use appropriate descriptive labels and clearly separate phases/conditions;
- use easily distinguishable data points and data paths; and
- use a 2:3 y-axis to x-axis ratio.

Ideally, data for every session in every phase of the study are plotted on the graph. Aggregating data (e.g. each data point in the graph is the mean/median of several sessions) can make variability in the data less apparent and distort the magnitude of any existing trends (Kazdin, 2011). Data should only be aggregated if this does not mask or distort variability in the data (Spriggs et al., 2014).

Examining SCED results graphically is advantageous for many reasons. If the data are plotted online as the study proceeds, major characteristics of the data (changes in level, trend, variability, and latency of response to intervention, described in Chapter 9), anomalies and unexpected features (possible effects attributable to maturation, history, cyclicity, or other threats to internal validity, described in Chapter 2) will be highlighted. Monitoring the data in this way facilitates what is known as the response-guided approach. That is, emerging changes in data level, trend, and variability, are used to inform the practitioner's decisions about when to introduce, withdraw, modify, or change interventions (Kazdin, 1980; Kratochwill et al., 2013). In other words, this online, close monitoring of the participant's response allows the practitioner to verify that the therapeutic effect of the intervention is progressing as expected, and, if necessary, to make adjustments to the intervention if, as is not infrequently the case, the course changes. Indeed, it has been persuasively argued that ongoing, systematic assessment of the participant's progress not only enhances clinical care, but should be an integral part of the therapeutic intervention, bridging the gap between clinical research and clinical practice (Kazdin, 1993; 2008). Moreover, online monitoring facilitates ongoing detection and evaluation of threats to internal validity. If anomalies or unexpected changes in the data become apparent, their source can be (hopefully) identified and controlled, thus increasing the reliability of the data. Finally, a plot of the study data provides a detailed quantitative summary of study results over time that forms the basis for subsequent visual analysis (Spriggs et al., 2014; see also Chapter 9 in this volume).

Standards of evidence

Horner, Carr, Halle, McGee, Odom and Wolery (2005) proposed quality indicators that SCED data must meet in order to be able to "determine if a specific study is a credible example of single-subject research and if a specific practice or procedure has been validated as 'evidence-based' via single-subject research" (p. 165). The standards specified the minimum requirements needed to establish a causal (i.e. functional) relationship between the intervention being investigated (independent variable) and the target behaviour being treated (dependent variable). In order to do this, the 'architecture' of the study design had to provide sufficient opportunities to demonstrate the experimental effect. There were also minimum requirements for the number of data points per phase. In essence, the standards enhanced methodological robustness of

SCEDs in order to safeguard against threats to internal validity. They were subsequently published with further elaboration as the What Works Clearinghouse Single-Case Designs Technical Documentation Version 1.0 (Kratochwill et al., 2010). Two sets of criteria were proposed: Design Standards to evaluate internal validity (Table 1.2), and the Evidence Standards to evaluate level of credibility of the data. The standards were reissued three years later, with some slight elaboration (Kratochwill et al., 2013), and it is this version that we discuss here.

The four Design Standards have been incorporated, to a greater or lesser extent, in critical appraisal scales developed to evaluate methodological quality in SCEDs (see Chapter 2). Each standard stipulates minimum requirements that SCEDs must meet in order to establish a functional relationship between the intervention and the target behaviour:

TABLE 1.2 Design standards for single-case intervention research

---

Design Standard 1: Manipulation of variables
 • Independent variable (intervention) must be systematically manipulated by investigator
 • Standard must be met in order for the study to meet Design Standards

---

Design Standard 2: Inter-assessor agreement
 • More than one rater/assessor measures target behaviour and all outcome variables throughout the study
 • Inter-rater reliability established on at least 20% of the data points in each condition (i.e. baseline, intervention)
 • Rate of agreement must meet minimum thresholds (e.g. 80% agreement or Cohen's kappa of 0.60)
 • At least one outcome measure must meet this standard for study to meet Design Standards
 • Standard must be met in order for the study to meet Design Standards

---

Design Standard 3: Experimental control
 • Study must provide at least three opportunities to demonstrate the experimental effect (i.e., the effect of the intervention) at three different points in time. Consequently:
  WRDs must have at least four phases A-B-A-B
  MBDs must have at least three tiers (or baselines)
  CCDs must have at least three criterion changes
 • For ATDs, Design Standard 3 is superseded by Design Standard 4. That is, ATDs must provide at least 5 opportunities (i.e., at least 5 repetitions of the alternating sequence) to demonstrate the experimental effect
 • Standard must be met in order for the study to meet Design Standards

---

Design Standard 4: Phase validity
 • A minimum of 3 data points (preferably 5) are required in each phase used to demonstrate experimental effect

---

Source: adapted from Kratochwill et al. (2013)

- *Design Standard 1* defines the fundament of experimental control in terms of the systematic manipulation of the independent variable. The introduction, withdrawal (and, if necessary, the modification) of the independent variable during the course of the study, must all be instigated by and under the investigator's control.
- *Design Standard 2* concerns data accuracy and dependability, and stipulates how the target behaviour and other outcome variables need to be measured and the reliability of the data established.
- *Design Standard 3* concerns the demonstration of the experimental effect. According to Horner et al. (2005), "An experimental effect is demonstrated when predicted change in the dependent variable covaries with manipulation of the independent variable" (p. 168).[4] All SCEDs need to provide at least three opportunities to demonstrate the experimental effect, either at three different points in time for the same participant or for three different participants.
- *Design Standard 4* stipulates that a phase cannot be used to demonstrate the experimental effect if it has fewer than 3 data points, preferably 5.

The evidence level furnished by the SCED in terms of how well it meets the Design Standards is then rated on a set of Evidence Standards and classified as follows: meets standards, meets standards with reservations, or does not meet standards. Standards for the four prototypical designs are as follows:

- WRDs: the experimental effect is demonstrated when there is a phase change, for example, from A to B or from B to A. Hence, a WRD needs to have at least four phases (A-B-A-B), and meets evidence standards if each phase has at least 5 data points. If the design contains four phases and each phase has 3–4 data points, it is classified as meeting the standards with reservations. Designs with fewer than four phases (e.g. A-B-A), do not meet evidence standards (either with or without reservations), even if each phase has at least 3 data points.
- MBDs: requirements for MBDs are that they must have at least three tiers, each containing an A-B sequence with at least 5

4 At face value, this may be taken to suggest that the experimental effect is only demonstrated if the intervention produces the expected changes in the target behaviour. Demonstrating the experimental effect consists of determining whether or not the intervention has had an effect when the independent variable is manipulated.

data points in each phase in order to meet evidence standards. If these designs contain 3–4 data points per phase, they meet evidence standards with reservations.

- ATDs: Design Standard 4 supersedes Design Standard 3 for ATDs. Designs with at least five repetitions of the alternating sequence meet evidence standards. ATDs with only four repetitions of the alternating sequence, meet evidence standards with reservations.
- CCDs: at least three criterion changes and at least 5 data points per phase are required for CCDs to meet evidence standards. There is no specification in the Standards as to requirements for CCDs to meet evidence standards with reservations. But following the formulation for the preceding designs, it would seem reasonable to propose that a CCD with three criterion changes and 3–4 data points per phase are necessary to meet standards with reservations.

Although the requirement for three demonstrations of the experimental effect provides a benchmark for experimental control, it is not empirically based, nor is a specific rationale given for its adoption. There is no 'gold standard' for the number of times the experimental effect needs to be demonstrated in order to be able to make valid inferences. The three-demonstration criterion conforms to what, according to Kratochwill and colleagues (2013), is "professional convention". They acknowledge that while Barlow et al. (2009) consider A-B-A withdrawal/reversal designs to be "experimental", for others, such as Kazdin (2011) a withdrawal/reversal is "experimental" only if it has at least four phases. It has also been suggested that demonstration of experimental control is less clear if there is a delay in response (Gast, Lloyd, and Ledford, 2014). It is not unreasonable to suppose, however, that some interventions (like some medications) might need to be implemented (i.e. 'taken') for some time before their effect is evident. Moreover, some behaviours may also respond more slowly than others to treatment.

There might be practical or ethical reasons, however, why in some instances these standards may need to be ignored. For example, if the intervention is being applied to treat extremely aggressive behaviour, it would be unethical to continue a baseline phase until stability is achieved and/or at least 3 data points have been recorded.

Further reference to Design Standards 3 and 4 is made in the specific context of the individual designs discussed in Chapters 5–8. Of course, standards of evidence for SCEDs also encompass other experimental features (e.g. how the dependent variable is operationally defined, measured, recorded, and evaluated; whether the intervention is implemented as intended) that also need to meet standards of evidence in order to ensure that threats to internal and external validity are adequately addressed. These issues are taken up in the next three chapters.

Concluding remarks

The antecedents of single-case designs pre-date the between-groups approach that subsequently laid the foundations for the randomised controlled trial (RCT). Yet, arguably, single-case studies in the neurorehabilitation field have been marginalised by the enormous sway that the RCT has exercised (particularly in the medical field). For example, in the American Academy of Neurology evidence table for interventions, the SCED is classified as Class III evidence (patients serving as their own control); the Australian National Health and Medical Research Council considers interrupted time-series data without a parallel control group (basically, SCED data) as Level III evidence.

Both RCT *and* SCED methods, however, proffer sound methodologies for evaluating intervention effectiveness. Moreover, single-case designs play an important role in evidence-based clinical practice. Well-designed and conducted SCEDs can, in fact, provide a stronger level of evidence than Class/Level III. According to the Oxford Centre for Evidence-Based Medicine (Howick et al., 2011; OCEBM, 2011), the randomised N-of-1 trial (which is essentially the SCED which is structurally and methodologically analogous to an A-B-A-B design; see Chapter 5), provides Level 1 evidence for treatment decision purposes, with the single RCT providing Level 2 evidence.

Well-designed SCEDs and RCTs can each demonstrate functional (i.e. cause–effect) relations between the independent (intervention/condition) and dependent (target behaviour) variables. Randomisation can be incorporated in both methodologies (albeit in different ways; see Chapters 2 and 10) to bolster internal validity. Although generalisation of results is considered to be a strength of RCTs and a weakness of SCEDs, both methodologies have problems in this regard (see Chapter 3). A clear limitation of RCTs is that they are not well suited to investigating rare conditions, where recruitment of sufficiently large numbers of participants to ensure adequate power, is problematic. SCEDs, however, are eminently suited to this circumstance. Moreover, unlike RCTs, SCEDs have the flexibility to modify and tailor treatment to individuals and to changing conditions during the clinical trial without compromising experimental control. And, unlike RCTs, SCEDs "fit hand-in-glove with day-to-day clinical practice and set it within the framework of evidence-based clinical practice" (Perdices & Tate, 2009, p. 905). Although in some quarters the RCT may be considered to be the 'gold standard' for intervention research to the exclusion of any other methodology, nonetheless "both single-case and between-group research methods have goals, methods of achieving them, and strengths and limitations. They share the goals, but their different methods, strengths and limitations underscore their complementary roles in uncovering knowledge" (Kazdin, 2011, p. vi).

2

MAXIMISING VALIDITY IN SINGLE-CASE DESIGNS

This chapter addresses issues related to the scientific rigour of single-case designs. Scientific rigour is important because the results of a study that has sound methodology provide more credible evidence than those from a study with methodological flaws. All intervention studies using between-groups and single-case methodologies aim to establish a cause–effect functional relationship between the independent and dependent variables: that is, Intervention X is responsible for changes in Behaviour Y. Such a link can only be firmly established, however, if threats to validity are minimised.

Moreover, evidence drives clinical practice. Consequently, if the evidence base includes flawed work, then this adversely impacts clinical decision-making. Regrettably, the scientific literature contains many studies (both between-groups and single-case) that are poorly designed, poorly conducted, and/or poorly reported, including in the neurorehabilitation field (Perdices et al., 2006; Tate, Perdices, McDonald, Togher, & Rosenkoetter, 2014). Happily, however, tools are now available to assist the investigator to plan, conduct, and report intervention (and other) studies at a high standard of scientific rigour.

The structure of the present chapter is in three parts: first, we consider validity in relation to single-case designs and strategies that can be implemented to address (and hopefully overcome, or at least minimise) threats to validity. We focus on internal and external validity and provide a worked example from the neurorehabilitation literature to illustrate how threats to validity can be addressed. We then review a selection of published critical appraisal scales that evaluate methodological quality of single-case designs and which are also useful for designing scientifically robust studies. Finally, we describe a reporting guideline for single-case designs that was developed within the CONSORT tradition, which assists authors to write their reports with clarity, completeness, and transparency.

Validity refers to the soundness of a research study; specifically, its credibility. There are many factors that can interfere with a study producing credible results, and these factors are generally classified in four domains (e.g. Shadish, Cook, & Campbell, 2002):

- *internal validity*: the capacity to attribute changes in the dependent variable (target behaviour) to the independent variable (intervention) rather than extraneous factors (i.e. to make causal inferences);
- *construct validity*: the higher-order construct/s underlying the variables of interest in the study and how they are measured;
- *statistical-conclusion validity*: drawing accurate inferences about the data. Given that both statistical and visual analytic techniques are used in SCEDs (see Chapter 9), this domain has a broader application in SCEDs, and Kazdin's (2011) term, data-evaluation validity, captures the breadth; and
- *external validity*: the applicability of the intervention in other contexts.

Each of these domains involves many individual threats that affect all types of research, including single-case research. Although the literature is in agreement about the individual threats to validity, variability exists regarding their classification within the four broader domains. In this chapter, we have largely followed the classification used by Domholdt (2005) and our previous work (Tate & Perdices, 2017). In the course of planning and conducting a study, the investigator will inevitably encounter situations and issues that threaten validity. Knowing about these threats is the first step to putting procedures in place to minimise them. Common threats to validity, as these apply to single-case methodology, are described and defined in Table 2.1; not forgetting that individual threats can be additive as well as interactive.

TABLE 2.1 Threats to validity as applied to single-case designs

Type of threat	Description
Internal validity	
History	Changes in the external environment (positive or negative) that coincide with the introduction of the intervention and may be mistaken for changes due to the intervention. These include one-off and recurrent (cyclical) events in the environment
Maturation	Changes (positive or negative) in the participant that may account for changes in the target behaviour. This may include recovery, deterioration, or cyclical internal changes (e.g. biological rhythms)
Attrition	Loss of data due to participant factors
Instrumentation	Unreliable methods/procedures used to collect data/implement the intervention may spuriously inflate/deflate the treatment effect
Testing	Effects of repeated assessment with the participant may spuriously affect (positively or negatively) performance
Statistical regression	Regression of extreme scores to the mean on subsequent test occasions are mistaken for/misinterpreted as effects of the intervention
Diffusion of treatment effects	In single-case studies this refers to treatment differentiation whereby elements of one condition (e.g. intervention) may be incorporated into another condition (e.g. baseline/different intervention)
Participant reactivity	Participant responds the way that he/she perceives to be expected; alternatively, under-performs due to lack of engagement or over-performs as a compensatory mechanism
Investigator reactivity	Investigator biases the implementation of the intervention and/or the recording/interpretation of participant responses in accordance with the investigator's expectation
Construct validity	
Construct explication	Poorly or inexactly defined constructs without an operational definition of the variable to be measured
Construct confounding	The extent to which constructs overlap with each other *Construct confounding with levels of construct:* a more general construct (e.g., leisure activity) is erroneously inferred from the more specific construct that is actually being studied (e.g., sporting activities)
Construct under-representation	*Mono-operation bias:* the measure/s (e.g. confrontation naming) do not adequately evaluate the construct (e.g. communication) *Mono-method bias:* the method of measuring the construct (e.g. fitness) is restricted in mode (e.g. self-report measures) and does not include other types of measures (e.g. performance-based) that may also be pertinent in valuation of the construct, such that the construct being measured is dictated by the method (e.g. self-reported fitness)

(Continued)

TABLE 2.1 (*Continued*)

Type of threat	Description
Treatment-sensitive factorial structure bias	The intervention itself may produce changes in the participant (e.g. increased awareness) that go beyond the intervention components (e.g. a memory intervention) yet which may affect measurement of the target behaviour (in either direction). For example, increased awareness of memory failures may affect the number of reported memory failures
Statistical-conclusion/data-evaluation validity	
Data evaluation	Excessive variability in the data, trends, insufficient data, mixed data patterns
Violated assumptions of statistical tests	Assumptions underlying the analytic techniques used are not met by the data being examined
Multiple comparisons	Increased likelihood of finding a significant result and erroneously conclude that the intervention is successful when it is not (type I error)
External validity	
Participants	The applicability of the intervention to other participants
Practitioners	The applicability of the intervention to other practitioners
Settings	The applicability of the intervention in other settings
Timeframes	The applicability of the intervention at other times of day
Adaptations of the intervention components	The effect of varying intervention components in producing in the same treatment result

Internal validity

Single-case methodology uses strategies that allay concerns about internal validity. The Standards of Evidence discussed in Chapter 1 help to diminish vulnerability to threats to internal validity. Multiple strategies need to be used and we suggest that a single-case intervention study that incorporates the seven features described below will have sound internal validity because the important threats are addressed:

i   *Use a strong research design*, defined as one that has experimental control and provides opportunity to repeatedly demonstrate the experimental effect; the rule of thumb is at least three repetitions of the experimental effect (Horner et al., 2005; Kratochwill et al., 2010, 2013; see also Chapters 1 and 5–8 in this book). This strategy addresses threats due to history and maturation.

ii *Apply randomisation* if feasible to determine the order and/or onset of the phases, which addresses threats caused by history and maturation.

iii *Incorporate blinding (masking)* wherever possible. Blinding, in both an RCT trial and a SCED, principally involves three people: the participant, the practitioner, and the assessor, although other people can be blinded as well (e.g. data entry personnel). Whereas in between-groups research, blinding refers to the person not knowing the condition to which the participant has been allocated, in single-case methodology, blinding refers to the person being blind to phase.

Blinding of the participant and practitioner to phase are very difficult to achieve with behavioural interventions. Some types of interventions (e.g. using technologies) may facilitate the condition of blinding the practitioner if the intervention can be implemented without the need for human involvement. Investigators could consider how to capitalise on this strength when using such interventions. For example, Klarborg, Lahrmann, Agerholm, Tradisaukas, and Harms (2012) used "intelligent speed adaptation" equipment to control driving speed in two participants with acquired brain injury. In this case, the equipment,[1] which was fitted to the participant's private vehicles, can be conceptualised as serving the role of the practitioner. In this and similar scenarios, we believe that it is reasonable to consider the practitioner as being blind when the practitioner is completely independent from and has no direct involvement in the delivery of the intervention. The risk of bias due to human factors is avoided when equipment is exclusively used to deliver the intervention. Successful blinding of the participant covers threats due to participant reactivity; successful blinding of the practitioner addresses treatment diffusion and investigator reactivity.

1   The equipment in the Klarborg et al. study delivered the intervention and was described as follows: "an onboard unit (OBU) that used the GPS [global positioning system] position of the vehicle to match its speed to the speed limit (retrieved from a digital map). A display mounted on the dashboard showed the current speed limit. If this speed limit was exceeded with more than 5 km/h the following voice message was given: '50 (the actual speed limit) – you are driving too fast'. This message was repeated every sixth second until the speed was below the activation criterion (speed limit +5 km/h)" (p. 58).

Blinding of the assessor is easier than blinding the participant and practitioner when using behavioural interventions. In a single-case study, the assessor of the target behaviour needs to be blind to the phase of the study (i.e. not know if the data assessed are from an intervention or baseline phase). Because of the usual chronological sequence of phases (baseline followed by intervention), successful blinding will usually require rating after the conclusion of the study. Hence a permanent product record of the target behaviour is required, session order needs to be taken out of chronological sequence by an independent person. The assessor then evaluates the data not knowing whether they come from the baseline or intervention phase. Successful blinding of the assessor controls for investigator reactivity and some of the threats due to instrumentation.

iv *Pay close attention to the target behaviour*; specifically, how and when it is measured (see Chapter 3) by using the following strategies:
    - operationally define the target behaviour;
    - carefully select the measure of the target behaviour so that it is objective, produces a quantitative index, and avoids practice effects. If equipment is used in assessments, it needs to be calibrated to ensure that it is reliable;
    - train personnel to mastery in data collection and coding procedures to ensure competence;
    - take repeated and frequent measures of the target behaviour *within phases*; the rule of thumb is at least three, preferably at least five times per phase (Kratochwill et al., 2010, 2013);
    - conduct frequent monitoring of the integrity of the data collection process to ensure consistency throughout the study;
    - use raters who are independent of the practitioner and blind to phase; and
    - empirically verify the reliability of data collection by examining inter-rater/observer agreement (explained in Chapter 3).

These procedures will address multiple threats to internal validity due to instrumentation, testing, statistical regression, and participant and investigator reactivity.

v *Develop the intervention so that it contains checks and balances*, particularly in terms of incorporating strategies to minimise participant attrition part-way through the intervention, ensuring practitioners are competent, and that treatment differentiation and adherence are monitored and maintained (see Chapter 4). If equipment is used to implement the intervention, practitioners need to be competent in its use. If the intervention is delivered by a person then it needs to be administered in a standard way which will be enhanced by the following procedures:

- draw up treatment manuals and session protocols;
- train personnel;
- provide supervision/mentoring sessions throughout the intervention; and
- empirically document treatment adherence against a protocol (explained in Chapter 4).

All these steps will address threats posed by instrumentation, diffusion of treatment effects, and investigator reactivity.

vi *Collaborate with the participant and family* in planning and implementing the intervention. This will encourage their involvement, motivation, and cooperation, and help to safeguard against threats involving attrition and participant reactivity.

vii *Document any pertinent issues/events* occurring throughout the study. This is an important, yet often overlooked, strategy regarding internal validity. Although documentation will not provide a control per se to any of the threats to validity, it may assist in understanding the data and reasons that might contribute to compromised validity. For example, change in family circumstance may contribute to internal validity threats involving history; illness or noncompliance may prevent the participant attending therapy and hence risk attrition; equipment failure may impact instrumentation; and so forth. Indeed, early detection can facilitate taking immediate action to prevent ongoing problems that may compromise the study (e.g. fix or replace equipment, address and rectify reasons for noncompliance, institute additional sessions).

Using the above seven strategies, a single-case study can minimise the main threats to internal validity allowing causal inferences to be drawn. Indeed, use of a strong single-case design (i.e. containing experimental control and adequate demonstration of the experimental effect), with randomisation and sufficient sampling will qualify as Level 1 evidence (OCEBM, 2011) for making treatment decisions in the individual person (i.e. "does this intervention help?").[2]

External validity and generality

In the context of single-case methodology, the term generality is often used in association with external validity. Both concepts refer to whether the effects of the intervention extend or transfer to other contexts (e.g. behaviours, settings, practitioners, participants) beyond those of the original study.

External validity is particularly apposite to single-case research because the method is designed for a sample/unit size of only N=1. It is clear that in this situation the grounds for generalisation are tenuous, although "logical generalisation" (Barlow et al., 2009; Edgington, 1967) suggests that an intervention may also apply to a different participant whose characteristics very closely resemble those of the original participant. Yet, as is often noted, between-groups research itself is not immune from threats to external validity. First, between-groups studies use strict selection criteria and participants in the experimental group (active intervention) and the control group (no intervention) are homogeneous within a relatively narrow range of relevant clinical characteristics. Consequently, the results of the study are, strictly speaking, applicable only to other individuals with similar clinical characteristics. Second, intervention effectiveness in the experimental group reflects the group mean score. However, the intervention is, almost always, not effective for a small percentage of participants in the experimental group. Hence, even *within* the group, results are not generalisable.

---

2   The 2011 OCEBM Levels of Evidence is a ranking system that was designed to help clinicians quickly answer clinical questions using the best available evidence (Howick et al., 2011). It recognises that different research methodologies contribute differentially to clinical questions regarding prevalence, diagnosis, prognosis, therapeutic effects, identification of harms, and screening. The medical randomised N-of-1 trial (a variant of the WRD described in Chapter 5), is regarded as providing Level 1 evidence, equal to the systematic review of multiple RCTs in the areas of treatment decisions and identifying harms.

Replication

The primary answer to the problem of external validity for all research designs is replication. In single-case research, replication serves two purposes relating to both internal and external validity (Barlow et al., 2009; Kazdin, 2011; Sidman, 1960). One type of replication, used to evaluate the *reliability of findings*, is direct *intra*-subject replication. In this within-subject application, replication occurs with the repetition of phases and conditions in the same participant. Direct intra-subject replication in WRDs occurs every time the intervention is introduced or withdrawn. In MBDs across behaviours or settings it occurs when the experimental effect is demonstrated across different tiers. Each alternation of the interventions being compared provides direct intra-subject replication in ATDs. In CCDs, it is achieved every time there is a criterion change. Thus, direct intra-subject replication relates to internal (rather than external) validity.

A second application of replication is used to evaluate the *generality of findings* (external validity), which is the focus of this section of the chapter. Following Sidman's (1960) seminal conceptual framework, two types of replication relating to generality are distinguished:

i *Direct inter-subject replication* refers to the exact (as possible) replication of the experiment with other participants who have similar characteristics to the original participant, but holding all other features of the experiment constant (i.e. the same target behaviour, same intervention, same setting, same practitioner). Direct inter-subject replication can be used in any of the prototypical designs where the entire experiment is repeated with other participants: WRDs (e.g. Beattie, Algase, & Song, 2004), ATDs (e.g. Rose & Sussmilch, 2008), and CCDs (e.g. Davis & Chittum, 1994). Direct inter-subject replication is also achieved in MBDs across settings and behaviours by including more than one participant in the study (e.g. Feeney, 2010; Savage, Ballard, Piguet, & Hodges, 2013 respectively). In the case of MBD across participants, it has been argued that if the design is used for the purpose of experimental control, then it cannot also be used simultaneously to demonstrate replication (Schlosser & Braun, 1994). In this case, replication would constitute another entire experiment of MBD across participants, as was done by Ouellett and Morin (2007). They applied an intervention to treat insomnia in 11 participants with traumatic brain injury who were randomly allocated to four subgroups with differing baseline lengths. Each subgroup contained three participants (apart from the final subgroup which contained two participants) for the three tiers of the MBD. Each subgroup thus represented a separate experiment of an MBD across participants.

ii *Systematic replication* alters some feature of the original experiment, usually a different setting, practitioner, behaviour, type of participant, or other feature, including component/s of the intervention. The variations are selected a priori and systematically, to be used, in Kazdin's (2011) words, as approximations of the original experiment. The aim here is to evaluate the intervention in other contexts to establish its generality. In the foregoing paragraph we noted that an MBD across participants requires replication of the entire experiment to qualify for replication. A similar logic holds for the MBD across settings or practitioners which would be pertinent to systematic replication – if this design is used to establish experimental control, then replication requires another entire experiment across settings or practitioners, as the case may be.

Systematic replications are conducted much less frequently in the neurorehabilitation literature than are direct inter-subject replications. Examples include that of Tate, Wakim, Sigmundsdottir, and Longley (2018) who studied the effects of an intervention to increase meaningful activity in participants with apathy after traumatic brain injury, using both direct inter-subject and systematic replication. Inter-subject replication was evaluated in three participants who had a similar (mild impairment) neuropsychological profile to the original participant. Systematic replication was evaluated in another three participants with apathy but who experienced major neurobehavioural impairments and functional disability. Besharati, Kopelman, Avesani, Moro, and Fotopoulou (2015) reported two systematic replications of a study originally published by Fotopoulou, Rudd, Holmes, and Kopelman (2009), addressing anosognosia for hemiplegia (denial of paralysis of the person's own limb). Fotopoulou and colleagues had evaluated an intervention (a single session of self-observation of video replay) in a patient with anosognosia in the acute stages after stroke. The systematic replication of Besharati et al. examined two variations of the original procedures with two participants with anosognosia after stroke: (i) the chronic stage post-onset (participant FG); and (ii) adding another component to the intervention protocol ("emotional support"; participant ED). The two participants were treated in separate locations (Italy and the UK) by two independent research teams.

Barlow et al. (2009) provide helpful guidelines for the steps involved in conducting a replication study. For direct inter-subject replication, they recommend the following:

- practitioners and settings to remain unchanged from the original;
- the target behaviour to be topographically similar to the original;
- participant characteristics to be closely matched to those of the original participant;
- the intervention and procedure of implementation to be unchanged from the original;
- in the event of failure to replicate the experimental effect, the investigator to analyse the variability to identify the cause by implementing "improvised and fast-changing experimental designs" (e.g. designs such as A-B-A-B-BC, where BC is a different therapeutic component). If this process is successful, then the alteration in the intervention (e.g. the BC component) needs to be tested on additional participants; and
- three to five successful replications of the original experiment are considered sufficient, in which case the generality of the intervention is further evaluated with systematic replication.

Guidelines for systematic replication are more difficult to formulate than those for direct inter-subject replication owing to the variety of factors involved (Barlow et al. 2009). Nonetheless, Barlow and colleagues proffer the following:

- systematic replication to build upon successful direct inter-subject replication;
- document, in detail, the differences that constitute the systematic replication;
- evaluate one variable at a time otherwise, in the event of failure to replicate, it is not possible to isolate the responsible factor (e.g. was it the change in practitioner or the change in setting?); and
- the guiding principle of systematic replication is that it is "a search for exceptions. If no exceptions are found as replications proceed, then wide generality of findings is established" (p. 334).

When sufficient successful replications have been achieved, it is appropriate to consider whether there is sufficient support for an intervention being classified as an evidence-based procedure. According to Horner et al. (2005), and reinforced by the WWC Standards (Kratochwill et al., 2010; 2013), an intervention can be considered evidence-based if: (i) a minimum of five SCEDs that either meet evidence standards or meet standards with reservations are used to evaluate intervention effects; (ii) at least three independent practitioners at different institutions conduct the studies; and (iii) the combined number of participants across the studies is at least 20. This is commonly referred to as the 5–3–20 rule.

Generalisation and social validity

Thus far, we have considered replication as being the arsenal to address external validity. Other constructs, including generalisation and social validity, have secondary relevance to the external validity and generality of a SCED. Whereas replication requires the implementation of a separate and independent experiment, generalisation and social validity can be evaluated within the original experiment by using measures additional to the target behaviour. For example, Guercio, Johnson, and Dixon (2012) treated problem gambling in three participants with traumatic brain injury. The intervention setting was a specially designed "gambling room" in the laboratory at the university. Generalisation was evaluated periodically throughout the baseline and intervention phases, by measuring the target behaviour in a genuine gambling establishment. Generalisation measures can be administered on as few as two occasions, before and after the intervention, as well as intermittently or continuously throughout all phases, which Schlosser and Braun (1994) advocate as recommended practice.

Social validity, referring to the practicality and social value of a study, is considered integral to SCED methodology, arising from the philosophy of applied behaviour analysis addressing socially important problems (see also Chapter 9). Horner et al. (2005) highlight four features of a SCED that enhance social validity: (i) the dependent variable should have high social importance; (ii) the intervention can be applied with fidelity by typical practitioners in typical settings, (iii) the typical practitioner finds the intervention procedures to be acceptable, feasible given their resources, effective, and would choose to continue using the intervention after study completion; and (iv) the intervention produced an effect that met the participant's clinical need.

Unlike target behaviour and generalisation measures, social validity measures are usually taken at the conclusion of the intervention. For example, in their study teaching five participants with dementia to use the telephone, Perilli et al. (2013), evaluated the social validity of both the intervention (a computer-aided telephone system) and control (staff assistance) conditions at study conclusion. Thirty-five staff members rated five questions on a 5-point scale (from 1=very low to 5=very high) regarding the participants' independence and comfort, whether the condition was practical and acceptable, and whether it promoted the participant's social image. In situations where social validity measures are taken throughout the study (see the example of Broach & Dattilo, 2001, described in the next section of this chapter), they allow the opportunity to immediately address potential problems.

In summary, the principal method of addressing threats to external validity is replication. This necessitates the conduct of another experiment, which may not always be feasible or possible. The judicious selection of generalisation measures where relevant and appropriate is desirable and should be possible in most SCEDs. This can be achieved by using probes throughout the phases to determine the effect of the intervention beyond the training setting, practitioner and/or target behaviour. Schlosser and Braun (1994) believe that generalisation should not only be incorporated into the treatment process, but also be a major dependent variable in its own right. Such documentation is an important first step in evaluating generality.

Case illustration: addressing threats to validity

Broach and Dattilo (2001) examined the effects of aquatic therapy to improve motor function and fatigue in four women (aged 30–53 years) with relapsing-remitting multiple sclerosis (MS). The authors conducted a concurrent MBD across participants, using the multiple-probe technique (see Chapter 6). Data on four target behaviours were collected throughout the study: walking up and down stairs (see Figure 2.1), pedalling both an upper extremity ergometer and a stationary bicycle, and self-report on the Fatigue Questionnaire. Trained observers were used to record performance, and also to evaluate the reliability of data collection and treatment adherence. The intervention was conducted over an eight-week period, with participants attending three sessions per week for measuring the target behaviours, and receiving the intervention of 45 min./session.

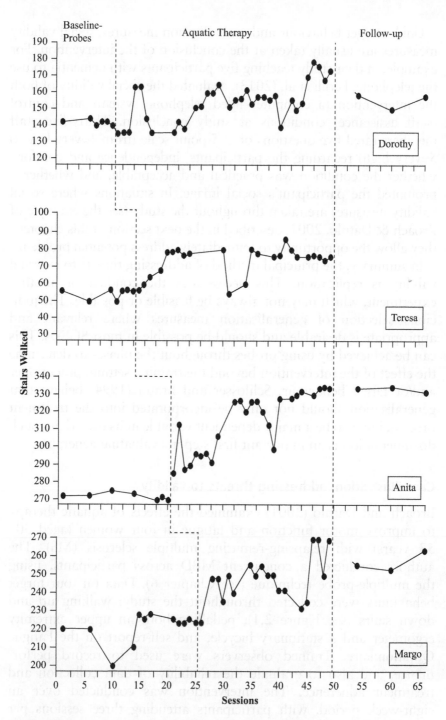

FIGURE 2.1 Frequency of stairs walked across participants
Source: Broach and Dattilo (2001); reprinted with permission

Threats to internal validity were controlled in the following ways:

History – changes in the external environment: the design of the study (MBD across participants) controlled for history because (i) the design was concurrent (data collection for all participants commenced at the same point in time), and (ii) the intervention was introduced in a staggered way across time for the participants (see Figure 2.1). The staggered introduction of the intervention combined with ongoing measurement of the target behaviours controlled for any external (history) or internal (maturation) events. In addition, randomisation was used to allocate participants to the tiers, which partialled out any known or unknown participant factors that may have influenced performance.

Maturation – changes within the individual participant: the three features of the design described for 'history' also controlled for maturation. In addition, the baseline (control condition) was measured for each participant until stability was achieved (although because it only occurred during baseline this does not ensure that maturation effects were not manifest in the intervention phase).

Attrition – loss of data: a common reason for loss of data in neurorehabilitation studies is participant nonattendance at sessions or nonadherence to task requirements. In this study, social validity data were collected on nine occasions throughout the intervention phase to see if the intervention was meeting participants' expectations. This strategy, while not directly addressing attrition, may have served a motivational purpose by keeping participants engaged and allowing opportunity for the investigators to intervene and address any concerns raised by participants. Results indicated high levels of satisfaction. There was no participant attrition, and the occasional missing data value coincided with medical issues (illness, back/knee pain, headache). Missing data values were not of such magnitude to compromise the results.

Instrumentation – unreliable treatment implementation and data collection methods and procedures: instrumentation refers equally to intervention implementation as well as data collection procedures. Instrumentation also refers to both inanimate instruments (tests, equipment), as well as 'human instruments' (i.e. practitioners/assessors). The intervention minimised threats to instrumentation due to unreliable administration procedures because the practitioner was an aquatic therapist who was a certified therapeutic recreation specialist, MS aquatic exercise instructor. Moreover, the intervention was directed by an Aquatic Exercise Association instructor. Treatment adherence (see Chapter 4) was also measured. Independent observers rated treatment implementation against the protocol, yielding a result of 80% adherence. This solid result strengthens confidence that the intervention was implemented as intended.

In terms of data collection procedures, one of the target behaviours (stair-step climbing) was measured by human observers, two behaviours (pedalling on the machines) used automated recording, and the final target behaviour (fatigue) was self-report. Observers, who were independent of the practitioner, were trained in data-recording procedures until they reached mastery (80% accuracy) and inter-observer agreement on the stair-step task was high (90%). No information was provided about calibration of the two machines, and it is not possible to establish inter-observer reliability (which is the critical type of reliability in this context) with self-report data. Other procedures used in the Broach and Dattilo (2001) study to address instrumentation included tight operational definitions of the target behaviours (see Chapter 3). A strong method to address threats to instrumentation is by blinding assessors to phase. Had stair-step climbing been videotaped, for example, then it would have been possible to alter the sequencing of phases and data collection occasions so that the assessor would not be able to tell the phase that was being rated, and hence be blind to phase. Being blind to phase is a stronger control of threats caused by instrumentation than the assessor simply being independent of the practitioner, which in turn is a stronger control than the practitioner being involved in both the assessment and the intervention.

Testing – effects of repeated assessment: threats caused by testing were a consideration in this study. The possibility exists that repeated performance on stair-step climbing and machine pedalling may by themselves result in improved motor function simply by virtue of repeated practice, as opposed to being due to the aquatic therapy. Use of the MBD, with sequential participants having extended baseline phases would allow the monitoring of any practice effects. Inspection of the data in Figure 2.1 shows that practice effects were not a problem.

Regression of extreme scores: continuing the baseline measures until stability was achieved controlled for statistical regression.

Participant reactivity: the social validity data gathered by the authors indicated that the participants were engaged and their expectations about the intervention were met. This procedure allowed the investigators to monitor participant reactivity factors. It is possible that participants underperformed on the physical tasks such as stair-step climbing (over-performance being unlikely – one cannot do better than one's best), although the data in Figure 2.1 do not suggest that this was a factor. There was some variability in performance within participants in the intervention phases, but the authors explained that this coincided with medical events.

Diffusion of treatment across conditions: this threat to validity was minimised because of the clear descriptions and very different conditions of the baseline versus intervention conditions and procedures.

Investigator reactivity – practitioner and assessor expectancies: the intervention was administered by a qualified aquatic therapist and the intervention directed by an Aquatic Exercise Association instructor. Treatment adherence data (80% agreement with the protocol) confirmed that the intervention was implemented as intended. Independent observers were trained to criterion and collected the data with high (90%) inter-rater agreement.

In summary, the preceding information indicates that threats to *internal validity* were well controlled in the Broach and Dattilo (2001) study. Consequently, we can have confidence that it was the aquatic therapy intervention, and not some other factor, that was responsible for improvements in the target behaviours. With reference to other types of validity, for *construct validity*, the authors did not make claims beyond the constructs that were being examined. Additionally, the constructs were clearly explicated, both for the target behaviours and the active intervention. The measures of the target behaviour were appropriate to the constructs. This lends confidence to the credibility of the study. In terms of *statistical-conclusion validity*, the authors used visual analysis of level, trend, and variability (see Chapter 9). Use of these techniques supported interpretation of the data. *External validity* was built into the study design, in that the study was a systematic replication of a similar study previously conducted by the authors. In that work they also evaluated the effects of aquatic therapy in participants with MS, with the present study including an extension, to examine the effects on fatigue.

Critical appraisal scales to measure scientific quality of single-case reports

The scientific literature contains many critical appraisal scales that are designed for different methodologies, including systematic reviews (e.g. AMSTAR, Shea et al., 2007, 2017), RCTs (e.g. Cochrane risk of bias tool, Higgins et al., 2011; PEDro scale, Maher, Sherrington, Herbert, Moseley, & Elkins, 2003), observational studies (e.g. Downs and Black Scale, 1998; MINORS, Slim, Nini, Forestier, Kwiatowski, Panis, & Chipponi, 2003). Critical appraisal scales have also been developed for single-case methodology.

Parenthetically, critical appraisal scales should be distinguished from the more familiar reporting guideline, such as the PRISMA Statement (Liberati et al., 2009) for systematic reviews and CONSORT Statement (Moher et al., 2010) for RCTs. A reporting guideline for single-case designs is described in the next section of the chapter. Whereas a reporting guideline makes recommendations about *what a study should report*, a critical appraisal scale evaluates *how well a study (as described in the published report) was conducted*. For example, a report of a study may state that a non-concurrent MBD across three participants was used because it was not possible to recruit patients with, say, prosopagnosia (inability to recognise familiar faces) at a single point in time due to the infrequent occurrence of prosopagnosia. This represents good reporting, because the reader knows exactly what type of design was used. Yet, such a study would be penalised on some critical appraisal tools (e.g. the Risk of Bias in N-of-1 Trials (RoBiNT) Scale; Tate et al., 2013a), because a non-concurrent MBD does not control threats to internal validity as well as a concurrent design.

A number of reports (e.g. Maggin, Briesch, Chafouleas, Ferguson, & Clark, 2014; Smith, 2012; Wendt & Miller, 2012) have compared the content of critical appraisal tools for SCEDs; some of the tools are published instruments, others appear on professional websites. Table 2.2 summarises the main features of five published critical appraisal procedures.

Horner et al. quality indicators: Horner and colleagues (2005), building on work in the special education field, were among the first to produce a set of "quality indicators" of single-case methodology in the context of developing evidence-based practices. The 21 items are

TABLE 2.2 A comparison of published critical appraisal tools for single-case designs

	Horner	Evaluative Method	SSRDQS	What Works Clearinghouse	RoBiNT
No. items	21	12 in 2 strata: • Primary (6 items) • Secondary (6 items)	14	4	15 in 2 subscales: • Internal validity (7 items) • External validity and interpretation (8 items)
Participants & settings	3	1	1	0	2
Design	2	1	1	2	2
Dependent variable/s	5	4	5	2	4
Intervention conditions	5	3	2	0	3
Data evaluation	1	1	4	0	2
External validity	1	1	1	0	2
Social validity	4	1	0	0	0
Scoring procedures and interpretation	No information	*Scoring*: Primary: 0, 1, 2; Secondary: 0, 1 *Interpretation*: algorithm –> strong, adequate, weak	*Scoring*: 0,1 *Interpretation*: strong: >10/14; moderate: 7–10; weak: <7	*Scoring and interpretation*: 3 levels – Meets standards; Meets standards with reservation; Does not meet standards	*Scoring*: 0, 1, 2 *Interpretation*: algorithm (in preparation)

(Continued)

TABLE 2.2 (*Continued*)

	Horner	Evaluative Method	SSRDQS	What Works Clearinghouse	RoBiNT
Psychometric properties					
Construct validity	No information	No information	No information	No information	Evidence of discriminative validity
Floor/ceiling	No information	No information	No information	No information	No floor/ceiling effects
Inter-rater reliability	No information	10 reports (random sample): • Primary: k=.69 • Secondary: k=.93	3 reports: Group agreement on overall classification (weak, moderate, strong): 75%	No information	20 reports (random sample) 2 pairs of raters (experienced and trained novices): • IV: ICC=.87-.88 • EVI: ICC=.87-.93 • Total: ICC=.88-.90
Test-retest	No information	No information	No information	No information	No information

Key: SSRDQS=Single-subject Research Design Quality Scale; RoBiNT=Risk of Bias in N-of-1 Trials; IV=internal validity; EVI=external validity and interpretation

tabulated in their report, but have not been formulated into a scale that has been evaluated psychometrically.

What Works Clearinghouse (WWC) Standards: Another influential publication, also from the field of special education, has been the development of standards of design and evidence (Kratochwill et al., 2010, 2013; also described in Chapter 1 in this book). The focus of their criteria is to evaluate four critical aspects of design rigour, rather than provide a comprehensive coverage of pertinent aspects of single-case methods. The WWC schema has been used by Maggin, Briesch, and Chafouleas (2013) to evaluate studies identified in a systematic review of self-management interventions to promote appropriate classroom behaviour in school students.

Evaluative Method: The 12-item Evaluative Method (Reichow, Volkmar, & Cicchetti, 2008) aims to identify interventions that are evidence-based, and hence its objectives are closely aligned with those of Horner et al. (2005). It uses a three-stage process, the first stage focusing on evaluating the research strength of the study. Psychometrically, inter-rater reliability was investigated in ten single-case articles with good results, particularly for the secondary variables.

Single-subject Research Design Quality Scale: The main aim of the 14-item Single-subject Research Design Quality Scale (Logan, Hickman, Harris, & Heriza, 2008) is to evaluate internal validity and adequacy of data analysis. The authors report some limited data for inter-rater agreement, using three single-case articles and obtaining a group agreement on the overall level of classification.

Risk of Bias in N-of-1 Trials (RoBiNT) Scale: The 15-item RoBiNT Scale (Tate et al., 2013a, 2015) focuses on internal and external validity. It is a revision of and replaces the original Single-Case Experimental Design (SCED) Scale (Tate, McDonald, Perdices, Togher, Schultz, & Savage, 2008). Psychometrically, the scale shows good results on a number of fronts: inter-rater reliability evaluated on 20 single-case articles, both for experienced and trained novice raters, is high; no floor or ceiling effects were found; and there is evidence of discriminative validity.

With the exception of the WWC Standards, items from the above instruments cover similar domains, but they vary considerably with respect to requirements to meet criteria and scoring procedures. Choice of a critical appraisal scale will depend on the purpose of evaluation. If the aim is to identify evidence-based interventions, for example, then instruments such as the Evaluative Method or the WWC criteria are a good choice. Alternatively, if the aim is to evaluate internal and external validity for a systematic review, for example, then the RoBiNT Scale is suitable. Strengths of the RoBiNT Scale are that it: (i) evaluates both internal and external validity in separate subscales; (ii) includes items on randomisation and blinding that are among the most powerful ways to control for many threats to internal validity; (iii) uses a 3-point rating scale which provides more sensitive discrimination among studies than the often-used binary (pass/fail) format; and (iv) has empirical evidence for high reliability and construct validity. Work is currently in progress to develop an algorithm to classify the magnitude of risk of bias. It also has a detailed manual (updated in Tate et al., 2015), which contains operational criteria for each of the items and their scoring levels, along with multiple examples for each of the scoring levels and rationale for the scoring decision. Items of the RoBiNT Scale and their correspondence with threats to validity are shown in Table 2.3.

A reporting guideline for SCEDs

What has reporting got to do with validity? Validity is about bias, and bias distorts the truth and credibility of the data. Bias can be introduced in a study via the written report, mainly due to omission and lack of clarity, and we have described these reporting biases elsewhere (Tate & Perdices, 2017). Sackett (1979), for instance, describes five types of reporting biases and it is easy to see how they are manifest in the literature: (i) bias of rhetoric; (ii) all's well bias; (iii) one-sided reference bias; (iv) positive result bias; and (v) hot stuff bias.

Having conducted and analysed a well-planned single-case study (see Chapter 10), the clinician or researcher should consider whether the study will contribute to the knowledge base. If so, it should be published. The neurorehabilitation literature, in particular, will benefit from more well-designed single-case experiments. Increasingly, neurorehabilitation journals are accepting studies using these methodologies, especially if it can be demonstrated that threats to validity have been controlled.

TABLE 2.3 The Risk of Bias in N-of-1 Trials (RoBiNT) Scale: item content and types of threats to validity addressed

No.	Item	Description	Type of validity threat addressed
Internal Validity subscale			
1	Design	The design incorporates experimental control to allow for adequate evaluation of the treatment effect	IV: history, maturation
2	Randomisation	Phase order or phase onset is randomly determined	IV: history, maturation
3	Sampling of behaviour	Adequate sampling of behaviour occurs in every phase (≥ 5 data points per phase)	IV: history, maturation, statistical regression
4	Blinding of participant and practitioner	The participant and practitioner are blind to the phase of the study	IV: participant reactivity (blind participant); treatment diffusion, investigator reactivity (blind practitioner)
5	Blind assessors	The assessor is independent from the practitioner and blind to the phase of the study	IV: investigator reactivity, instrumentation
6	Inter-rater agreement	Measurement of the target behaviour has demonstrated high inter-rater agreement (≥ 80%) in each condition (baseline/intervention) of the study	IV: instrumentation
7	Treatment adherence	The intervention is delivered as intended (≥ 80% adherence)	IV: instrumentation; investigator reactivity, treatment diffusion
External validity and interpretation subscale			
8	Baseline characteristics	An evaluation of the features that influence the behaviour being targeted for intervention is provided. This includes but is not restricted to functional status, sociodemographic and medical variables, as well as factors that serve to maintain the behaviour	EV: providing sufficient information for replication
9	Setting	The general location and specific environment of the study are described	EV: providing sufficient information for replication

(Continued)

TABLE 2.3 (*Continued*)

No.	Item	Description	Type of validity threat addressed
10	Dependent variable (target behaviour)	The target behaviour is specified in precise and operational terms, and its method of its measurement is described	IV: instrumentation EV: providing sufficient information for replication
11	Independent variable (intervention)	The content of the intervention is described, as well as the procedure of delivery, and any equipment/manuals used	EV: providing sufficient information for replication
12	Raw data record	The raw data record is provided, comprising all data collected on the target behaviour	SCV
13	Data analysis	Specification of data analysis and rationale, with results reported	SCV
14	Replication	Description of any replication: inter-subject or systematic, including settings, behaviours, practitioners, elements of the intervention	EV
15	Generalisation	Description of any measures additional to the target behaviour that are used for generalisation, with results reported	EV

Notes: IV=internal validity; EV=external validity; SCV=statistical-conclusion validity

Reporting guidelines, particularly those that have been developed in the CONSORT tradition, are helpful to authors to improve the clarity, completeness and transparency of reporting. The mid 1990s saw the emergence of reporting guides in response to concerns about the poor quality of reporting in the medical literature, where often the reader is "unable to determine exactly how the research was conducted, what was found, how reliable the findings are and how they fit into the wider context of existing knowledge" (Simera, Moher, Hoey, Schulz, & Altman, 2010, p. 35). Reviews of the single-case literature have found the same problem (Didden et al., 2006; Maggin, Chafouleas, Goddard, & Johnson, 2011; Smith, 2012; Tate et al., 2014). The EQUATOR network[3] contains no fewer than 358 reporting guidelines for a wide variety of methodologies in health research. Tate and Douglas (2011) summarised six reporting guidelines commonly used in the neurorehabilitation field, along with their corresponding critical appraisal scales: systematic reviews, RCTs, diagnostic investigations, observational studies, qualitative research, and SCEDs.

Two reporting guidelines are available for single-case studies: CONSORT Extension for N-of-1 Trials (CENT; Shamseer et al., 2015; Vohra et al., 2015) for medical N-of-1 trials and the Single-Case Reporting guideline In BEhavioural interventions (SCRIBE; Tate et al., 2016a, 2016b) for the variety of SCEDs used in the behavioural sciences. The SCRIBE is more relevant for the current purposes and is published in two complementary articles. A brief paper describes the methodology underpinning the development of the SCRIBE (Tate et al., 2016a). A more detailed article (Tate et al., 2016b) provides background to and rationale for each of the items, along with illustrative examples from the literature.

The 26 items of the SCRIBE are grouped into six domains that generally form the structure of a published report: (i) Title and abstract (2 items); (ii) Introduction (2 items); (iii) Method (14 items), including design (5 items), participants/units (2 items), context (1 item), approvals (1 item), measures and materials (2 items), interventions (2 items), analysis (1 item); (iv) Results (3 items); (v) Discussion (3 items); and (vi) Documentation (2 items). The SCRIBE checklist, which can be downloaded from the SCRIBE website[4] is reproduced in Table 2.4. Authors using single-case

3 www.equator-network.org; accessed 5 September, 2018.
4 www.sydney.edu.au/medicine/research/scribe; accessed 5 September, 2018.

TABLE 2.4 The SCRIBE checklist

Item number	Topic	Item description
TITLE AND ABSTRACT		
1	Title	Identify the research as a single-case experimental design in the title
2	Abstract	Summarise the research question, population, design, methods including intervention/s (independent variable/s) and target behaviour/s and any other outcome/s (dependent variable/s), results, and conclusions
INTRODUCTION		
3	Scientific background	Describe the scientific background to identify issue/s under analysis, current scientific knowledge, and gaps in that knowledge base
4	Aims	State the purpose/aims of the study, research question/s, and, if applicable, hypotheses
METHODS		
	Design	
5	Design	Identify the design (e.g. withdrawal/reversal, multiple-baseline, alternating-treatments, changing-criterion, some combination thereof, or adaptive design) and describe the phases and phase sequence (whether determined a priori or data-driven) and, if applicable, criteria for phase change
6	Procedural changes	Describe any procedural changes that occurred during the course of the investigation after the start of the study
7	Replication	Describe any planned replication
8	Randomisation	State whether randomisation was used, and if so, describe the randomisation method and the elements of the study that were randomized
9	Blinding	State whether blinding/masking was used, and if so, describe who was blinded/masked
	Participant/s or unit/s	
10	Selection criteria	State the inclusion and exclusion criteria, if applicable, and the method of recruitment
11	Participant characteristics	For each participant, describe the demographic characteristics and clinical (or other) features relevant to the research question, such that anonymity is ensured
	Context	
12	Setting	Describe characteristics of the setting and location where the study was conducted
	Approvals	
13	Ethics	State whether ethics approval was obtained and indicate if and how informed consent and/or assent were obtained

Item number	Topic	Item description
	Measures and materials	
14	Measures	Operationally define all target behaviours and outcome measures, describe reliability and validity, state how they were selected, and how and when they were measured
15	Equipment	Clearly describe any equipment and/or materials (e.g. technological aids, biofeedback, computer programs, intervention manuals or other material resources) used to measure target behaviour/s and other outcome/s or deliver the interventions
	Interventions	
16	Intervention	Describe intervention and control condition in each phase, including how and when they were actually administered, with as much detail as possible to facilitate attempts at replication
17	Procedural fidelity	Describe how procedural fidelity was evaluated in each phase
	Analysis	
18	Analyses	Describe and justify all methods used to analyse data
RESULTS		
19	Sequence completed	For each participant, report the sequence actually completed, including the number of trials for each session for each case. For participant/s who did not complete, state when they stopped and the reasons
20	Outcomes and estimation	For each participant, report results, including raw data, for each target behaviour and other outcome/s
21	Adverse events	State whether or not any adverse events occurred for any participant and the phase in which they occurred
DISCUSSION		
22	Interpretation	Summarise findings and interpret the results in the context of current evidence
23	Limitations	Discuss limitations, addressing sources of potential bias and imprecision
24	Applicability	Discuss applicability and implications of the study findings
DOCUMENTATION		
25	Protocol	If available, state where a study protocol can be accessed
26	Funding	Identify source/s of funding and other support; describe the role of funders

Source: retrieved from www.sydney.edu.au/medicine/research/scribe (date accessed 5 September, 2018)

methods are encouraged to use the SCRIBE checklist when preparing their reports. It will result in a clear, complete, and transparent report that will demonstrate to journal editors and journal reviewers that the study is well planned and conducted and the report carefully prepared.

Concluding remarks

A study that does not control threats to validity is at risk of bias. Studies with significant bias are of little worth and may, in fact, produce erroneous data and draw misleading conclusions. In this context, we are reminded of Greenhalgh's (1997, p. 243) startling editorial in the *British Medical Journal*:

> It usually comes as a surprise to students to learn that some (perhaps most) published articles belong in the bin, and should certainly not be used to inform practice . . . If you are deciding whether a paper is worth reading, you should do so on the design of the methods section and not on the interest of the hypotheses, the nature or potential impact of the results, or on the speculation in the discussion.

Investigators who address threats to validity in the design and planning stages, and who monitor the implementation and conduct of data collection and the intervention, are in a good position to produce a study with sound internal validity and low risk of bias. This, when other types of validity are maximised, will furnish the evidence base with reliable and credible data. Those critical appraisal scales that provide a comprehensive set of items with rigorous criteria lend themselves very well to guide the planning, conduct and analysis stages by incorporating features of the scale items. This will result in a high-quality study. The SCRIBE is a complementary resource that will assist authors to write SCED reports to a good standard.

3

THE DEPENDENT VARIABLE

Measuring the outcomes

The dependent variable in a study refers to the variable that is being measured. Accordingly, this chapter is about assessment, with particular focus on the target behaviour. Assessment is, in Kazdin's (2011) words, pivotal because it is a precondition for drawing inferences. Yet, as we have seen in Chapter 2, biases in the measurement process will threaten construct validity and internal validity (most notably, threats posed by testing, instrumentation, and investigator and participant reactivity). Thus, measures in SCEDs, as in other research methodologies, not only need to include quantifiable indices, but also provide data that are precise, reliable, and accurate, so that they are free from bias.

The structure of the present chapter covers the initial procedures in identifying, defining, and understanding the target behaviour (the primary outcome or dependent variable), followed by issues pertaining to its measurement, data fidelity and reliability. SCED studies often use additional outcome variables for specific purposes, such as measures of generalisation and social validity which are discussed in Chapter 2 in the context of measuring external validity (and specific aspects of social validity are addressed in Chapter 9). The role of other measures providing contextual information that will inform the intervention (e.g. psychosocial history, neuropsychological and functional status) are briefly addressed in Chapter 10. Throughout this chapter, we refer to a large number of SCED studies in the neurorehabilitation field that are summarised in the Appendix to this book. Inter alia, they illustrate the wide variety of dependent variables that are used in SCED research and differences in the way in which they are measured.

Identifying, defining, and understanding the target behaviour

SCEDs require a deep understanding of the target behaviour. This involves being able to articulate what constitutes a given target behaviour, as well as having intimate knowledge about the context in which it occurs. At the outset, however, the target behaviour needs to be identified. Participants can present with multiple problems and in the early stages of evaluation it may not be clear which behaviours of concern should be targeted for intervention. Initial interview with the participant and relevant others as appropriate (e.g. family members, clinical and residential staff, educators, employers), along with informal observations in situ, will assist in clarifying and identifying the potential behaviour/s that may be targeted for intervention. More formal interview, assessment and behavioural observations are conducted in subsequent stages.

Operationally defining the target behaviour

Roane, Ringdahl, Kelley, and Glover (2011) believe that defining the target behaviour is "the linchpin of the data collection process" (p. 133). Without an adequate operational definition of the target behaviour, the likelihood of inaccurate data recording is very high, thus posing threats to internal validity. Specifically, observers and data recorders need to know what does and does not constitute an occurrence of the target behaviour.

Three criteria that the operational definition of the target behaviour should meet are objectivity, clarity, and completeness (Kazdin, 2011). In the study of Broach and Datillo (2001) described in Chapter 2, for instance, one of the target behaviours, walking up and down stairs, was described as follows: "Participants stood facing a flight of eight 8" steps, used the handrail for balance, walked up eight steps, turned around, and walked down the steps when the observer stated 'go' on a cue of 'ready, set, go'. Participants were directed to complete this sequence as often as possible within 3-min. An event recording system was used to count each step" (p. 145). Locke and Mudford (2010) operationally defined their target behaviour (disruptive vocalisations made by a man with dementia and non-functional communication residing in a nursing home): "Vocalizing was defined as all sounds emitted by Mr S except involuntary noises such as coughing or sneezing" (p. 255). Similarly, Raymer et al. (2007) provide the necessary information regarding the range of acceptable responses of the target behaviour in their participants with Broca's aphasia and anomia: "The primary outcome measure for this training experiment was a picture naming task . . . A correct naming response was the target word, a synonym, an immediate self-correction, or a simple phonemic distortion/substitution of one phoneme" (p. 251). These operational definitions are objective, complete, and clear, even to the non-expert. They delineate the boundaries of the target behaviour and permit objective measurement (e.g. counting the number of stair-steps/sounds emitted/ pictures named). The reader of such a description knows precisely what the target behaviour entails and how it could be measured.

Morris (1985; cited in Roane et al., 2011, p. 133) poses three questions to evaluate the quality of an operational definition:

1. Can the number of times the behaviour occurs in a minute, or the number of minutes the behaviour was done be counted?
2. Would a stranger know exactly what to look for?
3. Can the behaviour be further broken down?

Morris's (1985) third question, whether the behaviour can be broken down into its most specific components, is critically important. The general domain of a behaviour (e.g. aggression, communication, depression, memory, mobility) is insufficient for an operational definition. Aggression, for instance, can be broken down into verbal aggression, which itself can be further broken down into threats, profanities, insults, and so forth.

As we have noted elsewhere, some abstract concepts, primarily related to private events (e.g. pain and other sensory functions, headache, self-esteem, urges, thoughts, planning, emotional processing, empathising, feelings) are difficult to operationalise in concrete terms. Yet, such constructs may be highly relevant to the problem at hand. Just because a construct is difficult to operationalise does not suggest that it is out of scope or should not be studied. Their operationalisation may "need to rely on the way in which they are measured. Usually, this will be with a self-report measure (e.g. pain with a 10cm visual analogue scale)" (Tate et al., 2015, p. 72).

Another consideration in defining the target behaviour is the distinction drawn between topographical and functional features of the target behaviour. Topographical features refer to the form of behaviour in terms of its physical properties. The aforementioned examples of operational definitions of target behaviours (stair-steps climbed, disruptive vocalisations, picture naming) describe topographies of behaviour, and this is a common perspective in neurorehabilitation. Behaviours can also be described in terms of their functional effects on the environment. Lancioni et al. (2010), for example, taught two participants with profound disability from acquired brain injury (one of whom, Giselle, had anoxic brain damage from a cardiac arrest), basic communication strategies via text messaging. To activate the messaging technology, Giselle could either touch her ear or the wheelchair tray table, both of which activated a micro-switch which triggered other events. In this case, the investigators were interested in function (i.e. movements which could activate the micro-switch), irrespective of their topography (viz., touching her ear vs the tray table).

Understanding the target behaviour

Several approaches are appropriate to gain a more detailed understanding of the target behaviour. This knowledge is critically important for selecting an appropriate intervention. Within the context of applied behaviour analysis, formal and tightly specified procedures are used (viz., functional behaviour analysis). This approach is well suited to target behaviours that are maintained by external, potentially changeable environmental influences, such as challenging behaviours. In specific neurorehabilitation situations, however, the traditional functional behaviour analysis approach may not be informative or appropriate. We address a neurorehabilitation perspective first, followed by the traditional functional behaviour assessment.

A neurorehabilitation perspective

This approach will provide justification for using a particular intervention with a specific target behaviour, and the context in which it occurs, both with respect to other associated impairments, as well as personal and environmental factors of the participant.

Theoretical models

These provide one avenue by which the investigator may identify where the breakdown of a target behaviour occurs. This, in turn, will inform the intervention that will be most appropriate given the pattern of impairment. This approach, however does not allow definitive functional cause–effect relations to be drawn regarding factors influencing the target behaviours that are proffered by the experimental analysis of behaviour described later in this section. But they certainly provide directional hypotheses and inform the type of intervention to be implemented. Identifying the level at which a behaviour breaks down, usually involves extensive and targeted assessment. Francis, Riddoch, and Humphreys (2001), for example, treated MGM who had complex cognitive disabilities resulting from a traumatic brain injury many years earlier. His presenting problem was alexia (a reading disorder), due to profound visual agnosia (failure to visually recognise or identify objects), and complicated by memory disorder. Extensive assessment, including of visual perception, reading, and writing, phonological skills, memory, as well as ophthalmology, identified MGM's "functional locus". On the basis of the pattern of the results, his good phonological and residual visual processing skills were "exploited in helping him to read" (p. 113), and a four-stage remediation programme to teach basic reading skills was developed.

Case formulation

This provides a clinical analysis, but does not necessarily fractionate the level of breakdown of cognitive function within a conceptual model. Nonetheless, case formulation provides a necessary justification for choice of the intervention to address the target behaviour. Fiksdal, Houlihan, and Buchanan (2012) for example, worked with an elderly man with progressive dementia who resided in an assisted living facility. The authors used a memory priming (with spaced retrieval) intervention to assist him to relearn memory facts, which was evaluated with a multiple-probe design across behaviours. Their "case conceptualisation" included the following description:

> The participant was considered a good candidate for the memory-enhancement intervention used in this study based on several criteria. First, he was able to engage in some activities independently. Second, he was very talkative, had the ability to talk in great detail about a few life events, was open to new experiences, and was not prone to negative affect such as frustration or anxiety. These characteristics were important because

memory priming required regular conversation about life events that could be recalled in some detail. Third, his memory impairment was in the moderate range of severity based on cognitive screening measures, although he was able to remember some information about his personal life. Previous research with other memory-enhancement interventions has demonstrated that success can be achieved even with those with cognitive impairment in the moderate range of severity [ref.].

(Fiksdal et al., 2012, p.396)

Functional behaviour assessment

Another method for obtaining a detailed understanding of the target behaviour is the functional behaviour assessment. It is integral to applied behaviour analysis and may take a number of forms, including descriptive analysis using direct observation, indirect assessment, and experimental analysis. Any of the assessment procedures can stand alone, or be conducted in combination.

Descriptive analysis

This refers to direct observations of the participant in a setting, either natural or contrived, to document events that serve as triggers for the target behaviour (antecedents) and to observe what happens after the target behaviour occurs (consequences). This process is thus often referred to as an ABC (antecedents – behaviour – consequences) assessment. It will lead to an understanding of the target behaviour within its environmental context and will furnish hypotheses as to the role of specific factors, which in turn will inform the intervention to be selected.

Stewart and Alderman (2010), for example, treated GD who sustained severe traumatic brain injury and was admitted to their specialised neurobehavioural unit. He exhibited verbal outbursts, which led to physical aggression directed towards objects, himself, and sometimes other people. The outbursts were particularly frequent during his personal hygiene routine. An ABC assessment was conducted, using the Overt Aggression Scale – Modified for Neurorehabilitation (OAS-MNR). This instrument, designed for use in their specialised setting, is a structured observational procedure for recording the type, frequency, and severity of aggression, along with the antecedents and interventions (consequences) instituted to manage the aggression. Data from the OAS-MNR indicated that the most common antecedent triggering the outbursts was verbal prompts from staff. Occurrence of the target behaviour prevented the staff from carrying out the personal hygiene pro-gramme, thus effectively resulting in GD's avoidance (escape) from engaging in the hygiene routine. Because of its descriptive nature, however, by itself, an ABC assessment does not allow definitive causal statements to be made. That can only be provided by an experimental analysis of behaviour, described later.

Indirect assessment

An understanding of the target behaviour can also be informed by indirect assessment. In this case, the data are reported by the par-ticipant or an informant, rather than being directly observed. Interviews, questionnaires, rating scales and other instruments may be used to collect data about the target behaviour. It is the case that for some target behaviours, most notably those concerning 'private events', indirect assessment may be the only source of information about the target behaviour. An example of indirect measures is that of Lundervold, Pahwa, and Lyons (2013) who treated social anxiety in RZ who had Parkinson's disease accom-panied by dyskinesia.[1] A diagnostic behaviour interview was con-ducted to evaluate the antecedents and consequences related to the anxiety and dyskinesia and to identify the target behaviour and treatment goals. Standardised questionnaires were also adminis-tered to measure anxiety (Clinical Anxiety Scale) and depression (Geriatric Depression Scale). RZ was trained in recording 'sub-jective units of distress' to evaluate the intensity of anxious periods during the phases of the study.

Experimental analysis of behaviour

Undoubtedly, experimental analysis of behaviour provides the most definitive information in identifying factors that may serve to maintain the target behaviour. As we note above, such an analysis

1 Dyskinesia is a disabling side effect of long-term use of some medica-tions, including levodopa for the treatment of Parkinson's disease. It involves involuntary gross motor 'wiggling or dance-like' movements generally affecting the upper and lower extremities. The movements can be exacerbated by anxiety.

may be appropriate in some neurorehabilitation situations, and we describe it here in some detail because of its heuristic value. This type of analysis is experimental in that variables are manipulated to determine their effect on the target behaviour. Information from the experimental analysis then guides selection of the intervention. In applied behaviour analysis, work largely conducted in the 1970s and 1980s provided a model and a methodology, with functional analyses focusing on response–reinforcer relations, and structural analyses on antecedent–reinforcer relations (Waker, Berg, Harding, & Cooper-Brown, 2011). A fairly uniform set of conditions has been identified (see review of Hanley, Iwata & McCord, 2003), including social–positive reinforcement (e.g. attention), social-negative reinforcement (e.g. escape from demands), automatic reinforcement, also referred to as non-social (e.g. alone), control (e.g. free noncontingent access to tangibles such as toys, magazines). The target behaviour is empirically evaluated under different conditions in an experiment. It is possible to conduct an experimental analysis in a single session of 90 min. (Betz & Fisher, 2011). The experimenter contrives an environment in which the target behaviour is observed under various of the above conditions in a multi-element design, usually presented in random order, for approximately 5 to 15 mins. The set of conditions is repeated five to ten times. The aim of imposing these conditions is to see which of them provokes occurrence of the target behaviour. Visual inspection of the data is generally regarded as sufficient, although Hagopian, Fisher, Thompson, Owen-DeSchryver, Iwata, and Wacker (1997) have developed a set of quantitative criteria to identify the condition maintaining the target behaviour. It is obvious that the best-case scenario is when a single condition consistently outperforms the others. But results may not be clear-cut, with some target behaviours being maintained by multiple conditions or, at the other extreme, no clear pattern emerging.

Dixon et al. (2004), for example, treated four males with traumatic brain injury who exhibited inappropriate verbal behaviour. The target behaviours for Matt, for example, were aggressive vocalisations to staff, including profanities and demands to be left alone. The authors conducted a functional analysis using a multi-element design with four conditions administered four times each for 10 min. In the attention condition, the experimenter responded to occurrence of the target behaviours within 2 to 3 secs with a reprimand (e.g. 'You should not say things like that'). In the escape from demand condition Matt was provided with prompts to talk about difficulties he had been having in rehabilitation. Every occurrence of the target behaviour resulted in termination of the conversation for 15 secs. For the alone condition, Matt was placed in a room alone and observed through a one-way mirror. The control condition consisted of free access to preferred activities (magazines, TV, radio) and the experimenter delivered noncontingent attention every 30 secs and no consequence for occurrence of the target behaviour.

Figure 3.1 shows the results of the functional analysis for Matt (top panel). The escape from demand condition (circles) resulted in a higher frequency of target behaviour occurrence than the other three conditions. These results guided selection of the intervention. Consequently, a differential reinforcement of alternative behaviours (DRA) intervention was implemented, using a B-A-B design (bottom panel of the figure) that addressed the escape from demand condition maintaining the target behaviour. The DRA intervention involved the practitioner asking questions about Matt's difficulties in rehabilitation every 15 secs, and if he gave an appropriate and content-relevant verbal response, the questioning ceased for 30 secs; inappropriate responses were ignored. In this way, alternative desirable behaviours that were incompatible with the target behaviour (i.e. appropriate and content-relevant verbal responses were incompatible with aggressive vocalisations and profanities) resulted in 'escape from demand' (i.e. questioning ceased). As a consequence, the target behaviours decreased (bottom panel of Figure 3.1).

Measuring the target behaviour

The measure of the target behaviour is critical and should be selected with the aim of, inter alia, minimising bias and threats to internal validity caused by instrumentation, testing, and participant and investigator reactivity. In particular, as mentioned in the previous section, the measure of the target behaviour needs to be specific, observable, and replicable (Barlow et al., 2009). Selecting a sensitive measure of the target behaviour meeting these requirements, however, is not always an easy task. A single measure of the target behaviour that is specific may come at the expense of it not comprehensively capturing all elements of the target behaviour. Thus, in Kazdin's (2011, p. 89) view, "multiple measures of the target behaviour are to be encouraged". Moreover, some areas of enquiry may

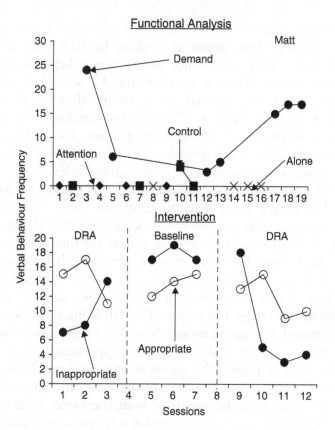

FIGURE 3.1 The number of verbal utterances during the functional analysis condition (top panel), and the number of utterances during DRA and baseline conditions (bottom panel), for Matt

Source: Dixon, Guercio, Falcomata, Horner, Root, Newell, and Zlomke (2004); reprinted with permission

involve target behaviours that are not directly observable, the so-called 'private events' described earlier. The challenge for the investigator here is to determine how the construct can be externalised and objectified, so that it can be measured in quantitative terms. Finally, the requirement in SCEDs for continuous measurement of the target behaviour throughout all phases, means that the measure needs to be amenable to frequent and repeated administration without adverse consequences. This generally precludes the types of standardised assessment batteries commonly administered in between-groups research because of their length, susceptibility to practice effects, and often the nonspecificity of each item to the target behaviour. That said, there are some exceptions. For example, SCED studies of unilateral spatial neglect often successfully use standardised instruments, such as subtests from Behavioural Inattention Test (e.g. Bailey, Riddoch, & Crome, 2002; Smith, Herbert, & Reid, 2007; Tunnard & Wilson, 2014); studies of motor function frequently include the Fugl-Meyer Assessment (e.g. McCrimmon, King, Wang, Cramer, Nenadic & Do, 2015; Slijper, Svensson, Backlund, Engström, & Sunnerhagen, 2014). It is usually the case, however, that most investigators develop tailor-made measures of the target behaviour (see Appendix for examples).

Repeated measurement in SCEDs is one of its distinguishing features. It contrasts with the between-groups study where the dependent variable is measured infrequently, on as few as two occasions, one before and one after the intervention. Why is continuous measurement of the dependent variable in a SCED necessary? Because a within-subjects approach is used to determine treatment effect, the naturally occurring variability of the target behaviour has to be documented, in both the baseline and intervention phases. Without this, the investigator does not know whether any changes in the dependent variable (target behaviour) are due to the effects of the intervention or simply the naturally occurring variability representing day-to-day fluctuations. This need does not occur in the between-groups design, because the variability is averaged across all the individuals within the group. Having a large number of data collection occasions allows the SCED investigator to determine whether those changes occurring during the intervention phase are above and beyond the variability observed in the absence of the intervention. It therefore stands to reason that the more occasions of measurement that are taken, the more reliable will be the sample of behaviour obtained.

Basically, there are two methods of measuring the target behaviour: direct and indirect. The 'gold standard' measure in SCEDs is regarded as the continuous and direct observation of overt behaviour. The reasons for this relate to the close correspondence that direct observation affords between the target behaviour and the intervention, as well as the precision and high reliability of the data that can be obtained from measures of overt or 'public behaviour' (e.g. walking, sitting, dressing, talking, swearing, hitting, initiating activity) when these are adequately operationally defined. On the other hand, target behaviours representing 'private events' that are not directly observable (the aforementioned sensory functions, mood states, abstract cognitive constructs) may have to be inferred from other data. Some of those 'other data' might be furnished from overt behaviours that bear a close relationship to the target behaviour (e.g. diminished activity levels in depression). Participants can self-record quantitative data (e.g. activities completed) or they can be directly observed by others. Reports, a source of indirect data, can also be used. Participants can self-report about their experiences or perceptions (e.g. feelings of sadness, low self-worth, disinterest in things, that generally accompany depression); significant others (e.g. clinician, family member) similarly can provide relevant data via report, interview, questionnaire, or behavioural ratings.

Direct measures

Continuous, direct measurement is described as a "recording of behaviour as it occurs without interference from other events . . . an uninterrupted, natural time flow" (Kahng, Ingvarsson, Quigg, Seckinger, & Teichman, 2011, pp. 119–120). Observations are usually taken in real time. Although challenging behaviours are most frequently associated with direct observation, many other types of target behaviours in different domains of neurorehabilitation are also amenable to direct measurement (including basic and instrumental activities of daily living, as well as cognitive, communicative, motor, and sensory functions), as shown in the Appendix. Common types of direct measures of overt behaviour/performance are event-based, time-based, and intensity.

- *Event-based measures* such as *frequency counts* are most suitable when the target behaviour consists of discrete responses. For example, in an intervention to decrease elopement behaviour in a man with dementia who attended an adult day care centre, Valle Padilla, Daza González, Fernández Agis, Strizzi, and Alarcón Rodríguez (2013) counted the number of times he approached the exit doors – operationally defined as within the area covered by the alarm sensors, approximately 2m from the doors. *Percentage* of occurrence is used in different ways. Many authors simply use percentage in lieu of frequency counts (e.g. the percentage of correct responses). The percentage, as used in this context, is not recommended if the total number is less than 20 (Ayres & Ledford, 2014). Use of the percentage, however, is necessary in situations where there is not a fixed number of trials or opportunities to demonstrate the behaviour. In this case it is needed to equalise the denominator. In their study on driving speed, for example, Klarborg et al. (2012) reported the percentage of time driving above the speed limit. The percentage was necessary, because driving distances for each trip varied in length, as well as duration.

As described above, event-based measures generally measure the same behaviour (e.g. counts of occurrence of approaching the exit doors, percentage of time driving above the speed limit, as per the above examples). Yet a target behaviour may also consist of a series of discrete steps which, taken together, mean that the target behaviour is accomplished. For example, using email requires completion of a number of distinct tasks such as turning on the computer, navigating to the email page, composing the text, retrieving the email address of the intended recipient. Discrete categories for task accomplishment are amenable to event-based measurement. For example, the number of steps correctly performed for the email task, as in the study of Ehlhardt, Sohlberg, Glang, and Albin (2005); McGraw-Hunter, Faw, and Davis (2006) calculated the percentage of steps completed independently from a 25-step task analysis for stovetop cooking.

- *Time-based measures* are best suited to the situation where the interest is in the entire *duration* of the target behaviour. For example, Engelman, Matthews, and Altus (2002) increased independence in dressing in residents with dementia who were living in a nursing home. The target behaviour selected was dressing independence and one of the measures was dressing time, measured in mins. Similarly, McCrimmon et al. (2015) used functional electrical stimulation to improve foot drop and gait after stroke, the primary target behaviour being gait speed as measured in m/sec over the mid 6-m section of a 10-m walkway. *Latency* is another time-based measure, and is calculated using the time between instructions to commence a task until its onset. Evans, Emslie, and Wilson (1998) used an external cueing system to assist a woman with stroke to initiate tasks, such as taking her medication. They measured latency, being the time difference between the message being sent by the paging system and the client's action in taking her medication.

- *Intensity* of the target behaviour refers to the "magnitude, strength, amplitude, force, or effort of a response" (Kahng et al., 2011, p. 121). Response intensity is highly salient in some areas of neurorehabilitation, such as dysphonia (volume and other dimensions of voice), muscle weakness, and challenging behaviours. In the absence of measurement using a machine (e.g. decibels to measure volume), human observers will have to use judgement in evaluating the strength or intensity of the response. This can be difficult to do with accuracy and consistency: when does a whisper, for example, become a conversational tone, a loud voice, a shout? These threshold judgements will introduce reliability problems for the data. Rating scales can be also used, as did Feeney and Ylvisaker (2008) in their treatment of challenging behaviours in two school-aged children with traumatic brain injury. They used 20 items from the Aberrant Behavior Checklist. Whenever an instance of one of the items occurred (e.g. boisterousness), it was rated for intensity on the 4-point scale (not a problem, slight, moderately severe, severe problem).

The preceding measures are not the only types of direct measures. *Rate* of occurrence is a hybrid of event- and time-based measurement. It needs to be used if time periods are of different lengths in order to adjust for duration differences. Rate is calculated by dividing the frequency by time (secs/mins). For example, in a man with non-fluent aphasia, LaFrance, Garcia, and Labreche (2007) calculated the rate of verbal and nonverbal communication behaviours, as operationally defined, that occurred per minute in the presence/absence of a therapy dog and dog handler. *Spatial displacement* is often used in measuring unilateral spatial neglect (a disorder characterised by failure to attend to one side of space). Tunnard and Wilson (2014) used the Line Bisection Task and measured spatial deviation from the midline in mm.

Discontinuous, direct measurement. The direct measures described above all use continuous measurement; that is, every event, or the entire time, or the full range of intensity is measured. *Discontinuous*, intermittent or interval recording[2] may be used for practical reasons (e.g. it is not possible for a rater to observe and record at the same time, particularly if the recording requires detailed/complex coding or the behaviour has a high rate of occurrence). In this situation,

2 Discontinuous/intermittent/interval recording in this context (i.e. *within* a data collection occasion) is to be distinguished from discontinuous data collection *between* occasions in the multiple-probe design, where data collection occasions might be scheduled to occur every day, for example, but are probed less frequently (see Chapter 6).

blocks of time are divided into smaller intervals. Observers then record whether an instance of the target behaviour did or did not occur during that interval, irrespective of the number of occasions the behaviour may have occurred within the observation interval.

Kahng et al. (2011) describe four discontinuous recording procedures. In the *whole-interval method* occurrence of a target behaviour is recorded if it continues throughout the entire duration of the interval. Locke and Mudford (2010), for example, divided 5-min blocks into smaller 10-sec intervals and observers recorded whether the entire 10-sec interval was free of vocalisation. The *partial-interval method* involves recording occurrence of the target behaviour if it occurs at any point within the interval. Arco (2008) treated compulsive counting in a man with traumatic brain injury, and an instance of compulsive counting (as operationally defined) was registered if it occurred at any point in the 60-min interval. The *predominant-activity method* is an intermediate method, whereby occurrence of the target behaviours is recorded if it occurs for more than 50% of the interval. *Momentary-time sampling* uses the procedure of recording occurrence of the target behaviour if its occurrence coincides with the precise end of the time interval. Tasky, Rudrud, Schulze, and Rapp (2008) used momentary-time sampling to measure on-task behaviour in three participants with traumatic brain injury. Recordings were always made between 10am and 11am each weekday. Within the 1-hour period, a block of 30 mins was randomly selected (e.g. 10.20–10.50am). The 30-min block was divided into 6 x 5-min intervals, and the final 10 secs of the 5-min interval was used to observe whether or not the on-task behaviour occurred. It was necessary for the on-task behaviour to occur for the entire duration of the 10-sec segment for it to be scored as an occurrence. The authors then calculated the percentage of intervals in each 30-min block in which the on-task behaviour occurred.

Interval recording has limitations. It uses an incomplete sample of behaviour, and so investigators need to ensure that the period selected is a representative sample. For this reason, some researchers use a time-sampling procedure by selecting a few different periods throughout the day in which to sample the behaviour. Hufford, Williams, Malec, and Cravotta (2012) treated a patient in the early stages of recovery from a fall causing traumatic brain injury, whose agitation was measured three times per day during the morning, afternoon, and evening nursing shifts. Depending on features of the behaviour (e.g. high/low rate, instantaneous/long duration), interval recording is subject to inaccuracy, either over and/or underestimating actual occurrence (Kahng, et al., 2011).

Indirect measures

Some SCED researchers are sceptical about the use of indirect measures because (i) inferences need to be drawn from the data, and (ii) some indirect measures provide inaccurate data. Kazdin (2011), however, reminds us that the direct measurement of overt behaviour, while desirable, is not a requirement for SCEDs: "any assessment method that provides ongoing data over time can be used" (p. 97). Moreover, having a range of different types of measures will minimise the threat to construct validity caused by mono-method bias (see Chapter 2). In the context of discussing physiological and behavioural methods of measuring the effect of treatments for headaches, muscle tension, stress, and pain, Kazdin comments that "as superb as these are as measures, there is no substitute for asking if the client in fact is experiencing fewer or no headaches, less muscle tension and stress, and no pain" (p. 85). Barlow et al. (2009) also recommend incorporating the participant's self-report: "For some outcomes, such as the occurrence of thoughts or feelings (e.g. suicide ideation, experience of fear or anxiety), the subjective experiences of the participant may be what is most important" (p. 64), and of course, as indicated previously, they may be the only way of measuring some behaviours (e.g. suicide ideation).

It is worth emphasising that indirect measures are not restricted to self- or informant report, and some indirect measures can provide great rigour and precision. When calibrated, machine-recorded behaviour produces highly specific, accurate, and quantitative data at the interval (and even ratio) level of measurement. Physiological measures are increasingly accessible for SCED research, including heart rate, blood pressure, body temperature, skin resistance, muscle tension, brain activity, blood-serum levels. Other machine-recorded data can involve pedometers to track walking activity, scales for measuring weight, computers for recording responses, and so forth. Whether these data are direct or indirect measures of the target behaviour will depend on the study question: heart rate as a cardiovascular index of the effects of exercise may be a direct measure, but heart-rate as an index of anxiety is an indirect measure of anxiety.

Permanent product recording is another form of indirect measure, where, in this context, data are gathered from (generally) audio/

visual recordings of the target behaviour, rather than direct observation. They also include inter-session records, such as completed homework, which may be part of the intervention. Permanent product recordings are often used for the purposes of scoring/coding target behaviour data, as did Douglas, Knox, De Maio, and Bridge (2014). This facilitated the rater keeping track of a large number (n=35) of possible communication-specific coping strategies for integrating into a single outcome measure using a visual analogue scale. Such permanent product records also lend themselves to evaluating inter-rater agreement and treatment adherence.

All measures, including direct measures of overt behaviour, are susceptible to error and bias, but self-report measures are additionally potentially prone to distortion from participant reactivity. Data cannot be verified, although as Kazdin (2011) points out, this does not necessarily imply that the data are inaccurate. Nor indeed that measures of direct behaviour are accurate either and even machine-based data can be inaccurate – it is well known that different pedometers, for example, vary in their reliability (e.g. Schneider, Crouter, Lukajic, & Bassett, 2003). Nonetheless, with self-report measures it is easy to produce a response that is not the true one, in an effort to provide socially desirable responses or succumbing to expectancy biases. They are also particularly susceptible to the Hawthorne effect, wherein behaviour changes simply as a function of the person being aware that their behaviour is being observed (which, of course, is not restricted to self-report). Responses can also be influenced by other factors of which the respondent may or may not be aware. In neurological populations, cognitive impairments in memory, judgement, or self-awareness may unwittingly distort a self-report; as may a significant other's levels of stress and distress impact upon his/her report of the participant's behaviour. Other respondents, such as clinicians, may only see a selection of the participant's behaviour in a single setting, which may not correspond with his/her behaviour in the home or community setting.

Data integrity and reliability

Having identified and defined the target behaviour/s, and then selected methods for measurement, two final measurement-related tasks remain: (i) maintaining data integrity during the data collection process; and (ii) verifying that the data are reliable. Data quality applies to all data collection, whether using equipment, direct observation, or indirect measures. Even measuring time with a stopwatch, for example, will require precision with respect to coincidence between the onset/offset of the actual behaviour and the observer's ability to capture it accurately.

Maintaining data integrity

Threats to internal validity caused by instrumentation can jeopardise the results of a study. Instrumentation, in this context, refers to the unreliability of methods and procedures used to collect data. It applies equally to the instruments themselves, as to the persons using/administering the instruments and recording the requisite measures. Practitioners need to be competent to use all the types of instruments and measures that are involved in a SCED study, including indirect measures such as questionnaires and interviews, direct measures in the form of test administration and behavioural observations, as well as scoring and coding procedures once the data have been collected. If any equipment or materials are required, practitioners also need to be competent in their operation. Equipment needs to be calibrated (and recalibrated, as required) in order to ensure that it is reliable and accurate.

Depending on the assessment procedures, training may be required to ensure competence. This will almost certainly be the case for observational procedures, even for experienced practitioners, because of the need to ensure that observers are able to identify instances of when a specific target behaviour does and does not occur, as well as demonstrate competency in any required coding of behaviours. Recommended training procedures are to use a representative sample of the target behaviours (in vivo or recorded) and to compare the trainee's ratings with those made by the trainer, who provides corrective feedback.

Having obtained the required standard of competence, it is then necessary to ensure the standard is maintained and that 'observer drift' does not contaminate the assessment/observation process. Observer drift refers to the slackening of adherence to the operational definitions of the target behaviour. It can occur for a number of reasons: fatigue, inattention, boredom, or some other factor. Observer drift will introduce error into data collection and studies need to have procedures in place to identify and counteract it, such as periodic reliability checks of data collection and booster retraining sessions.

Verifying data reliability

Largely because of (i) the use of tailor-made measures of the target behaviour and lack of standardisation and (ii) the measurement error when using human judges, obtaining inter-observer agreement is an "expected standard" (Kahng, et al., 2011). Inter-observer agreement can be established on all but self-report measures. Even if inter-observer agreement of a protocol has been established in a previous study, it is suggested that it still be evaluated using the data set from the current study to ensure reliability of the data set at hand.

Kratochwill et al. (2010; 2013) recommend that a sufficient sample of data (at least 20%) be selected from each condition (baseline and intervention), and that it be evaluated by two independent raters separately for each condition (Design Standard 2; see also Chapter 1). Inter-observer agreement is straightforward to calculate: the number of times the raters agree that the target behaviour occurs (e.g. 14 in baseline) is divided by the number of agreements + disagreements (e.g. 14+2=16). The result (in this case, 0.875) is then multiplied by 100 to obtain percentage agreement (i.e. 87.5% in the baseline condition). The rule of thumb is that inter-observer agreement of at least 80% is considered acceptable.

$$\frac{number\ of\ agreements}{(number\ of\ agreements) + (number\ of\ disagreements)} \times 100$$

Of course, as Kahng and colleagues (2011) point out, high inter-observer agreement does not necessarily mean that the figure reflects the correct score, because it is possible that both raters were incorrect. But certainly, agreement that is less than 80% should be followed up to ascertain the reason for the low inter-observer agreement and procedures that can be implemented to improve it. Inter-rater reliability can also be evaluated using the intraclass correlation coefficient (ICC) for continuous data and kappa/weighted kappa (k/k_w) statistic for categorical data. The advantages of these techniques are that they take into account the magnitude of disagreement as well as rank order (ICC/k_w) and agreement expected by chance (k/k_w). This is particularly important with behaviours occurring at the frequency extremes (very low or high occurrence).

Concluding remarks

The main dependent variable in a SCED (the target behaviour) serves the same role as the primary outcome variable in a between-groups study, but there are differences in both type and purpose. In the between-groups study, the ideal primary outcome measure is a widely used, standardised instrument, that has excellent psychometric properties. The primary outcome variable will be administered infrequently (usually pre- and post-intervention), and very rarely during the intervention itself. By contrast, the primary outcome variable in a SCED differs in two fundamental ways. First, the measure of the target behaviour will often be tailor-made for and unique to the study, so that it is proximal and highly specific to the behaviour targeted by the intervention. Indeed, it will often be deceptively simple, such as a frequency count of the number of occurrences of the target behaviour. Second, the measurement occasions will be continuous throughout the study, both during the baseline (pre-treatment) as well as the intervention itself.

Whether the measure of the target behaviour is tailor-made, or a standardised instrument is used, the measure needs to be selected with care, its method of measurement considered in the context of the need for repeated evaluation, practitioners trained and monitored in its administration, and reliability of observations demonstrated. It is only then that the investigator can be confident that threats to internal validity are controlled, or at least minimised. The present chapter has provided an overview of the relevant factors to consider regarding the dependent variable/s. The practicalities of selecting the target behaviour and other outcome measures and their implementation are dealt with in Chapter 10.

4

THE INDEPENDENT VARIABLE

Implementing the intervention

Textbooks on SCEDs generally consider the intervention within the context of the research design – that is, how the independent variable can be manipulated to demonstrate a functional cause-effect relationship with the dependent variable. We also include that approach (see Chapters 5–8 on prototypical SCEDs). But interventions encompass more than the research design of a study. They involve the content and procedural details of the components of the intervention, how they are to be delivered, under what conditions, at what dosage, in what setting, by whom, and to whom. A related issue, measurement of the effects of the intervention, involves the dependent variable, which is covered in Chapter 3.

A concerted body of work published between the mid 1970s and the early 1990s addressed concerns about inadequate descriptions and implementation of the independent variable. With some notable exceptions, that momentum has largely been lost. But the problems still persist. In the course of their systematic review of RCTs of cognitive rehabilitation treatments for non-progressive acquired brain impairment, for example, van Heugten, Gregório, and Wade (2012) reported that few studies provided sufficient information about the contents of interventions to enable them to be implemented in clinical practice. Similarly, Glasziou, Meats, Heneghan, and Shepperd (2008) found in their review of general medical practice that elements of intervention description were missing in a large proportion of reports, especially nonpharmacological treatments where less than

30% provided adequate description. In the past decade, however, there has been a revival of interest in the topic of the independent variable and some important advances made.

The present chapter is devoted to a consideration of the intervention per se: its components and its delivery. Of course, given the vast number of interventions available, the aim is not to describe specific treatments (but see the Appendix to the book, which contains a large selection of SCED studies in neurorehabilitation describing, inter alia, a range of behavioural interventions used in this field). Rather, the intent is to provide guiding principles about the types of information that the practitioner or researcher needs to know, from the preparatory stages of designing an intervention through to its implementation.

The structure of this chapter has been informed by the literature on reporting guidelines and treatment fidelity (also called treatment integrity, as well as procedural integrity). In brief, reporting guidelines are documents that recommend what should be written in a report so that it represents a clear, complete, and transparent account of the study (see Chapter 2). Treatment fidelity refers to the concept that implementation of the intervention needs to be done in such a way that the intervention is "fairly and faithfully represented" (Kazdin, 1986). The chapter addresses areas where these two bodies of work intersect, namely (i) defining the intervention and its theoretical underpinnings, (ii) describing the intervention, (iii) ensuring practitioner competence, and (iv) striving for treatment fidelity.

Defining the intervention and its theoretical underpinnings

"What we need is good theory", said Yeaton and Sechrest in 1981, in relation to identifying those interventions that are best suited to treat particular problems. And the requirement for theory as an initial step in defining an intervention has been echoed ever since (e.g. Bellg et al., 2004; Des Jarlais et al., 2004; Hoffman et al., 2014; Kazdin, 1986; Whyte & Hart, 2003). Indeed, Hart and colleagues (Dijkers, Hart, Tsaousides, Whyte, & Zanca, 2014; Hart et al., 2014; Hart et al., 2018) have developed a rehabilitation treatment taxonomy based on theories underlying the interventions. Although describing the theoretical underpinnings of the intervention may seem to be a rather esoteric requirement, Yeaton and Sechrest go on to explain that theory will assist in "an understanding of the mechanisms relating the causes and the problem as well as the presumed manner by which the treatment alleviates the problem" (1981, p. 157). It is not about theory for theory's sake; it is about the "conceptual relevance" of the intervention, to use their term. The advantages of this approach are that "they force researchers and clinicians to articulate their underlying hypotheses and beliefs about the mechanisms of treatment effects" (Whyte & Hart, 2003, p. 640). Hart (2009) makes the valid point that formal theory does not commonly underpin many interventions used in rehabilitation. In situations where theory is not apparent, empirical evidence or an explicit rationale for selecting a particular intervention to address a particular target behaviour can be used.

An example of how theory informed an intervention is that of Rose and Sussmilch (2008), who treated three people with Broca's aphasia and anomia after stroke. They compared three treatment conditions to improve verb retrieval deficits, one of which was a gesture-based intervention, using an ATD (see Chapter 7): "One potentially useful speech pathology treatment for word production deficits involves the use of arm and hand gestures [refs]. Recent production models [ref] suggest links between gesture and speech production. Gesture may facilitate lexical retrieval through acting as an additional semantic cue or through cross-modal priming [refs]" (p. 692).

A primary reason for articulating the conceptual relevance of the intervention for the target behaviour is to elucidate the component processes, including the so-called 'active ingredients'. Active ingredients are those aspects of the intervention that are not only unique to it, but also important and necessary, without which a valid evaluation of the particular intervention cannot be made. Ehlhardt et al. (2005), for example, trained four people with severe memory impairments and executive dysfunction to learn to use email in a multiple-probe across participants design (see Chapter 6). They developed an instructional package, TEACH-M, with a number of intervention components. Each of the components was described as they related to the intervention; for example: "Meta-cognitive strategy training-Part 1: The reflection–prediction technique was used to increase the participants' self-evaluation of performance. Specifically, they were asked to reflect on their performance during the phase described above, then based on that performance predict which email steps would be easy and which would be difficult during the subsequent phase (i.e., cumulative review/spaced retrieval)" (p. 576).

In the above example, we can speculate that a potential active ingredient of the metacognitive strategy instruction is the reflection–

prediction technique and it could be one of the purported mechanisms underlying behaviour change in this multi-component intervention. If this technique were omitted or not executed correctly, the intervention would not be implemented as intended (an issue related to treatment fidelity, discussed later in the chapter). The point we wish to emphasise here, however, is the importance of explicating all of the components of the intervention including any hypothesised active ingredients in order to define the intervention. The separate issue of identifying and confirming which of the component/s actually *are* the active ingredient/s is an empirical question and requires a specially constructed dismantling design for which SCEDs are eminently suitable (see Chapters 5–8).

It is just as important to define the baseline conditions as the active intervention (Lane, Wolery, Reichow, & Rogers, 2007). The SCRIBE Statement (see Chapter 2) recommends that the control condition be described with the same specificity as the active intervention (Tate et al., 2016b). It is neither helpful nor sufficient to describe the control/baseline condition in general terms, such as 'usual care' or 'standard treatment' (Des Jarlais et al., 2004; Hoffmann, et al., 2014). If the term 'usual care' or similar is used, then it needs to be operationally defined (Boutron et al., 2008). Moreover, in neurorehabilitation, it is not infrequently the case that the participant is receiving concurrent treatments that need to continue during the course of the SCED study. In this case, such interventions also need to be fully described, as did Freeman and High (2009), for example, in documenting the type and dosage of medication during the course of their behavioural intervention to treat self-injurious behaviour in a woman with traumatic brain injury.

Practitioner behaviours that are proscribed in the baseline condition need to be stipulated – in other words, what they are *not* permitted to do. For example, Feeney and Ylvisaker (2008) used a multi-component treatment package to improve challenging behaviours in two children with severe traumatic brain injury, using a WRD (A-B-A-B; see Chapter 5). Some of the behaviour supports used in the treatment (B) phases included daily routine, escape communication, graphic advance organizers, and so forth. They explicitly stated that "None of the supports offered in the B condition was provided [in the A, baseline, condition]" (p. 119).

A critical concept pertinent to the foregoing is that of treatment differentiation (Kazdin, 1986; Moncher & Prinz, 1991). Perepletchikova (2014) describes treatment differentiation as "treatments under investigation [that] differ from each other along critical dimensions (e.g. implementing procedures prescribed by the manual for Treatment A and avoiding procedures for Treatment B and vice versa)" (p. 136). Treatment differentiation is important in all design types, whether two or more interventions are compared (e.g. multiple-treatment designs, such as A-B-A-B-A-C-A-C or an ATD) or a single intervention is being evaluated (e.g. with WRD, MBD, or CCD). In the latter scenario, the baseline condition should not contain techniques that are used in the intervention, as in the above example from Feeney and Ylvisaker (2008). Inadequate treatment differentiation will risk compromising internal validity in terms of treatment diffusion (see Chapter 2). Unless the component processes and active ingredients are identified and explicated, complex rehabilitation interventions are, to use Whyte and Hart's (2003) descriptions, a "black box", whereas we need a "Russian doll" framework to uncover layers of increasing specificity of the intervention components.

Having identified, specified, and operationalised the intervention and its components, they can then be formulated into testable hypotheses. Continuing the example of Rose and Sussmilch (2008) from earlier in this section, they tested a number of hypotheses based on their theoretical formulation: "We further hypothesised that the combined semantic plus gesture treatment would be superior to the semantic alone, gesture alone and the repetition alone treatments for participants with impairment of verb word forms (access impairment)" (p. 693).

Describing the intervention

Many interventions used in neurorehabilitation are complex (Hart, 2009), and these will be the focus of this section. But the term 'complex' implies the existence of other 'simple' interventions. What are these? Boutron et al. (2008) draw a distinction between pharmacological and nonpharmacological interventions, noting that non-pharmacological trials (including rehabilitation) "usually test complex interventions, involving several components" (p. 295). Their complexity also comes about because of their requirement for expertise in the person implementing the intervention. Yet even within the group of complex interventions, complexity itself varies along several dimensions, including difficulty level (e.g. minimally conscious and profoundly disabled patients with acquired brain impairment learning to use technology to interact with their environment, as in the extensive work of Lancioni and colleagues (e.g. Lancioni et al., 2009; 2010; Perilli et al., 2013)), degree of abstractness (e.g. an intervention using Acceptance and Commitment Therapy), and number of components (e.g. combination packages comprising a set of discrete techniques, such as the intervention of Guercio et al. (2012) for problem gambling behaviour in participants with traumatic brain injury which included training in antecedent management, assertiveness, relaxation, alternative replacement behaviour, etc). Complex interventions can be difficult to describe, standardise, administer consistently, and reproduce (Boutron et al., 2008).

Types of complex interventions

The combination treatment package

Some interventions may comprise multiple components, which taken together provide a treatment package. Each of the components needs to be described in explicit detail. The aforementioned studies of Ehlhardt et al. (2005) and Guercio et al. (2012) used combination treatment packages to facilitate learning to use email and treating problem gambling respectively, as did Rasquin, van de Sande, Praamstra, and van Heugten (2009) in their treatment of depression after stroke. Their eight-session intervention included components of education for recording mood (sessions 1–2), relaxation training (sessions 2–4), cognitive restructuring (sessions 5–6), and pleasant event scheduling (sessions 7–8).

With other types of interventions, it may be a sequence of steps that has to be followed. For example, Wright, Marshall, Wilson, and Page (2008) treated two adults with conduction aphasia after left hemisphere stroke to improve their naming ability, using an MBD across behaviours. They used an intervention modelled on the Copy and Recall Treatment (CART) which relied upon a cueing hierarchy. Five steps were described, with information about subsequent steps based on the participant's performance:

1 The participant viewed a picture from the training set and was asked, 'Can you tell me what this is?' If the participant verbally produced the word correctly, she was asked to write the word. If the participant wrote the word correctly, the next picture was shown.

2   If the participant was unable to write the word correctly, the written form was shown and the participant copied it three times.
3   The examples were then removed and the participant attempted to write and verbally state the target from memory three times.
4   If the participant was unable to verbally produce the target word or if she produced it incorrectly, she was asked to write the word.
5   If the participant wrote the word correctly, then the next word was presented. If the participant wrote the word incorrectly, then steps 2 and 3 were repeated once.

(Wright et al., 2008, p. 527)

Multiple interventions

A number of designs, such as multiple-treatment WRD and ATD have as their aim the comparison of multiple interventions. Tunnard and Wilson (2014), for example, compared five conditions in treating a man, FP, with severe unilateral spatial neglect after a right hemisphere stroke, in a multiple-treatment design (A-B-A-C-A-D-A-E-A-F). A baseline (A) phase separated each experimental condition: B=musical stimulation, C=anchoring, D=vibratory stimulation, E=limb activation, and F=anchoring and vibratory stimulation combined. Anchoring, for example, was described as involving "the experimenter drawing a thick red line down the left hand side of the test page. F.P. was instructed to look for the red line before beginning the tests" (pp. 387–388). This technique was not used in the other conditions (treatment differentiation): for example "In the passive limb activation condition (D), vibratory stimulation was applied to the lower part of F.P.'s left arm using a MotivAider®. This device was set to vibrate at 10 second intervals, and provided a cue towards the left side" (p. 388).

Modifying existing treatments

In cases where an intervention is adapted from a standard intervention, all adaptations need to be described. The aforementioned study of Wright et al. (2008), for example, adapted the CART, that had been developed to improve spelling and writing skills, and applied it to verbal naming abilities. They described the way in which it was adapted: "Beeson and colleagues [ref] suggested that CART may be an appropriate treatment programme for facilitating verbal naming abilities, and recommended combining verbal repetition with CART to stimulate oral language as well as written language abilities" (p. 523).

Tailoring treatments to individual participants

Hoffman et al. (2014) write of this in relation to group designs, where it is of obvious importance that all members of the same group receive the same intervention. This is not so much an issue in SCEDs, where tailoring treatments to individual participants is virtually the raison d'être of SCED methodology. Nonetheless, when interventions are tailored to the individual, the changes should be explicitly described. Tailoring interventions, is, however, a consideration in SCED methodology in terms of replication (whether using MBD across participants or inter-subject replication in another type of design). Inherent in the notion of replication is that the intervention will be sufficiently similar to the model so that it does not morph into a different intervention.

In summary, the foregoing descriptions reflect a broad approach to the development/application of neurorehabilitation interventions used in SCEDs. It is not intended to represent any specific classification system. Earlier in this chapter we made reference to the important work of Hart and colleagues (Dijkers et al., 2014; Hart et al., 2014), in developing a system "to organize the controlled chaos of rehabilitation interventions" (Hart et al., 2014, p. S33). Their schema proposes that components of interventions are classifiable into mutually exclusive groups:[1] organ functions, skills and habits, and cognitive/affective representations, the last two of which are particularly pertinent to behavioural neurorehabilitation. Their now-entitled Rehabilitation Treatment Specification System (Hart et al., 2018) encapsulates treatment targets (the specific and measurable aspects of functioning that are targeted for change), active ingredients (known or hypothesised elements of interventions that produce change), and hypothesised mechanisms of action (processes underlying the active ingredients responsible for change). As Hart (2017, p. 559) notes, "Understanding what treatments work, and for whom, in remediating the psychological and cognitive effects of brain disorders is critically important for developing more efficient and effective methods and for translating them into widespread use in the clinic", which resonates with using the SCED approach in a clinical setting (see also Chapter 10).

1   Personal communication: Dr Tessa Hart, 18 January 2018.

Materials

Materials, in this context, refer to any resource that will be used to implement and evaluate the intervention. They range from a comprehensive manual through to specific equipment or paper-based materials. These include computers and other machines, software, applications, recording equipment, technological aids, and other devices; stimulus items and recording forms for the practitioner; handouts and worksheets for the participant; tests, questionnaires, ratings scales, and coding sheets for evaluating the effects of the intervention. Hart (2009) observes that the compilation of materials can be time-consuming and may require pilot-testing and refinement. Equipment always needs to be calibrated to ensure that it records accurately.

Written documentation about the intervention in the form of a manual, or at the least a protocol, is essential. This serves multiple purposes and has at least six advantages. First, all relevant parties know the scope of the intervention and what it comprises. Second, a manual is a useful adjunct to training practitioners in the intervention. Third, it assists the practitioner to implement the intervention as planned and intended. Fourth, preparation of reports and other forms of dissemination about the intervention can be written in detail, with clarity, precision, and completeness. Fifth, clinicians reading such published reports will be able to implement a successful intervention more readily. Finally, researchers investigating such interventions will be better equipped to replicate the study.

Intervention manuals need to be explicit (Moncher & Prinz, 1991) and written in an accessible and user-friendly style (Borelli, 2011; Hart, 2009). There is general agreement about the contents of a manual (e.g. Moncher & Prinz, 1991; Perepletchikova, 2014):

- the theoretical basis of the intervention/s;
- definition of the target population and target behaviours;
- the overall structure of the intervention/s;
- procedural details re duration of the intervention/s; number, duration, and frequency of sessions/observation periods; mode of delivery; location;
- a detailed, session-by-session structure and sequencing of techniques;
- specification of standards of practitioner behaviours to be implemented, along with examples of verbal statements to be made;
- specification of proscribed practitioner behaviours (i.e. activities/behaviours/statements that are *not* permitted);

- guidelines for handling deviations;
- materials needed for implementing and evaluating the intervention (for both the practitioner and participant), along with detailed instructions for their use; and
- procedures for monitoring the conditions (both baseline and intervention).

Moncher and Prinz (1991) point to the important balance between structure and flexibility in the composition of manuals – there needs to be sufficient flexibility for the practitioner to adapt the intervention to the needs of the participant when indicated. Hart (2009) goes further and suggests that a critical element is the purpose and type of the intervention. She recommends that manuals with higher specificity are particularly appropriate for time-based interventions that have narrowly focused outcomes/target behaviours. SCED studies generally fall in this category. By contrast, more flexible manuals are suited to general treatment approaches (e.g. counselling interactions). The latter scenario may comprise a toolkit of treatment methods, wherein specific techniques are selected depending on the issue at hand. Moncher and Prinz also make a convincing case for an "intermediate level of specificity, because specifications that are too molecular may present implementers with an overwhelming task and specifications that are too global may offer inadequate guidelines that endanger treatment differentiation" (p. 260).

Procedural details

Detailed information about all the procedures required to implement the intervention (e.g. dosage, mode, and location of delivery) need to be documented in the manual. Dosage, or exposure, refers to the quantity of the intervention that the participant receives and the time frame in which it is in operation. At minimum, information is required about four aspects: duration of the intervention, number of sessions, length of sessions, and frequency or schedule of the sessions.

Additional procedural details include information about the mode of delivery and the location. The mode of delivery may be individual or group-based, alone or in the context of other people, face-to-face or distance (e.g. via phone, email, internet). The setting of the intervention refers to both the general location and the specific environment in which the intervention will occur, which should be described with replicable precision. An example of the latter is provided by LaFrance et al. (2007) who examined the effect of a therapy dog on the communication function of a man with non-fluent aphasia after a left hemisphere stroke:

> the participant was accompanied by the observer who walked to the right and slightly behind the participant's wheelchair. All walks with the participant throughout the duration of these 11 weeks occurred at the same time and on the same day each week at the hospital. All observations used the same route through the centre, from the therapy room on the lower setting of the hospital through a fixed route of hospital corridors back to the ward.
>
> *(LaFrance et al., 2007, p.221)*

A final procedural detail relates to monitoring implementation of all the conditions of the study, an issue related to treatment fidelity (described later). The important point to highlight here is that the standard or quality of implementation should be monitored throughout the course of an intervention, rather than solely being an assessment that occurs at the conclusion of the intervention. This also applies to the baseline condition (i.e. ensuring that a technique related to the active ingredient/s of the intervention is *not* used). Information about how, when, where, and by whom treatment fidelity will be monitored during the course of the study needs to be documented in the manual. This will include not only the specific content that will be monitored, but also the methodological details about when and how it will occur (e.g. direct observation, audio/video taping of sessions for later review, interview, completion of feedback forms) and preparation of any such materials and equipment, along with the location in which it will occur (e.g. direct observations in the field or on the hospital ward, behind a one-way screen).

Practitioner competence

Practitioners need to be qualified and competent to deliver the intervention. Yet, in many situations, the intervention is implemented by other people who do not necessarily have the qualifications and specialist training in the particular intervention (e.g. a nurse implementing physical therapy exercises on the ward; a family member providing a behaviour support programme). In this case, they act in loco of the practitioner and should receive ongoing guidance from the practitioner. In all cases, the person implementing the intervention (or components of it), whether the practitioner or other person, needs to be adequately skilled and competent. Skill and competency can be achieved with training.

The study of Hickey, Bourgeois, and Olswang (2004) is an example of teaching non-professionals to implement an intervention. They trained university students in a communication sciences course to converse with nursing home residents with aphasia:

> The SVs [student volunteers] received training three times per week to increase their use of multi-modality communication in conversations with the RAs [residents with aphasia]. The experimenter (EH), a certified speech-language pathologist, administered the training, using a manual and data collection sheets to keep the training consistent [refs]. The training included five steps: (1) general education . . . (5) conversational practice of multi-modality communication without on-line feedback. Progress through the training was determined using a criterion for each step of the programme. (The detailed training manual is available from the first author.)
>
> *(Hickey et al., 2004, p.627-628)*

It is recommended that training is versatile (Moncher & Prinz, 1991; King & Bosworth, 2014). A training manual is critical, but by itself is insufficient. Other training methods include didactic sessions, role-play, modelling, rehearsal, feedback, supervision sessions, group meetings, and periodic booster sessions for skill maintenance (Moncher & Prinz, 1991; Perepletchikova & Kazdin, 2005). Following training, competency needs to be assessed using a "well-defined, a priori performance criterion" (Borelli, 2011, p. S56), which may involve knowledge assessment and observing the trainee's performance in the intervention. A valuable method of ongoing competency assessment will be in the form of evaluating treatment adherence throughout the course of the intervention. This also assists to rein in any 'therapist drift', a phenomenon Peterson, Homer, and Wonderlick (1982) describe as the intervention gradually altering over time due to changes in practitioner behaviour – whether becoming lax with timing and techniques, or adding other techniques that are not part of the protocol.

Training should go beyond the concrete content of the intervention. Competence also encompasses qualitative features, such as practitioner attitudes to the intervention, their motivation, and interactional style: a warm and engaging manner is likely to be well received by the participant, and assist in his/her engagement. Participants, particularly those with acquired brain impairment, can be difficult to engage, and this can be a challenge for practitioners. Several authors have made the point that treatment adherence can actually be high, but the quality of the intervention low due to practitioner factors, such as the way in which the intervention is delivered, which may jeopardise the effect of the treatment (Bumbarger, 2014; Gresham, 2014).

Finally, all interventions need to be implemented in a manner that meets ethical standards and standards of conduct (see Mechling, Gast, & Lane, 2014), with due regard to risks and harms. The Mechling et al. chapter provides helpful direction for conducting SCED research within a framework of ethical principles. All professional associations have codes of conduct and ethical behaviour with respect to research practices, with which investigators and all personnel involved in a SCED study need to be familiar. The chief investigator is responsible for the overall conduct of the study, but all other personnel involved also have obligations and responsibility for ethical behaviour. Such codes of conduct are written in strong language, which leave no room for ambiguity. Paramount among the clauses are always those to the effect of using 'stringent safeguards' to protect rights of participants.

Many participants with acquired brain impairment are vulnerable, and some may not have capacity to provide informed consent. The SCRIBE Statement (Tate et al., 2016a, 2016b) notes that although formal ethical approval to conduct a SCED is almost always required when the study is conducted within a research framework, such approval may not be necessary in some clinical situations. Nonetheless, the SCRIBE states that informed written consent from the participant is always required, and in the case where the participant is unable to provide consent (e.g. a minor or person legally unable to provide consent), a legal guardian needs to provide consent and the participant's assent also needs to be obtained. Participants are always entitled to withdraw from a study at any time for any reason.

Mechling et al. (2014) also make reference to affirming procedures, originally described by Bailey and Burch (2005), which investigators and practitioners should embrace:

- practice within your area of expertise, aiming 'to do no harm';
- respect the participant's autonomy and promote self-efficacy;
- use goals that are valued by participants;

- be fair and truthful;
- treat others with dignity and respect; care and compassion; and
- accept responsibility for your own behaviour.

Treatment fidelity

What is treatment fidelity?

Treatment fidelity is not about whether the intervention is effective – treatment effectiveness is what the research study will determine. Treatment fidelity is a multi-dimensional construct, defined as "the extent to which essential intervention components are delivered in a comprehensive and consistent manner by an interventionist trained to deliver the intervention" (Sanetti & Kratochwill, 2009, p. 448). Accordingly, treatment fidelity comprises three components: treatment differentiation, practitioner competence, and treatment adherence (Perepletchikova & Kazdin, 2005; Sanetti & Kractochwill, 2009).

In the previous sections of this chapter we discussed issues pertaining to the definition of the intervention and treatment differentiation, along with practitioner competence, which are two of the three components comprising treatment fidelity. In this section, we focus on the third component, treatment adherence; that is, how the independent variable is implemented, such that it does not depart from protocol. First, we consider definitional issues, then ways in which the independent variable can be compromised and enhanced, and finally the measurement of treatment adherence.

A note on terminology in this area – it is confusing. Not only are multiple terms used to refer to the same construct, but also one term in particular, treatment integrity, is used in two different ways. Treatment integrity is often used in a broad sense (similar to treatment fidelity) to encompass that field of study, but it is also used in a narrow context (similar to treatment adherence) to refer to the intervention being implemented as intended. In order to avoid confusion, we do not use the term treatment integrity, and instead use treatment fidelity to refer to the field in general, and treatment adherence to refer to the intervention being implemented as intended.

Another term, procedural fidelity, is also used in this area. It refers to all conditions of a research design, including the control/baseline condition. Because the control/baseline condition does not have a treatment per se (disregarding the concept of 'usual care'), the term procedural fidelity does serve as a useful reminder that fidelity needs to be monitored and assessed in all conditions, not just in the 'treatment' condition (Ledford, Wolery, & Gast, 2014). Indeed, Ledford and colleagues make the excellent point that if fidelity data are only collected in the intervention phases, then this is sufficient to demonstrate adherence, but not treatment differentiation. Hence, although the term procedural fidelity is probably the most apposite term of all, *treatment* fidelity/integrity is so entrenched in the literature, that *procedural* fidelity/integrity is unlikely to gain traction.

Concerns about treatment adherence in particular are long-standing and emerged in the behavioural intervention literature of the 1970s and 1980s. Peterson et al. (1982, p. 478) highlighted "a curious double standard" in that review of the literature indicated a general dissatisfaction with the assessment of the independent variable. Yet, this contrasted with the detailed attention given to issues involving the reliable and accurate measurement of the dependent variable, including observer reactivity, observer bias, observer drift, observational complexity, sources of inflating observer reliability estimates, and so forth. Regrettably, this disparity between the careful attention paid to the dependent variable and the concomitant disregard of the independent variable continues to occur in the extant literature (as demonstrated in the review of van Heugten et al., 2012). Moreover, evidence suggests that treatment adherence in the behavioural health literature is poor. Borelli et al. (2005) found that only 27% of articles described methods to evaluate treatment adherence. This figure, however, does not distinguish between those studies that did versus those that did not meet an acceptable standard of adherence, and one can assume that fewer studies would meet performance criteria. When this was addressed, as in the study of Perepletchikova, Treat, and Kazdin (2005), it was found to be the case: only 3.5% of articles were classified as adequately implementing treatment adherence.

Knowing about treatment adherence is of the utmost importance. Without it, "both internal and external validity are compromised, and professionals cannot assume that the treatment is responsible for changes in behavior (internal validity) or that treatment can be generalized to other settings (external validity)" (McGivern & Walter, 2014, p. 233). More specifically, if Intervention X is not implemented as intended, then what is actually evaluated in the research study is Intervention X+Y if additional components are added (or X-Y, if components are omitted). If the findings of the study show significant improvement in the target behaviour at the conclusion of the study, we would erroneously conclude that Intervention X was an effective treatment, whereas because it was Intervention X+Y (or X-Y) that was implemented, the result actually pertains to Intervention X+Y (or X-Y, as the case may be). Conversely, if the results of the study show no improvement in the target behaviour after the intervention, then we conclude that Intervention X is not an effective treatment. But again, such a conclusion does not follow, because what was evaluated was not Intervention X, but rather Intervention X+Y (or X-Y). Both errors are costly. In the first scenario, an ineffective intervention may be advocated and implemented in practice settings. In the second scenario, a potentially effective intervention will almost certainly not be implemented (or even possibly considered for further research).

Ways in which the independent variable is compromised and how to enhance fidelity

Perepletchikova and Kazdin (2005) identify three sources which are prime candidates for compromising the integrity of the independent variable: the intervention, the practitioner, and the participant. In terms of the intervention itself, they enumerate six factors that may contribute to independent variable vulnerability and poor fidelity: complexity of the intervention, resources and materials, number of interventionists (both practitioners and others who may be involved in implementing the intervention), time needed to implement the intervention, rate of change, and acceptability of treatments by practitioners and participants.

Two practitioner factors that may compromise the independent variable fidelity include (i) their motivation to engage with a particular participant who may be difficult to work with (see below) and (ii) their clinical experience. Perepletchikova and Kazdin (2005) make the counter-intuitive suggestion that highly experienced practitioners may not, in fact, be the best adherers to protocol. They may have "solidified therapists' working styles" which can cause a barrier to new learning. Moreover, because more experienced practitioners are likely to be skilled in multiple therapeutic techniques, they may be more susceptible to 'therapist drift' and incorporate techniques other than those prescribed. That said, however, practitioners do need to be trained in the skills and techniques required for the intervention so that they meet the necessary standard of competence.

Several participant factors may contribute to low intervention adherence. Individual differences will likely be encountered with respect to problem severity and duration, comorbidities, and responses and interactions (e.g. resistance, defensiveness, hostility, negativity). Within the neurorehabilitation context, other factors will operate, such as coexisting cognitive (e.g. in attention, memory, awareness, communication, executive function) and/or noncognitive (e.g. affective, psychiatric, fatigue, pain, sensory-motor) impairments, activity limitations, participation restrictions, personal and environmental factors. A number of authors have discussed effective instructional strategies and how to adapt interventions so that they are suitable for people with acquired brain impairment (Ehlhardt et al., 2008; Hart, 2009; Khan-Bourne & Brown, 2003; Ownsworth & Gracey, 2017; Sohlberg & Turkstra, 2011).

Standardising aspects of the intervention prior to implementation can overcome many of these barriers. Standardising the development of manuals and ensuring practitioners are trained and competent were covered in the previous two sections of this chapter. Careful planning prior to commencing the intervention provides a foundation to maximise treatment fidelity. Bumbarger (2014) proffers the following six areas for consideration:

- careful programme selection decisions;
- develop a deep understanding of the intervention;
- assess readiness for implementation;
- engage in formal pre-implementation planning;
- develop an infrastructure to support continuous quality improvement, including coaching and monitoring, peer support and reflective practice, safe avenues for giving and receiving feedback; and
- frame programmes in a larger public health context.

Measuring treatment adherence

Treatment adherence can be measured indirectly and directly (Gresham, 2014; Perepletchikova, 2014). Indirect measures include self-report, rating scales, and interviews with the practitioner and/or participant about what was done. But investigator and participant reactivity (e.g. demand characteristics of indirect measurement and pressure to provide socially desirable responses) may compromise reliability and accuracy, thereby calling the result into question.

Direct measures of treatment adherence are regarded as the gold standard. They comprise actual observations of practitioner behaviour, which may be obtained through observation (e.g. one-way mirrors, audio/video taping of sessions/observation periods). Although more labour-intensive than indirect measures, direct measures provide more objective data. Perepletchikova (2014) emphasises the importance of using representative sessions from which to evaluate treatment adherence, which may be achieved by evaluating all sessions (as in the example below), or selecting a random sample. It is not only the sessions (including A and B phases) that need to be representative, however, but also the therapists, situations, and participants (if there are more than one). Raters of treatment adherence need to be trained, and Perepletchikova suggests that the most suitable raters are likely to be those who also have competence in the specific intervention techniques themselves.

In developing the treatment adherence item for our critical appraisal scale for single-case reports, the Risk of Bias in N-of-1 Trials Scale (Tate et al., 2013a; see Chapter 2 in this book), we sought to identify adequate standards of treatment adherence. We used a direct method, with four criteria: (i) use of an independent rater who is not the practitioner, participant, or someone with a personal relationship with the participant (e.g. family member, friend); (ii) a specified protocol against which adherence is evaluated; (iii) adherence sampled from at least 20% of sessions; and (iv) adherence being at least 80%. Adherence is calculated with the following formula:

$$\frac{\textit{number of times an agreement is recorded between the rater's observation and the protocol}}{(\textit{number of agreements}) + (\textit{number of disagreements})} \times 100$$

An example of describing treatment adherence in a study is provided by Guercio et al. (2012), who evaluated treatment adherence in their study of problem gambling behaviour described earlier in this chapter:

> The integrity of the treatment training package was evaluated via audiotaped assessment of each of the eight sessions presented in the CBT [cognitive-behaviour therapy] component of the treatment package . . . The primary investigator and a trained graduate student coded the tapes using a reliability form that contained all of the elements of each week's therapeutic protocol to determine that the delivery of the independent variable was consistent

with the elements of the treatment package. Specifically, each individual was given a checklist that contained the active treatment component labels (Table 1) and was asked to score a 'yes' or 'no' as to whether this topic was covered by the therapist during the session. The independent integrity variable score for all eight sessions for Shiloh was 98% (range, 86% to 100%).

(Guercio et al., 2012, p.490)

Finally, a caveat about evaluating treatment adherence: low treatment adherence does not necessarily mean that the intervention is weak; it may simply be that the intervention implemented was not the one that was intended (Perepletchikova, 2014). Although this needs to be taken into account in interpreting the data, it does not detract from the main message regarding the critical importance of evaluating and striving for high levels of treatment adherence.

Concluding remarks

As will be evident from this chapter, rehabilitation interventions are not described as 'complex' without reason. A lot of effort and expertise needs to be expended in designing and implementing interventions in the neurorehabilitation field. The aim of this chapter was to draw multiple disparate threads together and provide guidance in the steps that need to be undertaken regarding the intervention/s, from initial conceptualisation through to evaluating the adequacy with which the intervention is implemented, with due regard to practitioner and participant factors.

5

WITHDRAWAL/REVERSAL DESIGNS

This and the following three chapters discuss four of the most commonly used designs in single-case research. In this chapter, the focus is on withdrawal/reversal designs (WRDs). Chapter 6 deals with multiple baseline designs (MBDs), Chapter 7 with alternating-treatments designs (ATDs), and Chapter 8 with changing-criterion designs (CCDs). The content format of each of these chapters is similar. First, the rationale and basic structure of each design is described. Then, the features that the design must incorporate in order to meet evidence standards (see Chapter 1) are reviewed, and threats to internal validity and strategies for addressing them are discussed. We describe common types and variants of a design, illustrate their application using examples drawn from the neurorehabilitation literature and consider the advantages and disadvantages of the designs.

The discussion of SCEDs in this and the following three chapters focuses on what might be called the 'architecture' of the design. That is, how baseline and intervention phases are structured and sequenced in order to investigate the effectiveness of the intervention. It is important to keep in mind, however, that in the broader sense, the design of single-case studies goes beyond this architecture. Other components of the overall design when the study is being planned include precise stipulation of the content and method of delivery of the intervention (independent variable; see Chapter 4), as well as duration and frequency of intervention and baseline sessions, clear-cut operational definitions of the target behaviour (dependent variable) and other relevant outcome measures, how they are to be measured, recorded, evaluated, and by whom (see Chapter 3). Adequate planning and formulation of all these other elements of the design will ensure that threats to internal validity are well controlled and risk of bias is minimised (see Chapter 2).

A brief note on terminology

The term WRDs encompasses two design types: withdrawal designs (WDs) and reversal designs (RDs). Although closely related structurally, and sharing the same fundamental rationale (Kazdin, 2011), they differ in important ways.[1] The distinction between the two is not often explicitly made, and the terms *withdrawal* and *reversal* tend to be used interchangeably, but inaccurately (Wine, Freeman, & King, 2015). The label 'withdrawal/reversal design' is used in many studies to describe designs that are, strictly speaking, withdrawal, not reversal designs. The confusion is, at least in part, arguably attributable to the initial description of withdrawal designs by Baer, Wolf, and Risley (1968). They referred to WDs as "the 'reversal' technique" (p. 94) because, they argued, any changes in the target behaviour caused by the intervention should be lost or *reversed* when the intervention was withdrawn and conditions *revert* to baseline. In other words, terms such as reverse or revert to baseline used in the context of a WD are confused with a RD. In this and other chapters we avoid use of both these terms, and instead use the term "return" to baseline. In the next sections we discuss the rationale of WDs, and later describe RDs, highlighting the difference between the two.

Rationale of withdrawal designs

The architecture of WDs consists of a sequence of interspersed A phases (baseline) and B phases (intervention) and its rationale was first described by Sidman (1960). The intervention is systematically introduced and withdrawn at different points in time during the study such that when an intervention phase is terminated, conditions return to baseline and so, presumably, does the target behaviour. Baer et al. (1968) described WDs as follows: "Here a behavior is

---

1   The same rationale also underlies the multiple-treatment designs discussed in a later section of this chapter.

measured, and the measure is examined over time until its stability is clear. Then, the experimental variable is applied. The behavior continues to be measured, to see if the variable will produce a behavioral change. If it does, the experimental variable is discontinued or altered, to see if the behavioral change just brought about depends on it" (p. 94). This encapsulates the basic rationale of WDs (and is also applicable to other types of SCEDs): intervention effects are evaluated relative to baseline performance.

Ideally, the initial A phase baseline is continued until measures of the target behaviour are stable. Baseline data then serve as a predictor of future target behaviour; that is, what can be expected if the target behaviour were left untreated. An intervention phase is then introduced, and measures of the target behaviour are compared with those obtained during the baseline phase. The effectiveness of the intervention is evaluated by examining the extent to which measures of the target behaviour differ from the pattern predicted by the baseline data (Barlow et al., 2009; Kazdin, 2011). The logic of WDs (indeed of all SCEDs) is based on consistent replication of the experimental effect; in other words, the effect of the intervention. Experimental control in WDs relies on intra-subject replication of the experimental effect. The experimental effect (i.e. effectiveness of the intervention, or lack of it) is evaluated by determining what happens to the target behaviour when the intervention is systematically introduced (i.e. changes in the expected direction) or withdrawn (i.e. return to baseline levels).

It is important to keep in mind that WDs should only be used when the intervention can be meaningfully withdrawn. They should not be used if the target behaviour is unlikely to return to baseline levels when the intervention is withdrawn (Barlow et al., 2009; Kazdin, 2011; Kratochwill et al., 2010). If, for example, the intervention under investigation consists of teaching the participant a strategy or skill to address the target behaviour (e.g. turn-taking in conversation), then once the strategy has been learned (internalised), it cannot be readily un-learned. In such instances, either MBDs (see Chapter 6) or CCDs (see Chapter 8) can be considered.

Evidence standards and internal validity

In order to meet standards of evidence each phase in WDs must have at least 5 data points (Design Standard 4; Kratochwill et al., 2013), and needs to incorporate at least four phases in order to provide three opportunities for intra-subject replication of the experimental effect (Design Standard 3). Designs with at least 3 data points per phase and at least four phases (i.e. at least three intra-subject replications of the experimental effect) meet standards with reservations.

Intra-subject replication of the experimental effect provides the means to evaluate and control for threats to internal validity. If the target behaviour changes in the predicted direction, relative to baseline *each time* the intervention is introduced and then returns to baseline *each time* that the intervention is withdrawn, it is unlikely that these changes can be attributed to either history or maturation (i. e. threats to internal validity). It is possible, however, that changes (or lack thereof) in the target behaviour when the intervention is introduced or withdrawn coincide with events in the participant's circumstances (history), such as moving residence, illness in a family member, or winning the lottery. Consequently, observed changes in the target behaviour cannot be exclusively attributed to the intervention. Similarly, events related to changes occurring within the individual (maturation), such as natural recovery or cyclical physiological processes, may also coincide with the introduction and/or withdrawal of the intervention. This would also raise the possibility that these extraneous factors, not the intervention, may account for observed changes in the target behaviour. The possible effects of history and maturation are, however, unlikely to coincide with *every occasion* that the intervention is introduced/withdrawn. Therefore, if the target behaviour consistently and repeatedly changes in the predicted direction *every time* the intervention is introduced and withdrawn, there is less probability that these changes are attributable to extraneous factors. Ascribing behaviour change to the intervention effect then becomes increasingly more plausible, particularly as the number of intra-subject replications increases.

Types of withdrawal designs

A-B designs

A-B designs are "in principle the irreducible unit of single subject research design" (Parsonson & Baer, 2015, p. 36). They consist of just two phases. The first is a baseline phase (A) during which the target behaviour is continuously and frequently measured (Figure 5.1). As noted above, this establishes the natural pattern of the target behaviour which serves to predict its future pattern if it were left untreated. The intervention is then introduced (phase B) during

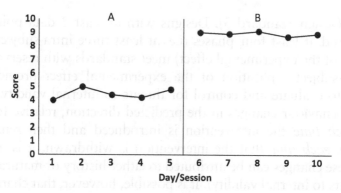

FIGURE 5.1 Hypothetical data for an A-B design

which the target behaviour is also continuously and frequently measured under controlled conditions. Data from the intervention phase are then compared to data from the baseline phase to determine if the intervention has changed the target behaviour in the expected direction.

Strictly speaking, A-B designs are not WDs, given that the intervention is only introduced once and is not subsequently withdrawn. Their main disadvantage is that even if each of the phases contain at least 5 data points, A-B designs cannot meet evidence standards because they provide only one opportunity (the change from A to B) to demonstrate the experimental effect. Control for threats to internal validity is poor. Consequently, A-B designs cannot be used to establish a functional (cause and effect) relationship between the target behaviour and the intervention. At best, A-B designs can be considered pre-experimental designs that demonstrate a correlation but not a causal relationship between the independent and dependent variables (Barlow et al., 2009; Byiers, Reichle, & Symons 2012; Gast & Baekey, 2014). They can, however be utilised in an exploratory manner to evaluate untried but potentially useful, interventions.

Douglas et al. (2014) used an A-B design with follow-up to improve communication-specific coping in two adults with traumatic brain injury. They used a novel communication-specific coping intervention (the CommCope-I programme) that incorporated strategies and principles from cognitive-behaviour therapy and context sensitive social communication therapy. The study consisted of a three-session baseline (phase A) for one participant and four sessions for the other. The intervention (phase B) involved twice-weekly sessions for six weeks. Both participants showed a change in the target behaviour (score on the Discourse Coping Scale) that reflected an improvement in communication coping skills. The investigators concluded that "The results of this study provide sound proof of concept support for the CommCope-I programme" (p. 199). The Douglas et al. study also illustrates an advantage of A-B designs, and that is that they can be utilised to investigate the effectiveness of interventions that are not withdrawable. The design can also include a post-intervention follow-up phase, as did the Douglas et al. study, to determine if the intervention effect has persisted. Follow-up at one week and one and three months post-intervention showed this to be the case.

A-B-A designs

Barlow et al. (2009) refer to A-B-A designs as the prototype of SCEDs. It is a straight-forward extension of the A-B design: a second baseline phase is added after the intervention phase (Figure 5.2). Like the A-B design, the A-B-A design allows the investigator to determine whether or not introducing the intervention affects the target behaviour in the hypothesised direction. Adding a second baseline phase after the intervention phase, makes it possible to determine whether or not the target behaviour returns to baseline conditions after the intervention is withdrawn.

Kazdin (2011) points out that the second A phase in an A-B-A design fulfils two related purposes. First, the B phase serves to predict what the target behaviour would be like in the future if it continued to be treated. By collecting data in the second A phase, we can ascertain if the target behaviour remains the same as it was during the intervention phase. If it does not and returns to the level of the first baseline, this suggests that intervention has had an effect. Second, if the target behaviour during

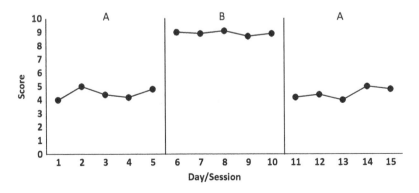

FIGURE 5.2 Hypothetical data for an A-B-A design

the second baseline returns to the level during the first baseline, it confirms the prediction made on the basis of data from the first baseline. That is, what the target behaviour would be like if untreated.

Experimental control is better in A-B-A than A-B designs because A-B-A designs provide two opportunities to demonstrate the experimental effect: in the first phase change from A to B and in the second phase change from B to A. Although on the critical appraisal RoBiNT Scale (Tate et al., 2013a; see Chapter 2 in this book), the A-B-A design is regarded as offering some limited experimental control (Item 1: Design criterion score of 1), they are not deemed to meet evidence standards given that there are insufficient opportunities to demonstrate the experimental effect (Kratochwill et al., 2013). Nonetheless, A-B-A designs allow conclusions about the effect of the intervention to be made with more certitude than is possible with A-B designs. If the target behaviour (i) changes in the predicted direction during the intervention and (ii) also changes in the predicted direction when the intervention is withdrawn, it is less likely that intervention effects may be attributable to extraneous factors such as maturation, history, or natural cyclic variation in the target behaviour (Gast & Baekey, 2014).

Klarborg et al. (2012) used an A-B-A design to evaluate the effectiveness of an intervention aimed at reducing driving speed in two adults with acquired brain injury. An assistive device was installed in the car to monitor driving speed and percentage of distance driven above (PDA) the speed limit was recorded. During the initial baseline (six weeks), the driver did not receive any alerts when the speed limit was breached. In the intervention phase (12 weeks) a voice message alerted driver if he/she drove over the speed limit. This was followed by a second baseline (12 weeks) during which the driver did not, again, receive any alerts. Data for the first participant in the study (GJ, a woman who had meningitis nine years earlier) presented in Figure 5.3 show that the intervention was effective. During the first baseline GJ's mean PDA was 8.7% and decreased to 2.4% when the intervention was introduced. After the intervention was withdrawn, GJ's mean PDA increased to 17.4% during the second baseline, returning to and surpassing initial baseline levels. The intervention effect was comparable for the other study participant.

The A-B-A design has been criticised because it ends in a baseline phase (Kazdin, 2011). The argument posited is that if the intervention has made the participant better, then returning the target behaviour to a baseline level at the end of the study is

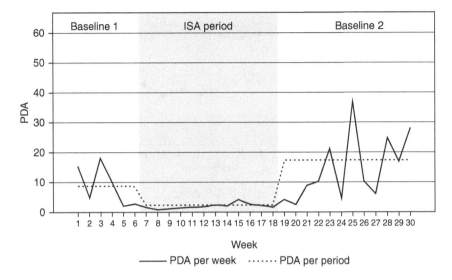

FIGURE 5.3 Driving data for participant GJ
Notes: PDA=percentage of distance driven above speed limit. Solid line shows PDA for each week of the study. Dotted line shows mean PDA for each phase
Source: Klarborg, Lahrmann, Agerholm, Tradisauskas, and Harms (2012); reprinted with permission

unethical, because it amounts to making the participant worse. The B-A-B design (an important variant of the A-B-A design) offers a way to address these concerns and is considered to be clinically superior to the A-B-A design because it begins and ends with a treatment phase (Barlow et al., 2009). Moreover, B-A-B designs are also appropriate when it might be unethical to hold back introducing the intervention until a baseline phase has been completed. For example, the situation where the target behaviour that needs to be treated may put the participant, or those around her/him, in danger or causes severe distress for the participant (e.g. self-harming). The shortcoming of these designs is that because the target behaviour has already been treated, the A phase cannot, strictly speaking, be used to directly ascertain the effect of the intervention on the natural pattern of the target behaviour.

A-B-A-B designs

A-B-A-B designs are, simply, extensions of the A-B-A design (Figure 5.4). After an initial baseline phase, an intervention phase is

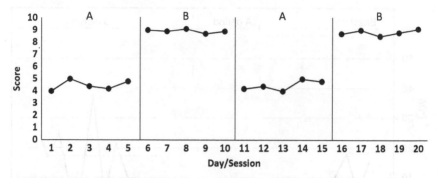

FIGURE 5.4 Hypothetical data for an A-B-A-B design

introduced. The intervention is then withdrawn, and a second base-line phase is commenced. Following the second baseline phase, the intervention is reintroduced. The same rationale that underpins A-B and A-B-A designs is applicable to A-B-A-B designs. That is, the pattern of the untreated target behaviour is established in the first A phase and this is compared with the pattern of the target behaviour during the first intervention phase. Data from the second A phase serve to determine whether or not the pattern of the target behaviour changes in the expected direction when the intervention is with-drawn. The second intervention phase serves to determine if changes comparable to and consistent with the changes observed in the target behaviour when the intervention was introduced after the initial baseline also occur when the intervention is reintroduced.

The primary advantage that A-B-A-B designs offer is that by having an additional intervention phase, they incorporate more systematic, intra-subject replication of the experimental effect. Consequently, if there are 5 data points in each phase, these designs meet the criterion for adequate experimental control (Kra-tochwill et al., 2013). For this reason, if other threats to internal validity are well controlled, A-B-A-B designs can demonstrate a cause–effect (i.e. functional) relationship between the intervention and any observed changes in the target behaviour. The design could, in theory, be extended to include additional phases, for example A-B-A-B-A-B-A-B, to further augment experimental con-trol, although in reality, this may not be practicable.

An example of an A-B-A-B design is that of Tasky et al. (2008) who examined the effect of choice on the ability of three adult women with traumatic brain injury to stay on-task, which they defined as "physical contact with one or more objects in a manner that could result in completion of a task" (p. 262). The occurrence of the target behaviour was recorded in the last 10 seconds of every 5-minute interval during a 30-minute session.[2] They used an A-B-A-B design and the results of their study are shown in Figure 5.5. In the initial baseline participants had to complete three randomly assigned common tasks (e.g. make a bed) in a set order. During the intervention phases participants could choose which tasks to complete and in what order. The second baseline phase was a yoked-control condition in which each participant was assigned the same tasks she had selected for the first intervention phase. The yoked condition provided another approach to evaluate if being able to choose the task, rather than task difficulty or preference for that task, influenced on-task time. As Figure 5.5 shows, the percentage of intervals with on-task behaviour increased relative to baseline during the first intervention phase for all three participants, then returned to baseline when the intervention was withdrawn and substantially increased when the intervention was reintroduced. In addition to using a design that controlled well for threats to internal validity, inter-subject replication of the experimental effect in Tasky's study also provided evidence for external validity.

Multiple-treatment designs

Multiple-treatment designs are variants of A-B-A-B designs that are used to compare and evaluate more than one intervention on the same participant (Birnbauer, Peterson, & Solnick, 1974). For example, an investigator wishing to compare the relative effectiveness of intervention B and intervention C, could use an A-B-C-B-C-A design. Multiple-treatment designs may also include interventions that are administered singly or in combination. For example, the phase sequence in the design might be A-B-A-C-A-BC-A, where phases B and C indicate administration of a single intervention and the BC phase indicates that the two interventions are administered simultaneously.

Like other SCEDs, multiple-treatment designs must provide at least three opportunities to demonstrate the experimental effect (Design Standard 3; Kratochwill et al., 2013). Because this involves evaluating changes that may occur *between the same phase pairs,* the sequence of, and component phases in a multiple-treatment design

---

2   The momentary time-sampling technique is described in Chapter 3.

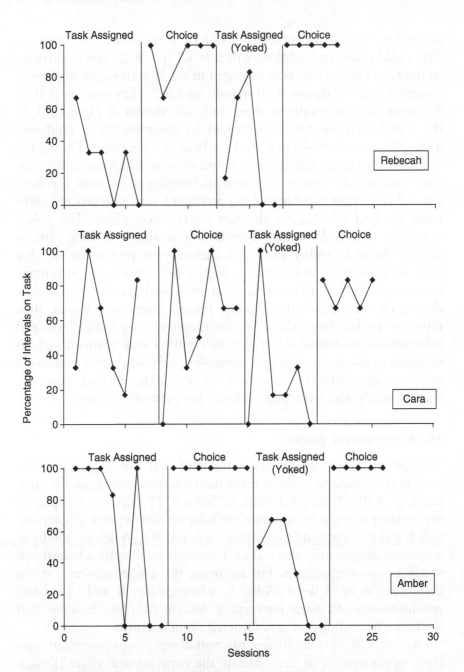

FIGURE 5.5 Percentage of intervals in which on-task behaviour occurred for each of the three participants in the study

Note: The Task Assigned and Task Assigned (Yoked) phases are baseline A-phases and the Choice phases are intervention B-phases

Source: Tasky, Rudrud, Schulze, and Rapp (2008); reprinted with permission

define the functional relationships that can be established. For example, an A-B-C-B-C-A design provides three opportunities to demonstrate the experimental effect, but only in terms of interventions B and C: (1) at phase change two/three from B→C; (2) at phase change three/four from C→B; and (3) at phase change four/five from B→C. Consequently, the design meets Design Standard 3 in terms of effectiveness of intervention B *relative to* intervention C. It does not, however, meet Design Standard 3 in terms of establishing the absolute effectiveness of either intervention B or C compared with baseline conditions. In order to do so the design would also have to incorporate at least three A→B/B→A phase changes as well as three A→C/C→A phase changes, which would make for a lengthy and rather unwieldy design.

The same threats to internal validity that apply to WDs also apply to multiple-treatment designs. In addition, these designs are vulnerable to the effects of multi-treatment interference; that is, the effect that intervention B may have on intervention C when they are administered to the same participant. Barlow and Hayes (1979) identified two types of multi-treatment interference applicable to multiple-treatment designs: sequential confounding and carry-over effects.[3] According to Hains and Baer (1989), however, the distinction between the two is perhaps a case of hair-splitting, because what is really at issue is the confounding effect of treatment sequence. Sequential confounding effects refer to the possibility that the *order* in which the interventions are implemented may affect the effectiveness of either or both of interventions. For example, the effect of intervention B may be enhanced or diminished *because* it is followed (or preceded) by intervention C (Wolery, Gast, & Ledford, 2014). Sequential confounding effects are addressed by either counterbalancing or randomising the intervention sequence and administering each sequence to a different participant (Barlow & Hayes, 1979; Barlow et al., 2009; Wolery et al., 2014). Counterbalancing (or randomising) the phase sequence serves to reveal, but not eradicate sequence effects. Hains and Baer argue that they are inevitable, but not necessarily disadvantageous. For example, it might well be that an intervention is effective, (or more effective) precisely because it is preceded or followed by a different

3   Multi-treatment interference is also a concern for ATDs, and for these designs, Barlow and Hayes also identified another possible confounder: alternation effects. See Chapter 7.

intervention. On the other hand, carry-over effects refer to "the influence of one treatment on an adjacent treatment, irrespective of overall sequencing" (Barlow & Hersen, 1984, p.257).

Wolery et al. (2014) suggest that multiple-treatment designs are not suitable to evaluate interventions designed to teach the participant new behaviours that are not already within their behavioural repertoire. Moreover, because they often include more phases than A-B-A-B designs, they require a longer time to implement. This increases exposure to threats to internal validity over longer periods. In addition, there might not be sufficient replications of the experimental effect for all the interventions to meet standards of evidence and enable the absolute (rather than the relative) effect to be reliably evaluated. That is, there might be sufficient replications to demonstrate that intervention B is more effective than intervention C, but it may not be possible to reliably demonstrate that either intervention is superior to no treatment.

A multiple-treatment design was used by Valle Padilla et al. (2013) to reduce the frequency of dementia-driven wandering in an 80-year-old man with a diagnosis of presumptive Alzheimer's disease. The target behaviour was the frequency of escape attempts from the adult day care centre the participant attended. An A-B-A-C-A-B-BC-B design was used to compare the effectiveness of environmental barriers (intervention B), cognitive training with differential reinforcement (intervention C), and a combination of both interventions (BC). In the baseline phase (A) escape attempts were not prevented. The first intervention (B) consisted of taping black plastic strips on the floor in front of the exit door and on the door's glass panel. The second intervention (C) consisted of differential reinforcement (verbal praise/physical contact) of incompatible behaviours (e.g. talking to other residents). The results of the study are shown in Figure 5.6. The data clearly demonstrate that there was a high frequency of escape attempts (between 20 and 42 per session) when there was no intervention (A phases). When intervention B was introduced, the frequency of escape attempts was significantly reduced (less than 10 per session). With a return to baseline conditions in the next phase, the frequency of escape attempts increased to near initial baseline levels. When intervention C was introduced in the next phase, the frequency of escape attempts was dramatically reduced once more (between 2 and zero). Upon withdrawal of intervention C, escape frequency again increased to a level comparable to that of the previous baselines. Reinstating intervention B drastically

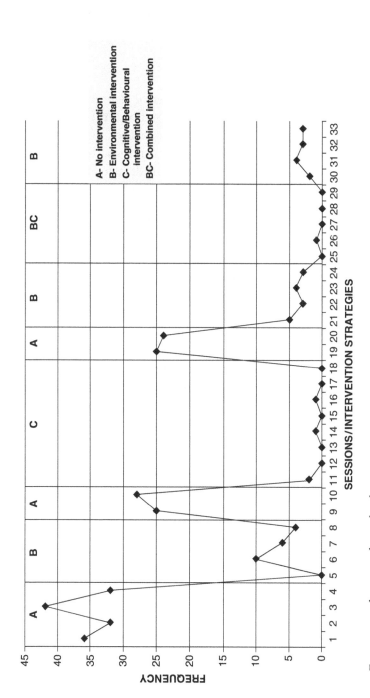

FIGURE 5.6 Frequency of escapes from the day care centre

Notes: A=no intervention; B=environmental barriers; C=cognitive training; BC=combined B and C interventions

Source: Valle Padilla, Daza González, Fernández Agis, Strizzi, and Alarcón Rodríguez (2013); reprinted with permission

reduced the frequency of escape attempts, as did combining the two interventions.

Rationale of reversal designs

The distinction between withdrawal and reversal designs was introduced by Leitenberg (1973). The structure of both WDs and RDs designs consists of a single, linear sequence of phases that constitute different conditions, either baselines or interventions. In WDs, the intervention is introduced and subsequently withdrawn so that conditions *return to baseline* (i.e. no intervention). The intervention continues to be applied to the same target behaviour and the experimental effect is demonstrated if the target behaviour *also returns to baseline levels*. By contrast, in RDs, the intervention is applied to one target behaviour (TB1), and then in the following intervention phase applied to another target behaviour (TB2) that is (usually) incompatible with the first target behaviour (Barlow et al., 2009; Gast & Beakey, 2014). That is, in RDs the intervention is never withdrawn, but its application to a given target behaviour is *reversed*, such that it is applied to a different (and incompatible) target behaviour in the next phase (Figure 5.7).[4] Although RDs are well suited for investigating interventions that are based on an operant conditioning paradigm, they are not often used in applied behavioural research (Barlow et al.; Gast and Beakey).

Kratochwill and colleagues (2010; 2013) do not discuss RDs and it is a moot point as to whether or not the evidence standards they propose for WDs are also applicable to RDs. Presumably, each phase in RDs that is used to demonstrate the experimental effect is also required to have at least 5 data points (Design Standard 4). It would seem reasonable to assume that the intervention effect needs to be demonstrated separately for each target behaviour. A design such as A-B_{TB1}-A-B_{TB2}-A-B_{TB1}-A-B_{TB2} would provide four opportunities to demonstrate the intervention effect on one target behaviour (i.e. A→B_{TB1}, B_{TB1}→A, A→B_{TB1} and B_{TB1}→A) and three opportunities to demonstrate it on the other (i.e. A→B_{TB2}, B_{TB2}→A and A→B_{TB2}). If it is assumed that phase B_{TB1} acts as a 'baseline' for phase B_{TB2} and vice-versa, then a design such as A-B_{TB1}-B_{TB2}-B_{TB1}-B_{TB2} provides three opportunities to demonstrate

---

4   Some studies use the notation C to refer to the reversal phase, and this needs to be distinguished from C as used to denote a different intervention. We refer to the reversal phase as follows: B_{TB1}→ B_{TB2}

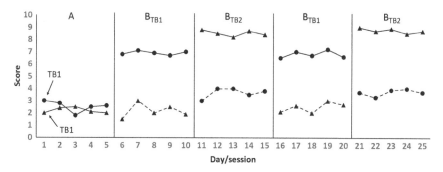

FIGURE 5.7 Hypothetical data for a reversal design

Notes: B_{TB1} indicates a phase where the intervention is applied to one target behaviour (TB1 – solid line) while an alternate target behaviour (TB2 – dashed line) is untreated. B_{TB2} indicates a phase where the intervention is applied to TB2 while TB1 is untreated

the intervention effect at three phase changes between target behaviours (i.e. $B_{TB1} \rightarrow B_{TB2}$, $B_{TB2} \rightarrow B_{TB1}$ and $B_{TB1} \rightarrow B_{TB2}$).

The medical, randomised N-of-1 trial

We make brief comment on the medical, randomised N-of-1 trial (see Kravitz & Duan, 2014; Nikles & Mitchell, 2015a), which is the particular design that the Oxford Centre for Evidence-based Medicine now classifies as Level 1 evidence for treatment decision purposes and for detecting harms (OCEBM, 2011). This methodology uses the A-B-A-B paradigm (see Figure 1.1), and gained popularity in the medical community in the mid 1980s (e.g. Guyatt et al., 1986; 1988; 1990; Keller, Guyatt, Roberts, Adachi & Rosenbloom, 1988). Its application has predominantly been with a pharmacological or other agent that is injected, ingested, inhaled, or topically applied. That community adapted the methodology to meet their needs and there are some differences from the standard A-B-A-B design.

N-of-1 trials are defined as "multi-cycle within-patient, randomised, double-blind, cross-over comparisons of a drug and placebo (or another drug) using standardised measures of effect" (Nikles & Mitchell, 2015b, p. 1). There are some terminological differences between SCEDs and N-of-1 trials: a 'phase' is termed 'period', and an A-B sequence is termed a 'cycle'. Hence, an N-of-1 trial using the familiar A-B-A-B-A-B design would be described as three cycles of A-B pairs. Within each cycle, the A-B periods are randomised. Often but not invariably, there are multiple replications across participants, and sometimes there is a very large number of replications where the intent is to generate population estimates. For example, Mitchell et al. (2015) conducted 43 N-of-1 trials of the effects of methylphenidate on fatigue in patients with advanced cancer; Nikles, Mitchell, Del Mar, Clavarino, and McNairn (2006) reported on 86 N-of-1 trials of stimulants for attention-deficit/hyperactivity disorder; and Zucker et al. (2006) conducted 58 N-of-1 trials of amitriptyline and fluoxetine for fibromyalgia. When pharmacological interventions are used, there is generally the need for 'run-in' and 'wash-out' intervals; the former so that the medication has time to initiate and stabilise, the latter so that the effects of the medication can dissipate and not carry-over into the next period. For this reason, an a priori decision is made to disregard any data collected in the specified run-in/wash-out intervals. Data from the medical N-of-1 trial are not usually graphed, as occurs in a standard SCED, and the analytic approach taken is not dissimilar to some ATD studies (see Chapter 7). All the data from one period (e.g. A) are aggregated and compared statistically with all the data from another period (e.g. B).

An example of a medical N-of-1 trial is that of Nikles et al. (2014) who examined the effects of stimulants (methylphenidate or dexamphetamine versus placebo) to treat attentional, executive, and behavioural symptoms as a consequence of traumatic and other acquired brain injury in seven children. Each participant received three cycles of placebo (A period) and active drug (B period) in treatment blocks of 1 week for each period. A wash-out period of the first two days of the week was specified a priori and data were *not* collected for those intervals. The period within each cycle was randomised, and everyone involved in the study (practitioner, participants, parents, teacher) was blinded. Medications, which were identical in appearance, were prepared in the pharmacy in individual Webster packs as per the participant's computer-generated randomisation schedule. Three standardised instruments were completed at the end of each one-week period: the Connors'3, Behavior Rating Inventory of Executive Function, and the Eyberg Child Behavior Inventory. Data were aggregated across the periods and analysed statistically, and Bayesian random effects models were used to combine the studies to obtain estimation of treatment effect for the group.

The N-of-1 trial is structurally analogous to an A-B-A-B design. The main difference between N-of-1 trials and SCEDs is that periods can be incorporated between phase changes in order to allow the effects of a drug to dissipate (washout period) or to take effect (run-in period). Apart from this, there is, essentially, little difference between the medical N-of-1 trial and a behavioural SCED, other than a labelling issue.

Concluding remarks

Withdrawal/reversal designs are the prototypical SCED. They provide a varied and flexible format for investigating the effectiveness of withdrawable interventions not only in applied research, but also in a rehabilitation setting. Although A-B and A-B-A designs might be rigorously implemented, they lack sufficient experimental control to establish credible cause–effect relationships between the intervention and its effect on the target behaviour. Nonetheless, they are useful tools.

An issue pertinent to WRDs is that designs ending in a baseline phase are unethical, particularly if an intervention has been effective and the participant improved. Kazdin (2011) notes that "Return to baseline conditions is unacceptable if this means making the client worse" (p. 128). This is, however, unavoidable within the framework of WDs. Every time there is a change from B to A it can, arguably, be considered unethical to withdraw the intervention if the participant seems to be benefiting from it. However, the fundamental rationale of and evidence standards applicable to these designs require returning to a baseline phase after an intervention phase on at least one occasion (i. e. A-B-A-B) in order to establish adequate experimental control. It would be unscientific not to do so and hence compromise internal validity to the extent that the therapeutic effectiveness of the intervention cannot be reliably determined. This is analogous to the situation in an RCT where participants in the non-intervention (placebo) arm may not receive the therapeutic benefits of the intervention (and may, indeed, be getting worse). Yet, it is necessary to have placebo control arms in order to determine if the intervention works.

Even if a study ends with an intervention phase, there are still ethical issues. What happens after the last (intervention) phase when the study ends? If the intervention is truly withdrawable, the participant will, essentially, return to a no-treatment condition after the study concludes. Ethical considerations should therefore be extended beyond the limits of the study. Clearly, it is ethically preferable that a study ends with an intervention phase, but whether it does or does not, it is also ethically important that procedures are put in place to plan for continuance of the intervention effects after conclusion of the study.

6

MULTIPLE-BASELINE DESIGNS

Withdrawal/reversal designs provide a powerful tool for investigating the effectiveness of rehabilitation interventions. Well-conducted, methodologically robust designs with sufficient intra-subject replication, such as A-B-A-B, have the necessary experimental control to establish a functional relationship between the intervention and observed changes in the target behaviour. It doesn't get better than that! There are, however, two concerns about these designs. First, they cannot (or should not) be used if the intervention under investigation is likely to produce permanent changes in the target behaviour, such that it will not, or is unlikely to, return to baseline conditions when the intervention is withdrawn. Second, even if the effects of the intervention can be withdrawn, there might be ethical or practical reasons that returning to baseline conditions during the investigation may not be desirable (the undesirability of returning to a baseline phase such that the target behaviour worsens was discussed in the previous chapter). Multiple-baseline designs (MBDs) proffer a way to address both of these concerns, and have the added advantage that they can also be used to investigate withdrawable interventions.

Rationale of MBDs

The structure and rationale of MBDs was proposed by Baer et al. (1968) in the same paper where they described what they termed the "reversal technique" (see Chapter 5). MBDs consist of several, chronologically anchored A-B sequences, with each A-B sequence constituting a baseline or tier of the design.[1] This generic architecture is illustrated in Figure 6.1, using hypothetical data and a three-tiered design. The defining characteristic of MBDs is that the target behaviour is simultaneously and continuously measured over time across each of the tiers and only one intervention is evaluated. That is, the onset of phase A occurs concurrently across all the tiers. The onset of phase B is then sequentially staggered over time across the different tiers, such that baselines become progressively longer in subsequent tiers. The two shaded areas in Tiers 2 and 3, labelled 'verification' are discussed below. Occasionally, published reports erroneously describe A-B designs as MBDs because the target behaviour in the initial baseline is measured on several occasions (i.e. more than one data point in the first A phase; see Tate et al., 2016c).

There are three main types of MBDs and they all share the same generic architecture shown in Figure 6.1. Each is discussed in more detail in the section on types of MBDs. One type is the *multiple baseline across participants*. In this design, the same target behaviour is measured for a different participant in each tier. Another is the *multiple baseline across behaviours*. Here, each tier of the design measures a different target behaviour for the same participant. The third type is the *multiple baseline across settings*. In this instance, the same target behaviour is measured for the same participant, but in each tier the target behaviour is measured in a different setting or situation. There are also two variants of the above designs and these are discussed in more detail in the section below on variants of MBDs. The first variant is the *multiple-probe design*, which can be across participants, behaviours, or settings. It has the same generic architecture as the standard designs described above. The difference is that in some tiers usually, but not always, the last one, the target behaviour is intermittently measured (i.e. probed) rather than continuously measured during the baseline and intervention phases. The second variant is the

---

1   In the broad context of SCEDs, the term *baseline* specifically refers to a 'non-intervention' phase. In the narrower context of MBDs, the term *baseline* is also used to refer to each of the A-B sequences that make up the design. To avoid ambiguity, our preference when discussing MBDs is to use the term *tier* to refer to the number of A-B sequences in the design, and use the term *baseline* to refer exclusively to the initial A-phase in each *tier*. Some authors refer to tiers as legs, levels, or data series.

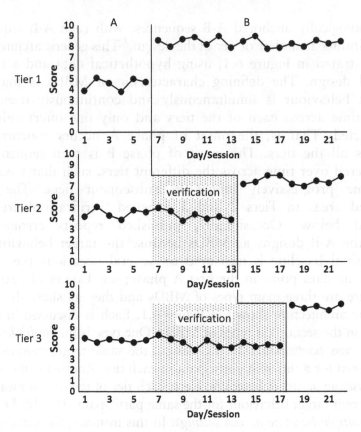

FIGURE 6.1 Hypothetical data for a generic multiple-baseline design

non-concurrent MBD across participants. In this instance, onset of the baseline phase in each tier is not simultaneous.

As described in Chapter 5, *experimental control* (see Chapter 1) in WRDs necessitates intra-subject replication of the *experimental effect* (i.e. when there is a phase change from A to B, or from B to A). In MBDs, whether across participants, behaviours or settings, the experimental effect is evaluated by examining what happens to the target behaviour when there is a phase change; that is, when the intervention is introduced across the different tiers of the design. The central element of experimental control in MBDs is demonstrated when "change occurs when, and only when, the intervention is directed at the behaviour, setting or participant in question" (Barlow et al., 2009, p. 202). Figure 6.1 shows two shaded areas labelled 'verification'; one between days 7 to 13 in tier 2, the other between days 7 and 17 in tier 3. It is during this period that the prediction that the untreated target behaviour will not respond when the intervention is introduced in another tier, is verified (Carr, 2005). *Experimental control* is then established either by inter-subject replication of the *experimental effect* across participants, or by intra-subject replication of the *experimental effect* across behaviours or settings within a single participant.

Evidence standards and internal validity

In their paper introducing MBDs, Baer et al. (1968) made no specific recommendations regarding the number of tiers that should be incorporated in the design. According to them, it was up to the investigators (whom they referred to as "the audience" p. 95) to decide on the number of tiers. Current recommendations are that MBDs meet standards of evidence if each phase has at least 5 data points (Design Standard 4; Kratochwill et al., 2013) and there are at least six phases (i.e. three A-B tiers) in order to provide three opportunities for replication of the experimental effect (Design Standard 3). Designs with at least three A-B tiers but only three to 4 data points per phase meet standards with reservations.

The staggered introduction of the intervention in MBD tiers provides good control for threats to internal validity (see Chapter 2) such as history, maturation, cyclicity and extraneous environmental factors (Kazdin & Kopel, 1975). This control strengthens the conclusion that any observed changes in the target behaviour are attributable to the intervention and helps to reduce the plausibility of alternative explanations. Consider, for example, an MBD across three participants. If the intervention is introduced and produces a change (in the expected direction) in the target behaviour for the first participant, it is still possible that the change might have coincided with 'natural' improvement (bias attributable to maturation). Or it might be that continued monitoring of the target behaviour during baseline has caused the first participant to focus on it and thus, begin to spontaneously modify it towards the desired goal (bias attributable to participant reactivity). Alternatively, some event unrelated to the intervention, such as a significant event in the participant's life or a change of routine in the rehabilitation setting (bias attributable to history) might have influenced the change in the target behaviour. It is also possible that the change in the target behaviour for the second and third participants also coincided with, and was attributable to, some extraneous factor, but this would be a rather improbable series of coincidences (Kazdin & Kopel, 1975; Kazdin, 2011). A similar logic applies to MBDs across behaviours and across settings.

The experimental effect in MBDs is clearly demonstrated when, after introducing the intervention in the first tier, there is little or no change in the as yet untreated target behaviour of the other two tiers. This bolsters the conclusion that the change in the target behaviour is attributable to the intervention.

The internal validity of MBDs also depends, to a considerable extent, on the functional independence of participants, behaviours, or settings across tiers. In other words, participants, behaviours, or settings need to be sufficiently independent to ensure that introducing the intervention in one tier will not influence the target behaviour in tiers that are not yet being treated (Barlow et al., 2009; Gast et al., 2014). Such generalisation to untreated tiers (also referred to as behavioural covariation) threatens internal validity because the experimental effect is not consistently demonstrated when and only when the intervention is introduced in each tier. At the same time, the participants, behaviours, or settings investigated in each tier need to be sufficiently similar to ensure that the intervention effect can be replicated across tiers.

Advantages and disadvantages

All MBDs offer two main advantages over WRDs. First, they can be used whether or not the intervention is likely to have an irreversible effect on the target behaviour. Second, because the intervention is not withdrawn, there are no ethical concerns about suspending treatment for target behaviour that, if left untreated, may have a detrimental impact on the participant (Barlow et al., 2009; Kazdin, 2011; Plavnic & Ferreri, 2013).

There are significant disadvantages associated with the extended length that some baselines in MBDs (especially the later tiers) may reach. Repeated measurement of the target behaviour during prolonged baselines, might pose risks to internal validity due to participant reactivity (Gast et al., 2014; Kazdin, 2011). Moreover, continuous and repeated measurement of the target behaviour over an extended time period during the baseline focuses the participant's attention on a pattern of erroneous performance. To that extent, this may inadvertently serve to reinforce such erroneous performance which might then be harder to eradicate once the intervention is introduced. Furthermore, limited resources for recording might render continuous and repeated baseline measures of the target behaviour across several baselines over long periods of time impractical or difficult. In addition, preliminary evidence from the first tiers in the design might suggest that the intervention is effective. This raises ethical concerns about delaying the introduction of the intervention to other tiers if baselines are extended for long periods of time, particularly if the target behaviour needs to be treated with celerity (Gast et al., 2014; Kazdin, 2011). The risks and difficulties posed by all the issues discussed above, obviously increase as the baseline duration increases. As we will see in the discussion below, multiple-probe designs address these issues. Kazdin (2011) also suggests that baseline length could be reduced if the intervention was simultaneously introduced in more than one baseline at a time. For example, in a six-tier design the intervention could be simultaneously introduced to two tiers at a time: 1 and 2, 3 and 4, 5 and 6. Such a design would still meet evidence standards, given that it provides three separate opportunities to demonstrate the experimental effect, albeit each opportunity involves two tiers simultaneously.

As we noted in the preceding section, MBDs should have least three tiers with 5 data points in each phase in order to meet current standards of evidence, or at least three tiers with 3 to 4 data points in each phase to meet standards of evidence with reservations. Either way, three-tiered designs are a requisite minimum. On the one hand, having more tiers in the design helps to strengthen internal validity by providing more opportunities to demonstrate the experimental effect. On the other hand, having more tiers also means that the later tiers are likely to be quite long, thus increasing the risks of threats to internal validity associated with prolonged baselines. There are no specific guidelines on how to resolve the conundrum posed by these two potentially conflicting effects on internal validity. A practical consideration would be to run the trial as two or more three-tiered MBDs instead of adding more tiers to a design. The resources needed to run either a single six-tiered trial or two three-tiered trials, and the logistic issues involved should be fairly comparable. Having two separate three-tiered trials also has the advantage that it essentially constitutes a direct replication of the first trial, crucial evidence for evaluating external validity.

Timing of the staggered interventions across the tiers also needs to be considered. According to Kazdin (2011), there is no fixed rule in terms of the number of days or sessions for each baseline. He recommends that the intervention should be introduced when the target behaviour in the tier has stabilised with little or no trend. Carr (2005) suggests that the intervention should be first introduced in the most stable initial A-phase (this then becomes the first tier), then introduced in the most stable of the other initial A-phases, and so forth. Roane et al. (2011) recommend that at least 3 data points should be taken in the baseline of a given tier after the intervention has been introduced in the preceding tier, before the intervention is introduced in that tier. An additional consideration would be to introduce the intervention when the target behaviour begins to trend in the opposite direction than that expected under the intervention (Gast et al., 2014). The latter is also equally pertinent to WRDs. Alternatively, the commencement of the intervention in each tier can be randomly assigned (Marascuilo & Busk, 1988). Participants, behaviours, or settings can be allocated to different tiers in the design in no particular order, or they can also be randomly allocated. Moreover, this can also be combined with random allocation of initial A-phase duration (Ferron & Sentovich, 2002; see also Chapter 9 in this book).

Another important issue is that the demonstration of the experimental effect may not be consistent across all tiers of the design. If the design has three tiers and the experimental effect is only evident in two of them, the functional relationship between intervention and response in the target behaviour cannot be clearly established. One approach to minimise this risk is to incorporate more tiers in the design (Kazdin & Kopel, 1975), although as we have seen, that may also increase other risks to internal validity. Having more tiers, however, means that even if the experimental effect is not clearly evident in one tier, the credibility of results will not be seriously compromised, particularly if the intervention effect is consistently evident in enough (hopefully at least three) of the remaining tiers (Kazdin, 2011). The downside is that the probability of obtaining inconsistent results across tiers also increases as the number of tiers in the design increases. Kazdin and Kopel also suggest that a withdrawal phase may be introduced in one or more tiers, converting them, in effect, into an A-B-A sequence. If the target behaviour in those tiers then returns to baseline levels when the intervention is withdrawn, it helps to bolster the conclusion that it was the intervention which caused the change. The limitation of this strategy is that it cannot be utilised if the intervention under investigation is not truly withdrawable.

A final consideration about MBDs is the way in which the results are displayed. Graphs in most concurrent MBDs studies plot sessions along the x-axis and then align session data points down the tiers (Carr, 2005). This implies that any given session, say, session 5, occurred on the same day for all tiers, whereas session 5 in the first tier might actually have occurred on a different day than session 5 in tiers two and three. Using hypothetical data for a two-tiered design, Carr showed that the number of data points that 'appear' to fall within the 'verification period' in the second tier (see Figure 6.1) can vary, depending on the metric used in the x-axis. If the data are plotted by session on the x-axis, the number of data points displayed in this section of the graph can be substantially higher than if the data are plotted on a real timeline. Carr recommends that data for MBDs should be plotted on a real-time metric so that "at best readers will have the necessary information to make a proper visual evaluation of the experimental control demonstrated by MB designs across participants, and at worst the procedural and data reporting will be more precise" (p. 223).

Types of MBDs

MBDs across participants

In MBDs across participants the same intervention is sequentially applied and staggered over time to different participants. Internal validity in these designs is established through inter-subject replication of the experimental effect. A relative strength of MBD across participants is that because the experimental effect is replicated on more than one participant, they also provide a measure of external validity, or generalisability of the effectiveness of the intervention. Presumably, the fact that different individuals participate in each tier would ensure functional independence across tiers. It does not, however, protect against behavioural covariation. In MBDs across participants, there is a risk that changes in the target behaviour for the first participant when the intervention is introduced could trigger changes in the target behaviour of as yet untreated participants (particularly if the study is being conducted in a clinical or residential setting where the participants have frequent contact with each other). That is, observation, imitation, and modelling of the treated participant's behaviour, influences the untreated participant's behaviour. Such behavioural contamination is a significant threat to internal validity.

In order to ensure functional similarity among the baselines, it is advisable that wherever possible participants have similar relevant characteristics, including comorbidities (Gast et al., 2014). For instance, both traumatic brain injury and focal strokes in the left anterior temporal lobe may impair anterograde memory. In the case of traumatic brain injury, the memory problem is likely to be primarily attributable to retrieval deficits, while with stroke it is likely to be attributable to encoding deficits. An intervention suited to treat day-to-day difficulties with memory which have one underlying mechanism (e.g. retrieval deficits) may not be as effective in treating a memory problem which has a different underlying mechanism (e.g. encoding deficits). In this vein, it is critical that, as far as possible, participants have the same repertoire of cognitive, behavioural, emotional, functional, and sensory-motor abilities required to attempt the performance of the target behaviour and engage in and comply with requirements of the intervention. In as much as possible, baseline and intervention phases also should be implemented in the same setting in order to exert better control for extraneous variables.

Guercio et al. (2012) used an MBD across participants to investigate an intervention aimed at reducing pathological gambling in three individuals with traumatic brain injury. Participants (one female and two males aged 31 to 49 years), met the South Oaks Gambling Screen criteria for pathological gambling. The intervention used was a multi-component cognitive-behaviour therapy programme to teach participants "the identification of specific 'triggers' or antecedents that occasioned gambling, alternative reinforcing activities, problem solving, assertiveness training to say no to peers who wished to gamble, and dealing with relapses" (p. 488). Baseline phases in the first, second and third tier comprised four, eight, and 11 sessions respectively. The intervention phase consisted of eight weekly one-hour sessions. The study was conducted in a 'gambling room' that was purpose built in the investigators' laboratory.

Each participant was given $20 for each gambling session, which they could supplement with their own money if they wished. The target behaviour for the female participant, Shiloh, was the number of lottery tickets (maximum of ten at $1 each) bought at the end of each session. For the male participants, Jerry and Jatar, it was the number of poker chips (maximum of ten at $1 each) bought in a simulated gambling situation held at the end of each session. On several occasions during the baseline and intervention phases, measures of the target behaviour at the end of the intervention session were taken in real-world situations (e.g. a casino), and these data were used to assess treatment generalisation. The results of the study are shown in Figure 6.2. The authors do not provide information about how the duration of baselines was determined, but it is clear from the graphed data that

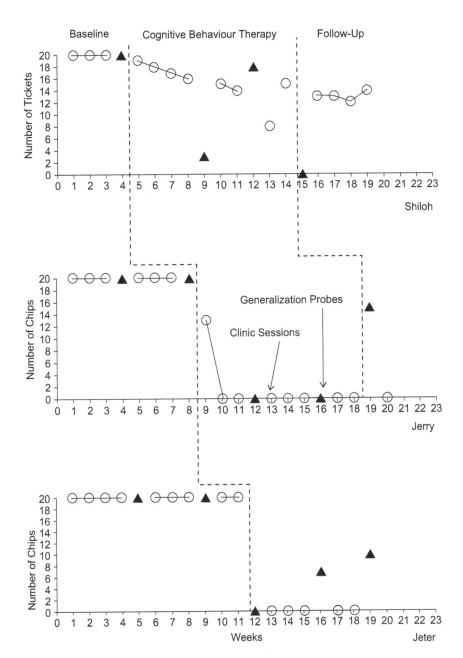

FIGURE 6.2 Number of tickets or poker chips purchased after weekly sessions by each participant

Notes: ○=indicates data collected in clinic; ▲=indicates data collected in real-world environment

Source: Guercio, Johnson and Dixon (2012); reprinted with permission

performance was at ceiling level and stable during baseline on all three tiers irrespective of whether the target behaviour was measured in the clinic or in a real-world situation. After the intervention was introduced, the amount of money all participants spent to either buy lottery tickets or poker chips was markedly reduced. For Shiloh, this reduction was mostly gradual and progressive over the intervention phase. Jerry's gambling expenditure was reduced to $0 on the second session of the intervention phase (session 10), while for Jatar's this occurred on the first session of the intervention phase (session 12). Thereafter, gambling expenditure for both participants remained at $0 for the reminder of the intervention phase.

MBDs across behaviours

In these designs, the same intervention is applied, in a sequentially staggered manner, to different target behaviours in the same participant. Internal validity is established by intra-subject replication of the experimental effect. On the one hand, the behaviours selected for each tier should be functionally independent. This reduces the possibility that when the intervention is introduced in one tier, it will also influence the target behaviour in tiers that are not yet being treated. If target behaviours are functionally similar, there might be diffusion of the intervention effect such that treatment of one target behaviour might affect an as yet untreated target behaviour (behavioural covariation). This generalisation of treatment effects is a well-documented phenomenon in behavioural research (Ducharme & Ng, 2012; Parrish, Cataldo, Kolko, Neef, & Egel, 1986; Russo, Cataldo, & Cushing, 1981; Wells, Forehand, & Griest, 1980). Consider the situation where two apparently independent target behaviours are being treated: verbal aggression directed to staff and other residents in the rehabilitation unit and participation in group activities. If the intervention reduces the individual's verbal aggression, this might also increase participation in group activities before that behaviour is treated. A possible reason for this could be that compliance with participation in group activities was also disrupted by verbal aggression. If behavioural covariation is a significant issue an MBD may not be the most suitable design to adopt. One strategy would be to include additional baselines (i.e. target behaviours) in the design (Gast et al., 2014). Doing so might help to reduce the possibility that behavioural covariation would occur across all the target behaviours. Another strategy would be to consider using other designs. Barlow et al. (2011) suggest using an ATD in these circumstances, but provide no rationale for doing so. A further alternative suggested by Gast and colleagues (Gast et al., 2014; Ledford & Gast, 2014) is to use an MBD across participants with an MBDs across behaviours embedded within each tier of the design.

As well as being functionally independent, target behaviours in each baseline also need to be sufficiently functionally similar to ensure that the intervention will be effective across behaviours. If the experimental effect is not consistently demonstrated across tiers because target behaviours are either not functionally independent or are functionally dissimilar, internal validity will be compromised. Achieving the right balance between functional independence and functional similarity of target behaviours is not necessarily an easy task.

Savage et al. (2013) used an MBD across behaviours to investigate the effectiveness of a home-based, word-relearning method aimed at improving word production in four males with semantic dementia. The basic intervention consisted of training the participant to name photographs of household objects (e.g. kitchen utensils, food, clothing, tools) presented either on a computer screen or on paper, and was administered in two self-paced formats. The first format consisted of a 'look–listen–repeat' procedure, in which the participant was trained to name objects using a hierarchy of steps involving visual presentation of pictures of the object to be named, combined with written and/or aural presentations of the object's name. The second format was similar to the first but in addition the participant was also required to use the object's name in a sentence. The target behaviour in each instance was the percentage of correctly named objects in the absence of a verbal label or description. Two participants were assigned to each intervention format.

Three object lists (i.e. stimulus sets) were used across the three tiers in the study (as well as in both intervention formats) and an identical structure MBD was used for each participant. Baseline data for the first list were collected for three weeks. The intervention was then introduced and implemented for a further six weeks. Baseline data for the second list were collected for six weeks before the intervention was introduced and implemented for a further three weeks. The third list was untreated for the duration of the study and used as a control condition. Follow-up data were collected at four and seven weeks after the intervention ended. Figure 6.3 shows the naming performance of one of the participants assigned to the first intervention format. As the graph demonstrates, naming accuracy in the

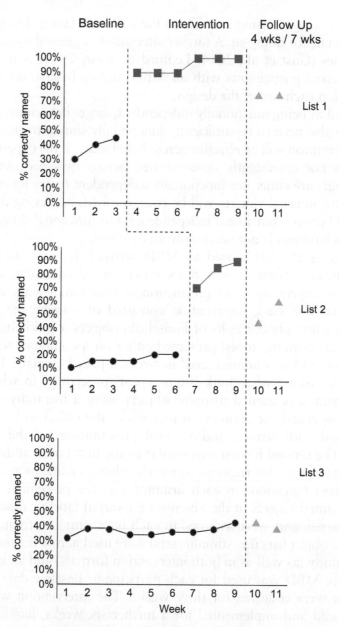

FIGURE 6.3 Object naming accuracy of a 61-year-old male with semantic dementia
Source: Savage, Ballard, Piguet, and Hodges (2013); reprinted with permission

baseline phase on all three tiers was fairly stable, ranging between 10% and just below 50%. Naming accuracy then increased to 90–100% when the intervention was introduced in the first tier, while remaining unchanged in the untreated tiers. Similarly, naming accuracy increased to 60–90% when the intervention was introduced in the second tier, while remaining consistently low in the third-tier control condition. Follow-up at four and seven weeks post-intervention showed that although naming accuracy was lower compared with the intervention phase, it was still notably above baseline levels. Comparable results were obtained for the other participants in the study.

MBD across settings

In MBDs across settings the same intervention is sequentially applied, to the same participant across different settings/environments. Alternatively, the setting may refer to the same physical environment but reflect different times of day (e.g. morning and afternoon) when the intervention is administered (Kazdin, 2011). This is a useful design in a rehabilitation setting when the question of interest is whether or not an intervention can address a behavioural, cognitive, or functional problem in the context of different environmental settings (e.g. at the clinic and at home). Like MBDs across behaviours, internal validity in these designs is based on intra-subject replication of the experimental effect. Settings need to be functionally independent to ensure that introducing the intervention in one setting will not influence the target behaviour in settings that are not being treated. Conversely, settings need to be functionally similar to ensure that the intervention effect can be replicated across tiers.

Feeney (2010) used an MBD across settings to examine the effectiveness of an intervention to reduce physically (e.g. hitting) and verbally (e.g. threatening) aggressive behaviour in the classroom. Study participants were two children aged 10 and 17 who had respectively sustained a severe traumatic brain injury five and two years earlier. Functional assessment prior to the commencement of the study revealed that the participants used aggression as an escape behaviour to avoid assigned work in the classroom. The intervention consisted of a multi-component cognitive-behaviour therapy programme that included learning effective strategies to negotiate daily work commitments, communication alternatives to replace aggression, and self-regulation skills. The intervention was implemented on a daily basis and the study was conducted across three classroom settings: English–language–art, maths, and science. The target behaviours were the frequency of aggressive behaviours (operationally defined), and the intensity of aggressive behaviours as measured by the Aberrant Behavior Checklist. Percentage of work completed by the participants in each classroom setting was also measured.

The structure of the MBD was the same for both participants. Baseline duration in the first, second, and third tiers was five, ten, and 15 sessions respectively. Figure 6.4 shows the results for frequency of aggressive behaviours for Jason. During the baseline phase, the frequency of Jason's aggressive behaviour was relatively high (8–15 occasions), stable and comparable across all three classroom settings. When the intervention was introduced in the English–language–art setting, there was a very marked and virtually immediate effect such that there were less than five instances of aggressive behaviour on any given day, and no instances of aggressive behaviour on most days of the intervention phase. Meanwhile, the frequency of aggressive behaviour in the maths and science classrooms remained high, and relatively stable. When the intervention was introduced in each of these settings a similar reduction in the frequency of aggressive behaviour was observed. Jason's score for intensity of aggressive behaviour was in the "moderately to very disruptive" range in the baseline phases, decreasing to the "minor problem" range when the intervention was introduced in each setting (p. 422). Percentage of work completed in each classroom setting increased from an average of 20% during the baseline phase to more than 85% when the intervention was introduced. Jason's results were very closely replicated by those of the other participant.

Variants of MBDs

Multiple-probe designs

The concept of the multiple-probe MBDs was introduced by Horner and Baer (1978). As mentioned earlier, these designs have the standard MBD format and they can be implemented across participants, behaviours, or settings. What distinguishes them from the standard format is that instead of taking continuous measures of the target behaviour during the baseline, the target behaviour is probed (or intermittently sampled) in order to establish its pattern/ level before the intervention is introduced. Because the introduction of the intervention is staggered over time, the baselines in each tier become progressively lengthier. As indicated in the section discussing advantages and disadvantages of MBDs, this has

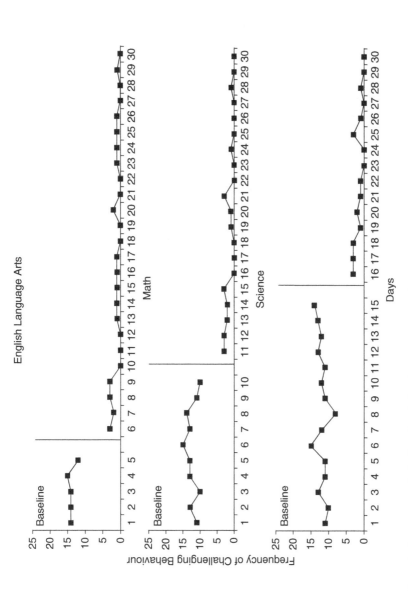

FIGURE 6.4 Jason's frequency of challenging behaviours across settings

Source: Feeney (2010); reprinted with permission

potential drawbacks which threaten internal validity. According to Horner and Baer, by reducing baseline length, the multiple-probe technique helps to control these threats. The multiple-probe technique is also particularly apt if, on the basis of prior evidence, there is good reason to assume that the target behaviour is likely to be stable during the baseline (Horner & Baer, 1978).

Horner and Baer (1978) used two published studies on which they superimposed hypothetical probe data to demonstrate the multiple-probe technique. They recommended that the target behaviour should be probed at the commencement of the baseline phase in each tier, that there should be a series of a "so-called true baseline sessions conducted just before each introduction of the independent variable" (p. 190), and that there should be an additional probe at the end of the intervention phase immediately after the performance criterion is met.[2] They noted that in their second example where the observed data were fairly stable and had little if any trend, baseline stability could possibly have been established with five or fewer probes. Gast et al. (2014) recommend that the target behaviour should be probed at least every five days and for at least three consecutive days (or sessions) immediately before introducing the intervention.

Although probes are generally used during baseline phases, Barlow et al. (2009) suggest that they should also be used during intervention phases if concerns about reactivity are prominent. Gast et al. (2014) also propose that probes can be used during the intervention phase in a subtype of the multiple-probe design they refer to as the *multiple-probe design (conditions)*. According to them, this variant is well suited to situations when there is not sufficient time each day in clinical settings to assess the target behaviour across all tiers. In a three-tiered design, across participants, behaviours, or settings, they recommend that the initial baseline in all tiers is probed consecutively on a minimum of three occasions over a minimum of two days. The intervention is introduced in the first tier when the data are stable; at this point the target behaviour is not probed further in the second or third tiers. When the target behaviour in the first tier reaches a

2   In Horner and Baer's (1978) first example the intervention is aimed at achieving a certain level of competence in the target behaviour. The same probing schedule can still be implemented, however, even if there is no requirement for the target behaviour to reach a pre-set criterion in order to end the intervention phase.

predetermined criterion,[3] another three consecutive probes are taken in all tiers. If the yet-untreated target behaviour in the second tier is stable, the intervention is introduced in this tier and the phase is continued until a predetermined criterion is reached. During this time, the target behaviour is not probed in either the first or third tiers. When the criterion has been reached in the second tier, another three consecutive probes are taken in all tiers. The intervention is then introduced in the third tier and no further probes are taken in the first or second tiers. When performance reaches a predetermined criterion in the third tier, a final three consecutive probes are taken in all tiers. Gast et al. (2014) suggest that this design is particularly suitable for investigating instructional interventions that are therapist-paced.

A multiple-probe, MBD across participants was used by Ehlhardt et al. (2005). The four participants had sustained a traumatic brain injury due to a motor-vehicle accident, 16 to 31 years previously. They all had severe impairment of anterograde memory and executive function, confirmed on standard neuropsychological tests at the commencement of the study. The investigators developed an instructional package (the TEACH-M programme) to teach participants a seven-step email task. A computerised email interface (designated as the instructional interface) was used to implement the TEACH-M instructional package. An alternative email interface with rearranged existing buttons, additional buttons, and additional hypothetical email partners was also used to assess generalisation. The email task was chosen because, apart from being complex and requiring completion of several steps, it was an ecologically valid task which "has the potential of reducing the social isolation experienced by individuals with acquired brain injury" (p. 571). According to their caregivers, participants had significant difficulty learning new multi-step procedures, and none of them had prior experience using email.

The investigators used an MBD across participants with probes, to investigate the effect of the TEACH-M programme on the

3 Gast et al. (2014) describe the *multiple-probe design (conditions)* in the context of interventions aimed at achieving a certain level of competence in the target behaviour. It is reasonable to assume, however, that the procedure could be adapted to rehabilitation interventions when there is no pre-set criterion that the target behaviour must reach. In that situation, interventions across the tiers could be introduced when the target behaviour has stabilised.

participant's procedural accuracy completing the seven steps of the email task. Measures of the target behaviour were operationally defined as: (i) the number of correct email steps completed in sequence; and (ii) the number of correct email steps completed regardless of sequence. An a priori decision was made to use a minimum of four and a maximum of six probes in the baseline phases. The upper limit was set at six for two reasons. First, because it was assumed that the target behaviour would not change during baseline. Second, to minimise the risk that mistakes made repeatedly during the baseline would be difficult to eliminate during the intervention phase. Probes were taken at the beginning of each training session. Training sessions with the TEACH-M program consisted of four phases involving task analysis, errorless learning techniques, spaced retrieval practice, and metacognitive strategy training. Training sessions were continued until the participant met the criterion for mastery: three consecutive sessions with 100% accuracy. A follow-up probe was also taken one month after the intervention ended in order to assess maintenance of the intervention effect.

Results for the number of correct email steps completed in sequence by each participant are shown in Figure 6.5. As the graph demonstrates, the target behaviour was continuously sampled during the baseline for participants 1 and 2; thus, the data points in these phases are not probes. The target behaviour for participants 3 and 4, however, was probed on two consecutive sessions at the beginning of the baseline, then on three consecutive occasions prior to the introduction of the intervention, and the inter-probe interval did not exceed four weeks. Given that despite their different duration, each participant was assessed on a comparable number of occasions during baseline, the risk of any potential confound attributable to reactivity would have been similar for all participants.

Four features are clear from Figure 6.5. First, baselines in all tiers were reasonably stable. Second, the experimental effect was consistently and immediately demonstrated across all participants. Moreover, all participants attained the mastery criterion within a comparable number of sessions. Third, the probe technique was also able to demonstrate generalisation for all participants. Performance on the alternative email interface, as shown by the probes at the end of each baseline (circular data point), did not differ from the performance on the instructional interface. Probes of performance on the alternative interface taken three days after the completion of the

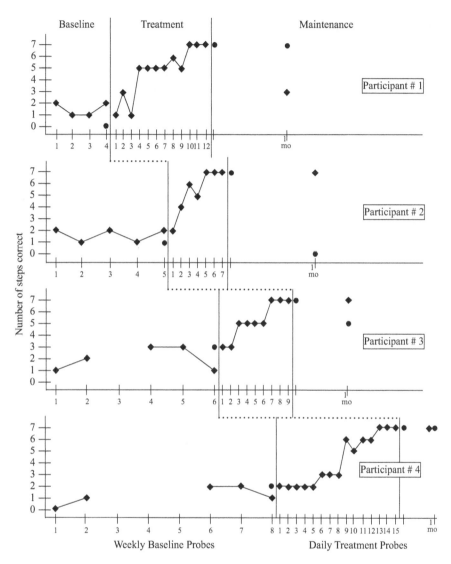

FIGURE 6.5 Number of correct email steps completed in sequence by each participant

Notes: ◆=instructional interface; ●=alternate interface

Source: Ehlhardt, Sohlberg, Glang, and Albin (2005); reprinted with permission

intervention phase, also showed 100% accuracy. This strongly demonstrated that the skills acquired on the instructional email interface had generalised to the untrained, alternative interface. Fourth, the follow-up probes one month after the intervention ended showed that skills acquired during training were maintained for participants 2, 3, and 4.

Non-concurrent MBD

Watson and Workman (1981) were the first to propose the concept of non-concurrent MBDs. Their contention was that studies across participants could be conducted either in the traditional manner, or as non-concurrent designs. Like the concurrent designs, which are those that we have discussed so far, non-concurrent designs also consist of a series of A-B tiers, with baselines of different duration. Unlike concurrent designs, the baseline phases in each tier do not commence at the same time, hence the non-concurrent label. Instead, the baseline phase in each tier commences at a different point in time, perhaps days, weeks, or even months apart. It is even possible that all data for one or more tiers in the design might have been collected before some tiers in the design have commenced. In one sense, non-concurrent MBDs are like a series of A-B studies that are implemented at different times. The length of the baseline phase in each tier is determined a priori, and then as participants are recruited they are randomly assigned to a particular tier (Watson & Workman, 1981).

Non-concurrent MBDs are useful when participants with the condition and/or the specific functional deficits being treated are relatively rare (e.g. functional problems due to visual object agnosia) and several participants cannot be recruited into the study at the same time and hence are not available to commence the study at the same point in time. A relative strength of non-concurrent designs is that risks to internal validity posed by behavioural covariation across participants may be minimised, if participants do not share the same environment when the study is being conducted. Otherwise, if participants share the same environment, the risks to internal validity posed by behavioural covariation would likely be higher than if they do not share the same environment, and comparable to those encountered in concurrent MBDs. Their major drawback is that they provide poor experimental control. Gast et al. (2014) argue that the interval between the introduction of the intervention in the first tier and the introduction of the intervention in subsequent tiers is critical in evaluating such threats to internal validity and establishing experimental control in MBDs. This so-called verification period (Carr, 2005) provides the opportunity to verify that the as yet untreated target behaviour in the other tiers has not been affected by the introduction of the intervention in the first tier. If tiers are non-concurrent, it cannot be adequately demonstrated that introducing the intervention to one participant does not cause any change in the target behaviours of other participants who are not yet being treated. Hence non-concurrent MBDs are considered to have poorer experimental control than concurrent MBDs (Barlow et al., 2009; Gast et al., 2014; Tate et al., 2015).

Non-concurrent MBDs are also considered to be more vulnerable than concurrent MBDs to threats to internal validity posed by history, maturation, or other extraneous factors (e.g. changing staff, change in medication regimen). Gast et al. (2014) argue a change in the target behaviour can only be exclusively attributed to the effect of the intervention when two conditions are met: first, the change in the target behaviour is observed when and only when the intervention is introduced; second, at the same time, no changes in the target behaviour are observed in the other, untreated tiers. By contrast, Watson and Workman (1981) argue that changes in the target behaviour when the intervention is introduced in non-concurrent MBDs cannot be readily attributable to extraneous factors, because it is unlikely that they would exert an influence at different, randomly determined time points. This is the reason that it is critically important for participants to be randomly allocated to baselines in non-concurrent MBDs. Christ (2007) demonstrated that the probability that history effects will be evident precisely at the point when the intervention is introduced becomes increasingly small as the number of tiers in the design and the number of observations in the phase of the study increases (p=0.002 for a three-tiered design with 6 data points in each phase). Harvey, May, and Kennedy (2004) acknowledge that because baselines are non-concurrent, the potential effects of history cannot be readily identified, either at the point that the intervention is introduced in a tier or at other time points during the study. Hence, it is possible that history can affect the target behaviour in one, but not necessarily all tiers of a non-concurrent MBD.

Concluding remarks

MBDs are extremely versatile and useful in the context of neurorehabilitation. They are the 'go-to' design when the effect of the intervention on the target behaviour cannot be withdrawn, which may often be the case in the neurorehabilitation setting. They can, however, also be used with withdrawable interventions. They are particularly useful when for ethical or practical reasons it is not desirable to remove an intervention.

MBDs are the only designs that provide the means of simultaneously evaluating the effectiveness of an intervention on the same individual across different settings, thus more comprehensively addressing the participant's needs. Moreover, it is not unusual that several aspects of an individual's behavioural repertoire are affected following acquired brain injury. Because MBDs can also be used to simultaneously evaluate the intervention across different behaviours for the same individual, these designs also provide an efficient means of developing rehabilitation strategies to comprehensively address the participant's needs. Evaluating interventions across different settings or different behaviours can also be accomplished using consecutive WRDs (if the effect of the intervention is withdrawable) for each setting or behaviour. In that instance, each design would require at least four phases in order to meet evidence standards (i.e. A-B-A-B) or many more phases if they are set up as multiple-treatment comparison designs (see Chapter 5). MBDs not only provide a more effective means of accomplishing this in terms of time and resources, but meet evidence standards using just three tiers.

Finally, because the target behaviour is simultaneously measured across all tiers of the design and the introduction is staggered across tiers, concurrent MBD offer excellent control for threats to internal validity. Despite these advantages, they are not as frequently used in neurorehabilitation (Tate et al., 2016c; Table 1.1 in this book) compared with fields of clinical psychology, sport psychology, and education research where they are the most commonly used type of SCED (Barker et al., 2013; Hammond & Gast, 2010; Shadish & Sullivan, 2011; Smith, 2012).

7

ALTERNATING-TREATMENTS DESIGNS

Alternating-treatment designs (ATDs) have two primary uses: comparing two (or more) interventions with withdrawable effects and comparing an intervention with no intervention (Barlow & Hayes, 1979; Barlow et al., 2009; Kazdin & Hartman, 1978). Their central design feature is that two or more[1] interventions are presented to the same participant in rapid alternation either on the same day (e.g. within the same session or different sessions, such as intervention 1 in the morning, intervention 2 in the afternoon) or different days/occasions (e.g. intervention 1 on one day, intervention 2 on the next) (Barlow et al., 2009). It is important to keep in mind that one of the interventions being compared might, in fact, be a no-intervention condition, equivalent to a baseline phase. So, when we refer to intervention 1 and intervention 2 in the context of ATDs, one of the interventions could well be a baseline condition. ATDs have been variously referred to as simultaneous-treatments designs, multiple-schedule designs, and multi-element baseline designs. Barlow and Hayes first

---

1 Kazdin (2011) notes that comparing more than three interventions is rare and would complicate the alternation schedule. It would also make it more difficult to evaluate the impact of multi-treatment effects. For illustrative purposes in our discussion, we will refer to studies comparing just two interventions. The arguments and issues raised are, however, still applicable if more than two interventions are being compared.

proposed the name, alternating-treatments design, to help dispel the confusion in terminology.

Rationale of ATDs

WRDs, MBDs, and CCDs are useful for determining whether or not a single intervention is effective for treating a specific target behaviour. Clearly, MBDs cannot be used to compare a single participant across interventions. Intervention 1 would be implemented in the first tier of the design, and the implementation of intervention 2 in the second tier would occur while intervention 1 was still active in the first tier. It would not be possible to disentangle the likely interaction between the two interventions and evaluate the specific effectiveness of each one. Nor is it easy to visualise how two interventions could be evaluated within the framework of CCDs (see Chapter 8). WRDs such as A-B-A-B-A-C-A-C can be used to compare two interventions, B and C. Like ATDs, they are vulnerable to sequencing effects (see section below on advantages and disadvantages). In addition, there is exposure to threats to internal validity over longer periods of time and there might be insufficient experimental control to reliably demonstrate the absolute (rather than the relative) effect of all the interventions being evaluated (see Chapter 5).

A fundamental methodological strength of SCEDs is that the participant is used as his or her own control. A design that allows this strength to be exploited when comparing two interventions is very useful, and ATDs provide the means to do this. The central feature of all ATDs is that two (or more) interventions are compared on an alternating schedule. Each intervention should be administered the same number of times (Barlow & Hayes, 1979). Interventions should be sequentially presented in either a counter-balanced or randomised sequence on each occasion, particularly if they are being administered on the same day, to avoid order effects (Wolery et al., 2014). Preferably, the alternating sequence should be randomised (but avoid having more than two consecutive sessions of the same intervention) to protect against threats to internal validity due to cyclical variability and for control of sequential confounding (Barlow et al., 2009; Wolery et al., 2014). Figure 7.1 illustrates the three common ATD subtypes: comparison phase only (Figure 7.1 A); comparison phase with initial A-baseline (Figure 7.1 B); and comparison phase with initial baseline and 'best treatment' final phase; no initial A-baseline is also an option

A: Comparison phase only

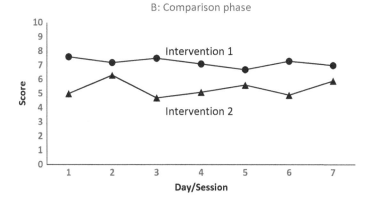

B: Initial baseline and comparison phase

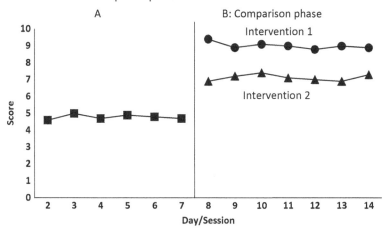

C: Intial baseline, comparison phase and best treatment follow-up

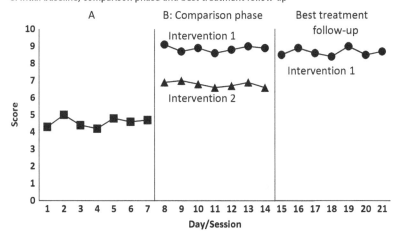

FIGURE 7.1 Hypothetical data for the three main variants of ATDs

(Figure 7.1 C). They will be discussed in more detail in the sections below. The interventions are compared simultaneously, or, more accurately speaking, within a short interval of time, often no more than a day (Hains & Baer, 1989) in the same participant.

In ATDs the level of the target behaviour under a given intervention is used to predict the level of the target behaviour when that intervention is next applied. That next application of the intervention serves to verify this prediction and (hopefully) to replicate the effect that the intervention previously had on the target behaviour (Cooper, Herron, & Heward, 2007). The effect of each intervention on the target behaviour is evaluated across conditions, where condition 1 refers to all the data for intervention 1 and condition 2 refers to all the data for intervention 2. For that reason, as Figure 7.1 shows, all data points for intervention 1 are joined, even though the intervention was not delivered on contiguous occasions. Data for intervention 2 are also graphed in this manner.

Evidence standards and internal validity

Experimental control in ATDs is achieved by intra-subject replication of the experimental effect. Good experimental control is established and the experimental effect is clearly demonstrated when one intervention consistently shows a better effect on the target behaviour than the other intervention. That is, the line joining all the data points for intervention 1 does not cross or overlap the line joining all the data points for intervention 2. According to Design Standard 3 (Kratochwill et al., 2013) single-case designs must provide at least three opportunities at three different points in time to demonstrate the intervention effect (i.e. the experimental effect). Design Standard 4 also requires that any phase used to demonstrate the experimental effect must have a minimum of 5 data points. For ATDs, Design Standard 3 is superseded by Design Standard 4, which means that the comparison phase in ATDs must have at least five replications of the alternating sequence in order to provide at least five opportunities to replicate the experimental effect. Designs with four replications meet standards with reservations, and fewer than four replications fail to meet standards (Kratochwill et al., 2013).

How useful a particular design is for answering a particular question is also largely determined by how robust the design is to internal validity threats when applied in that manner. The main strength of ATDs is that they provide excellent control for history, maturation, cyclicity, or changes in environmental confounds (e.g. commencing/ending other therapies unrelated to the study) that could threaten internal validity (Barlow & Hayes, 1979; Barlow et al., 2009; Kazdin & Geesey, 1977). According to Barlow and Hayes, "the testing of two treatments in the same subject within the same time period produces one of the most elegant controls for most threats to internal validity" (p. 203). Because the same participant is receiving both interventions within a short time frame, it is reasonable to expect that any confounding influences from extraneous factors would have a comparable impact on either intervention. The main downside is that ATDs are vulnerable to intervention interference effects. In other words, it might be difficult to determine how much the effects of intervention 1 might have been modulated by intervention 2, and vice versa. This might also make it difficult to determine how effective each of the interventions would be in isolation. This is important because if the data suggest that a given intervention is the preferred option, we would want to be confident that its effectiveness is as 'potent 'as the results of the ATD indicated when it is used as a monotherapy in the clinical setting. There are, however, strategies to control for these confounders, or at least estimate the magnitude of their potential impact, which are discussed later in the chapter.

In addition to controlling for intervention interference effects, three other fundamental requisites help to strengthen the internal validity of ATDs. First, the intervention effects must be withdrawable, otherwise the risk of multi-treatment interference effects is increased. Second, the target behaviours being treated should respond quickly to the intervention so that the differential effectiveness of two interventions can be demonstrated clearly. Clinical experience would guide this choice, but it is not unreasonable to expect that there might be occasions when the target behaviour under investigation is not as responsive as anticipated a priori. Sufficiently large inertia in the target behaviour would significantly increase multi-treatment interference and substantially threaten validity. Third, the interventions should be sufficiently different procedurally so that the participant can readily distinguish between them. Although these requirements help to increase the robustness of ATDs, they somewhat limit the types of interventions and types of target behaviours that can be investigated with these designs.

Types of ATDs

Comparison phase only

The most basic design contains a single comparison phase during which the two interventions are delivered in an alternating fashion (Figure 7.1 A). Initial baselines have a less critical role in ATDs than other type of SCEDs. An initial baseline makes it possible to assess the stability (trend and variability) of the target behaviour. If the target behaviour is unstable, it would be reasonable to assume that confounding effects due to this will have a comparable impact on both interventions. Hence, having no initial baseline does not invalidate plausible conclusions about which intervention is more efficient. A baseline also serves to make predictions about the level of the target behaviour if left untreated. Without a baseline such predictions can be neither made nor verified when the intervention is introduced. In these circumstances, although the *absolute* magnitude of intervention effects cannot be reliably evaluated, it is still possible to determine the *relative* effectiveness of two interventions (irrespective of their *absolute* effectiveness). Not requiring an initial baseline to demonstrate experimental control means that interventions can be commenced immediately. This may be very desirable in the clinical setting, particularly if the target behaviour is harmful to or distressing for the participant and those around her or him. Sometimes a 'no treatment' intervention is compared with an 'active' intervention. If it is assumed that the level of the target behaviour during the 'no treatment' intervention in the comparison phase was the same as it would have been during an initial baseline (had there been one), this would allow the *absolute* magnitude of the active intervention effect to be estimated.

Comparison phase with initial baseline

A second variant of the design includes an initial A-phase baseline prior to the comparison phase of the basic design (Figure 7.1 B). If two 'active' interventions are being compared, the inclusion of an initial baseline allows the clinician to draw reliable conclusions about both the *absolute* and *relative* effectiveness of the interventions. Also, including a 'no treatment' intervention in the comparison phase facilitates evaluation of multi-treatment interference. If the pattern and level of the target behaviour during the 'no treatment' intervention in the comparison phase is similar to that observed in the initial baseline phase, it suggests that the likelihood of multi-treatment interference is low (Wolery et al., 2014).

Comparison phase with 'best treatment' phase

In a third variant of the design, the comparison phase is followed by a 'best treatment' phase in which only the intervention that has been demonstrated to be more effective during the comparison phase is delivered. A 'best treatment' phase makes it possible to estimate the magnitude of intervention interference effects and thus strengthen internal validity. If the pattern of the target behaviour is the same during the comparison and the last phase of the study when the 'best treatment' is administered, it suggests that intervention interference effects are not a concern. Conversely, a marked change in the response of the target behaviour during the 'best treatment' phase would suggest that the interventions have interacted. This variant of the design can be implemented with or without an initial A-phase baseline. Including an initial baseline in the design also helps to further establish how effective the 'superior' intervention is when administered.

Mechling (2006) used this variant of the design to investigate use of assistive devices to allow individuals with profound intellectual disability and limited mobility to more extensively interact with their environment. Operating such assistive devices primarily requires the individual to physically operate a switch, and, more importantly, to be cognisant that operating the switch has an effect, namely, that it provides access to an assistive device. Mechling investigated the effectiveness of three interventions using different stimulus classes of reinforcement to teach this cause–effect relationship to three males aged 5, 6, and 18 years with profound intellectual disability. The three interventions comprised Treatment A (adapted toys and devices), Treatment B (cause–effect commercial software), and Treatment C (instructor-created video programmes). Each intervention was 3 minutes long and all three interventions were implemented during a single occasion on the same day. There were nine alternations in the comparison phase, and the final, best treatment phase had 3 data points. Alternation order was counterbalanced within sessions to minimise interference effects. The target behaviour in this study was number of times the individual pressed a switch (stimulus activation) during the intervention session.

The results of the study are shown in Figure 7.2. For the most part, the interventions did not show a clear, strong pattern of

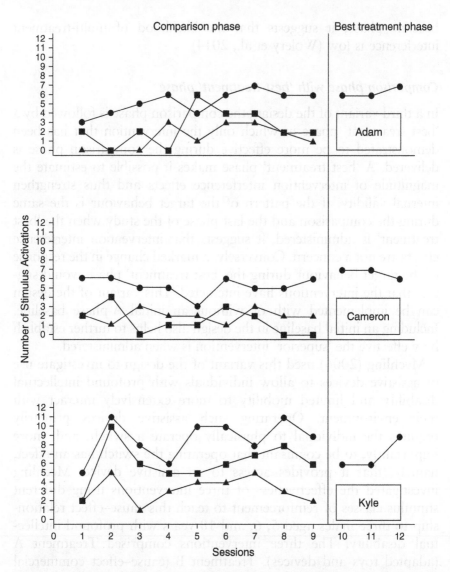

FIGURE 7.2 Number of switch activations for three participants under three intervention conditions

Notes: ▲=Intervention A: adapted toys and devices; ■=Intervention B: cause–effect commercial software; ●=Intervention C: instructor-created video programme

Source: Mechling (2006); reprinted with permission

improvement in the target behaviour over the sessions. Differences among interventions, however, were well demonstrated: Treatment C was clearly more effective in improving the target behaviour than the other two. For Cameron and Kyle neither of the other interventions overlapped with Treatment C, and for Adam this occurred on only one occasion. Moreover, when Treatment C was administered as monotherapy in the best treatment phase, the level of the target behaviour remained the same as or better than during the comparison phase for Adam and Cameron. This suggested that multi-treatment interference during the comparison phase was minimal. This was not so evident for Kyle for whom there might have been slight multi-treatment interference. In his case, the level of the target behaviour during the 'best treatment' phase dropped slightly below the comparison phase level. It did, however, remain generally above the level of the other two interventions.

Advantages and disadvantages

As we noted above, the principal advantage of ATDs is that they are very robust to the detrimental impact on internal validity that diffi-cult-to-control extraneous variables (e.g. history, maturation, target behaviour variability, cyclicity, and other factors) might have. This is primarily because, even if an initial baseline and best treatment phase are included, the same participant is exposed to exactly the same effects of such factors over a relatively short period of time. It can be reasonably assumed that potential confounders will have a similar impact on all the interventions being administered, particularly given that this is occurring within a brief time frame (Barlow & Hayes, 1979). The design is also considered to be less sensitive to baseline fluctuations or trends in the target behaviour, because it is assumed that any underlying baseline instability will affect all interventions similarly. Consequently, the effectiveness of interventions 'relative' to each other should be unaffected, and if there is a difference, it should be demonstrable despite underlying baseline stability.

Another advantage is that if target behaviours are selected on the a priori expectation of being able to respond quickly and interventions selected on the expectation they have a fast effect, it might also help to further minimise the impact of extraneous fac-tors. If changes in the target behaviour related to the intervention effect occur in a faster 'time frame' than changes related to extra-neous factors, the latter might not have a salient effect over a briefer time interval. This would include changes in underlying baseline trend and variability. Moreover, as noted above, if there is trend and/or variability in the target behaviour it presumably has a comparable impact on all interventions. For instance, a baseline trend in the therapeutic direction might inflate the apparent intervention effect, but it will do so for both interventions. Even so, it might still be possible to obtain a fairly credible estimate of the relative effectiveness of each intervention. Absolute and relative intervention effects, if any, should become clearer within five repetitions of the alternating sequence, a brief time interval. And that is an advantageous aspect of ATDs that is clinically important. On occasion, clinicians might be called upon to provide an intervention to address behaviour that is either emotionally and/or physically extremely distressing, hurtful or dangerous to the individual or those caring for him of her. ATDs can not only furnish quick, reliable data, but an initial baseline phase is not crucial. Consequently, interventions can be started immediately thus addressing the therapeutic urgency of the situation. Moreover, interventions are not withdrawn and the study can (and preferably should) end with a 'best treatment' phase.

Multi-treatment interference is the Achilles heel of ATDs. The very structure of the design virtually guarantees that this is going to be an issue (Tawney & Gast, 1984); a big one. Barlow and Hayes (1979)[2] identified three types of multi-treatment interference applicable to ATDs: sequential confounding, carry-over effects, and alternation effects. Hains and Baer (1989) consider that the distinction between three types of multi-treatment interference is perhaps a case of hair-splitting; "Sequence, carry-over, and alternation effects are usually discussed separately; however, they all refer to the same problem" (p. 60). Nonetheless, different specific strategies can be implemented to minimise the impact of each.

Sequential confounding refers to the possibility that the order in which interventions are implemented may affect the effectiveness of each intervention. That is, the effect of intervention B might be confounded because it precedes or follows intervention C. In ATDs this is controlled by counterbalancing or randomising the alternation sequence (Barlow & Hayes, 1979; Hains & Baer, 1989). Although this might require adding more alternations to the design, it would not make it unwieldy because more administrations of both interventions can be delivered in a shorter time (Barlow & Hayes, 1979). Sequential confounding, per se, may be less of a problem in ATDs than in other multiple-treatment designs

2   Sequential confounding and carry-over effects also occur with multiple-treatment designs and they are described in this context in Chapter 5.

because each intervention is presented briefly (i.e. on one occasion) rather than consecutively over many occasions, as in WRDs.

Carry-over (or contextual) effects refer to the influence of one intervention on a contiguous intervention regardless of sequencing order. Barlow and Hayes (1979) distinguished two types of carry-over effects: contrast and induction. Contrast effects refer to changes in the target behaviour in an opposite direction than expected due to contrast between interventions. Induction refers to the transfer of one intervention's effect to the other, as if there were a synergetic interaction between interventions. To illustrate contrast and induction carry-over effects we provide a hypothetical example. Imagine an ATD comparing three interventions to improve social communication (specifically, turn-taking) after traumatic brain injury: intervention 1 (video replay of social communication behaviours), intervention 2 (verbal feedback about social communication behaviours), and intervention 3 (repetitive practice of social communication behaviours without feedback). Induction could occur because intervention 2 (verbal feedback) primes or favourably predisposes the participant to the receipt of intervention 1 (video replay). In this case, the effect of intervention 1 would be greater *because* of the existence of intervention 2, than if intervention 1 were used in isolation. Contrast operates somewhat differently. Here, the participant may find intervention 3 (repetitive practice) so arduous and boring, that by its mere existence as one of the interventions it adversely affects the other two interventions, such that their effectiveness is actually opposite to that expected. According to Barlow and Hayes induction effects are, however, transient. Barlow and Hayes recommend two strategies for minimising these carry-over effects. First, to counterbalance or randomise alternation sequence (even though carry-over effects are not, by definition, order dependent). Second, to implement each intervention on alternate days, rather than in the same day or session.

Alternation effects are produced by the interventions being administered within a relatively brief time of each other. This tends to increase carry-over effects, particularly contrast. Barlow and Hayes (1979) recommend that a slower alternation sequence is preferable for this reason, but warn that the alternation speed also needs to be sufficiently quick to enable the participant to discriminate between interventions. This is an important issue in the context of neurorehabilitation. Consider a situation where the participant in question has, inter alia, significant impairment of anterograde memory. He or she might have some difficulty remembering sufficient intervention details to enable him/her to accurately discriminate between interventions. Reducing the alternation speed might exacerbate this problem. There are, however, no hard and fast rules on how to accomplish this balance satisfactorily (Hains & Baer, 1989).

Barlow and Hayes (1979) also suggest three ways to estimate multi-treatment effects via independent verification. The first way is to evaluate one of the interventions using a simple A-B design under the same conditions as the original ATD. If the effect of B is different than it was during the ATD study, the magnitude (and direction) of the differences will provide an estimation of interference effects. A second approach is to adapt the ATD, so that a single intervention is delivered on several occasions prior to commencing the comparison phase. Changes in the effect of B between the 'alone' and comparison phases would, again, reflect multi-treatment interference effects. A third approach, and one which Barlow and Hayes consider to be more elegant, is to use functional manipulation to evaluate multi-treatment interference. In this instance, the 'dosage' (i.e. intensity, duration, frequency) of one intervention is increased. If the effect of the second, unchanged intervention then varies after the dosage of the first intervention has been increased, the change could be attributable to carry-over effects.

Concluding remarks

ATDs provide a sound methodology for single-case applied research which also has practical clinical advantages. Internal validity is strengthened by intra-subject replication of the experimental effect and the strength of ATDs is their relative immunity to threats to internal validity. Major risks such as history, maturation, baseline instability, and cyclicity are assumed to have a comparable effect on all interventions. Changes under one intervention are less readily attributable to extraneous factors if changes do not also occur in the other interventions at the same time. ATDs should, however, only be used with interventions that are withdrawable and target behaviours that are likely to respond quickly to the intervention.

Unfortunately, multi-treatment interference is a significant concern with these designs. Although distinctions can be made between sequential confounding, carry-over effects, and alternation effects, they all essentially refer to the same problem: the mutual and simultaneous interference between interventions. Various strategies are, however, available to estimate the magnitude of multi-treatment interference. Selecting suitable target behaviours (i.e. target behaviours that are likely to respond quickly to the intervention) and interventions (i.e. fast acting), and manipulating the order and frequency of alternations helps to minimise these effects. Moreover, including an initial baseline phase, continuing to include the baseline as an intervention during the comparison phase, and including a final 'best treatment' phase, provide data to help detect and evaluate multi-treatment interference effects. Clinically, ATDs are practical because the intervention can be started immediately without a preceding baseline, interventions are not withdrawn, and the design yields clinically useful data in a relatively short time.

8

CHANGING-CRITERION DESIGNS

The changing-criterion design (CCD) was introduced into the field of behavioural research by Hall (1971; Weis & Hall, 1971). CCDs are modelled on operant conditioning schedules suitable for gradually shaping behaviour, and are focused on a single target behaviour. Following a baseline phase, the intervention is applied to the target behaviour over a series of treatment phases. The reinforcement schedule that comprises the intervention is incremented (accelerated) or decremented (decelerated) in a stepwise fashion at each treatment phase change. Apart from this standard format, there are two other variants (the range-bound CCD and the distributed CCD) that are discussed in the sections below. While MBDs and WRDs are frequently used in applied behavioural and clinical research, by contrast, CCDs account for less than 5% of the designs reported in the literature (Perdices & Tate, 2009; Shadish & Sullivan, 2011; Smith, 2012; Tate et al., 2016c; see Table 1.1 in Chapter 1).

Rationale of CCDs

The CCD is considered to be a variant of the MBD (Hartmann & Hall, 1976), and, as with most other single-case designs, CCDs start with a baseline phase during which the untreated target behaviour is repeatedly and continuously measured over a period of time. As is advisable with baselines in other design types, the baseline in CCDs should be continued until stability in the target behaviour has been achieved; that is, there is little or no perceptible trend or variability in the data. At this point the intervention phase is commenced. The intervention phase consists of a series of what Kazdin (2011) refers to as subphases, which he designates as b_1, b_2, b_3 ... b_n. In other words, a CCD is essentially an A-B design with an extended B phase consisting of several b subphases. Once the intervention is introduced, it remains constant throughout all the b subphases. A performance criterion for the target behaviour is set, a priori, for each b subphase, and the criterion is incremented/decremented in a stepwise manner in each successive subphase.

In other SCEDs the intervention is systematically manipulated with the aim of eliciting changes in the target behaviour. By contrast, in CCDs, the intervention is not withdrawn, and the same intervention is applied across all the subphases. It is the performance criterion of the target behaviour that is systematically manipulated in stepwise increments or decrements. Performance in the initial baseline serves to predict the level of target behaviour performance in the first intervention subphase (b_1) when the first criterion becomes operational. The level of target behaviour performance in each intervention subphase then becomes the 'baseline' against which performance in the next intervention subphase is compared. Figure 8.1A shows a hypothetical CCD where the aim of the criterion changes over the intervention subphases is to increase (accelerate) the level of the target behaviour. CCDs can be equally used if the therapeutic intention is to reduce (decelerate) the level of the target behaviour as, for example, might be the case with aggressive behaviour. In those instances, the graph would show a series of descending, rather than ascending 'steps' (Figure 8.1B). In either case, the discussion in the following sections is equally applicable.

As we can see in Figure 8.1, the performance criterion in each subphase is usually indicated by a horizontal line. The central aspect of the CCD is that the onset of the next intervention subphase is triggered when the level of the target behaviour reaches the predetermined criterion of performance that was set for the current subphase. Reaching the criterion of performance usually entails not only reaching the level of performance that was set a priori, but also maintaining that level for a specified number of consecutive sessions (usually three or more). It is possible that the target performance might reach criterion at some point during a subphase, then drop below criterion over the following sessions. Requiring that the performance criterion is maintained for several consecutive sessions helps to verify that reaching the performance

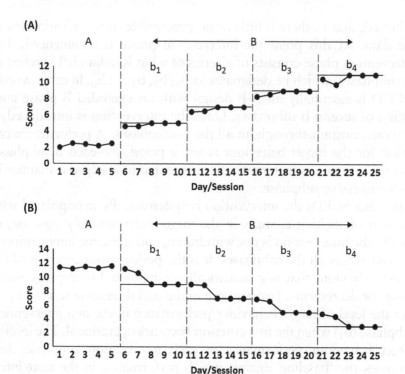

FIGURE 8.1 Hypothetical data for a CCD

Notes: the horizontal arrows at the top of the graph indicate that the B intervention phase consists of several subphases, designated as b_1, b_2, b_3 and b_4. Solid horizontal lines within each intervention subphase indicate the criterion level. The top graph (A) shows an accelerating criterion; the bottom graph (B) shows a decelerating criterion.

criterion on a given session does not just reflect inherent variability in the target behaviour.

Evidence standards and internal validity

Experimental control in CCDs is demonstrated when the performance level of the target behaviour changes with each stepwise change in the performance criterion (Hartmann & Hall, 1976). That is, the experimental effect is demonstrated when the performance of the target behaviour changes accordingly when, and only when, the next criterion for performance is introduced in the next subphase. Experimental control is unambiguously demonstrated when the target behaviour changes in a clear stepwise manner corresponding to the criterion changes.

According to Kazdin (2011), a baseline and two intervention sub-phases are a minimum requirement for CCDs. This format incorporates two changes in the criterion which provide two opportunities to replicate the experimental effect. Nonetheless, he recommends using three or more criterion changes, which Hartmann and Hall (1976) also endorse. In order to meet current standards of evidence, each subphase must have at least 5 data points (Design Standard 4; Kratochwill et al., 2013) and the experimental effect is replicated on at least three performance criteria (i.e. three stepwise changes in criterion), in order to provide three opportunities for replication of the experimental effect (Design Standard 3). It is, however, unclear if in order to meet evidence standards, the replication of the experimental effect on at least three criteria includes the change between baseline (phase A) and the first intervention subphase. If so, then the design need only include three intervention subphases. Otherwise, four intervention subphases are required. There is no specification in the standards of the requirements CCDs must fulfil in order to meet standards with reservations. However, as we proposed in Chapter 1, following the rationale of other designs, it would seem reasonable that a CCD with three criterion changes and 3 to 4 data points per phase would meet standards with reservations. In a recent review of 267 individual CCDs reported in 106 studies published between 1971 and 2013 in 57 journals primarily in the fields of applied behaviour and special education research, Klein, Houlihan, Vincent, and Panahon (2017) found that the majority of CCDs (68.6%) utilised three or more criteria and, hence, clearly met Design Standard 3. In 10.1% of CCDs two or less criteria were used, and for 21.3% the number of criteria used was unknown.

Threats to internal validity from maturation, history, or other confounding factors are minimised by intra-subject replication of the experimental effect at each criterion change. It is possible that a change in the target behaviour when the performance criterion is changed might coincide with the occurrence of an unrelated event which influences the target behaviour. In these circumstances, the change in the target behaviour cannot be unequivocally attributed to the intervention effect. If the target behaviour consistently and repeatedly changes in the predicted direction every time the performance criterion is changed, however, it becomes increasingly less likely that the observed changes on each of several occasions reflect the influence of extraneous factors. Attributing behaviour change to the intervention effect becomes more plausible. Intervention subphase lengths are likely to differ. If they are constant, they "should be preceded by a baseline phase longer than each of the separate treatment phases"[1] in order to ensure that changes in the target behaviour are not attributable to factors unrelated to the intervention effect (Hartmann & Hall, 1976, p. 530).

Types of CCDs

The standard design

The standard CCD was used by Skinner, Skinner, and Armstrong (2000) to improve reading persistence in a 26-year-old man with paranoid schizophrenia who was living in a community-based treatment facility. He was unable to read continually for more than very brief periods of time, and asked the investigator (a staff member at the facility) for help in improving his reading persistence. The intervention was a contingency schedule in which the participant could 'earn' a soft drink if he was able to read the required number of pages continuously (the criterion, as operationally defined). Baseline and intervention sessions were carried out on a daily basis. The reading criterion was set at one page for the first intervention subphase (indicated in Figure 8.2 as B1), and increased by one page at each subsequent intervention subphase. When the participant had met the reading criterion on three sessions during the intervention subphase, the criterion was increased by one page.

As Figure 8.2 shows, the participant consistently met the reading criterion across all eight intervention subphases (B1–B8). The eight occasions in subphases B2–B6 where reading performance was zero pages indicate days when the participant chose not to do any reading. Otherwise, he met criterion on all but one of the days he decided to read. The intervention was ceased at the participant's request after approximately six weeks. Follow-up approximately one week later showed that the participant surpassed the reading criterion (eight pages) that had been set at the last intervention subphase (B8).

Withdrawal features can be embedded in CCDs to strengthen internal validity if the effectiveness of the intervention becomes unclear. In these circumstances, if the target behaviour returns to pre-intervention levels, it bolsters the plausibility of the intervention being responsible for observed changes. This is particularly so if the target behaviour returns to criterion, or near criterion, levels when the intervention is

1 Admittedly, this will be difficult to predict and implement at least until the end of the second intervention subphase.

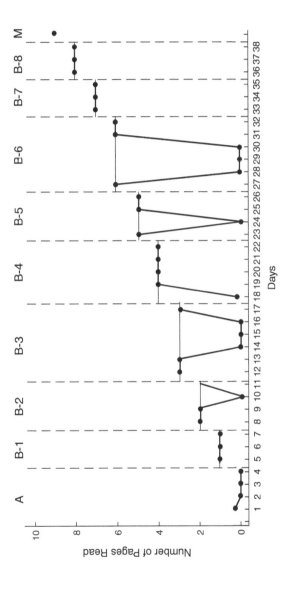

FIGURE 8.2 Number of pages read by participant each day

Notes: horizontal lines in intervention subphase denote the criterion (i.e. number of pages the participant was required to read continuously)

Source: Skinner, Skinner, and Armstrong (2000); reprinted with permission

reintroduced. Davis and Chittum (1994) used contingency and graphic feedback of performance to increase leisure activity levels (e.g. time spent playing cards, socialising) in six individuals with traumatic brain injury living in a residential facility. A CCD was used to deliver the intervention to each participant. For three participants, a second A-phase was introduced in the design after the first two intervention subphases. Target behaviour for two of the participants returned to baseline and then returned to criterion levels in the next intervention subphase. This provided a clear demonstration of the experimental effect. For the third participant, however, the effect was not observed: the target behaviour during the initial baseline was above the criterion for the first treatment subphase, remained well above criterion levels on all intervention subphases and did not diminish in the second A-phase. CCDs are also sometimes incorporated within MBD and ATDs (Klein et al., 2017; Shadish & Sullivan, 2011).

Range-bound CCD

The strength of experimental control might be compromised if there is gradual improvement in the target behaviour that is not clearly connected to criterion changes. In these circumstances, the criterion magnitude could be decreased and/or the duration of the intervention subphases could be increased in order to establish a clearer correspondence between changes in the target behaviour and the performance criterion (Kazdin, 2011). Rapid changes in the target behaviour that are not clearly connected to the criterion changes or may exceed the magnitude of change required by the criterion may also weaken experimental control clarity. The design variant proposed by McDougall (2005), the *range-bound* CCD, addresses this problem. In the standard CCD, criteria are defined as point measures of performance. For example, a 70% increase (if accelerating) or decrease (if decelerating) in target performance relative to the mean of the previous subphase. In the range-bound variation, criteria are defined as performance ranges, but other aspects of the design remain unchanged. For example, a 60–70% change or a 15 ± 3 score change in the target behaviour. This offers three advantages. First, a performance range makes allowances for inherent variability in the target behaviour which may not, of itself, indicate that the intervention is ineffective. Second, focusing on a performance range may help to improve the consistency of the participant's performance (Kazdin, 2011). Third, percent of days in which performance was in-range can be scored with these designs. This may be a useful clinical measure that helps to characterise the participant's progress during the study.

Distributed criterion CCD

McDougall, Hawkins, Brady, and Jenkins (2006) proposed a CCD variant, the distributed criterion CCD which incorporates features of MBDs and WRDs. This design variant is particularly suitable for investigating multi-tasking strategies where the participant needs to allocate time to several independent and mutually exclusive tasks (McDougal et al. offer the example of an investigator allocating time to work on three different research manuscripts simultaneously). The design has multiple tiers, as if several CCDs were being implemented simultaneously. Different target behaviours are treated in each tier, and return to an A baseline phase can be incorporated in each tier. Because of its narrow application, the distributed criterion variant is not likely to have wide relevance in neuropsychological rehabilitation.

Design issues

The level and magnitude of change in criteria, is an important design factor in CCDs. The criterion for the first intervention subphase is generally set as a percentage of the A phase mean above (for ascending designs) or below (for descending designs) the A phase mean. For example, if the mean score for baseline target behaviour is 10, the performance criterion for the first intervention subphase could be set at 15, which is 50% above the baseline mean. At the same time, the magnitude of the criterion change should be larger than the variability range of the untreated target behaviour. Roane et al. (2011) suggest that the full range of criteria that will be utilised in other phases should be available in each subphase of the design. This avoids artificially creating a ceiling effect if the participant surpasses the performance criterion in a given phase. In addition, it should reflect the anticipated degree to which the target behaviour might be resistant to change (Hartmann & Hall, 1976). Hence, the criterion magnitude should be large for target behaviours with high variability and small for those with low variability. And it should be small for target behaviours resistant to change and large for those that are not.

Advantages and disadvantages

A central advantage of CCDs is that the intervention is not withdrawn so, unlike WRDs, there are no ethical concerns regarding withholding treatment. There is a single baseline phase in CCDs, which means that, unlike MBDs, potential threats to internal validity associated with undue prolongation of baselines are not a concern. In terms of neuropsychological rehabilitation, CCDs offer a very practical advantage. Behaviours targeted for intervention in individuals with acquired brain impairment may be more amenable to gradual change. One possible reason for this might be that due to significant depletion of cognitive resources as a consequence of brain impairment, it might be difficult for an individual to modify a behaviour in one fell swoop. With CCDs, behaviours can be shaped gradually towards a desired goal. Moreover, the magnitude of the criterion change can be adjusted to best suit the resistance to change of the behaviour being treated (see the design issues and variations section above).

According to Ledford and Gast (2014) CCDs have two 'weaknesses'. First, they are applicable to a relatively small range of behaviours (although they give no justification for this claim) and these must be amenable to treatment within the framework of an operant conditioning paradigm. Second, criterion-change size can strongly influence how well experimental control is demonstrated. Criterion-change size needs to strike a balance so that the required changes in the target behaviour are not only detectable, but also achievable. Criterion size magnitude is, however, set a priori, and "there is always some degree of subjectivity or 'professional guess-work' involved" (Ledford & Gast, p. 349). One strategy for dealing with this is to set the criteria 'on the go' such that the criterion for an intervention subphase is set as a percentage of the performance level (usually the mean) of the previous intervention subphase. There is no reason why the magnitude of the criterion change should remain constant. Kazdin (2011) suggests that the magnitude of criterion change might need to be varied in response to the data and, if necessary, it should be varied.

Concluding remarks

CCDs are well suited to rehabilitation practice, and for evaluating interventions to address behavioural, functional, and cognitive consequences of acquired brain injury. The CCD offers at least two advantages in this context. First, the intervention does not need to be withdrawn, so ethical concerns about withholding treatment are not an issue. Second, the operant conditioning paradigm that underpins CCDs is eminently suited to modify behaviour in a gradually achievable manner. They are especially suitable when the target behaviour that is being treated cannot reasonably be expected to have an immediate or large response to the intervention. These may well be circumstances that characterise the dynamics of behaviour change in individuals with acquired brain injury. According to Klein and colleagues (2017) "The utility of the CCD as a behavior change agent is evident. It is a flexible design that can be used with any population, on a diverse range of behaviors, in a variety of settings, while maintaining adequate experimental control" (p. 60). It is surprising how underutilised they seem to be in neurorehabilitation.

9

DATA EVALUATION

Debate regarding the appropriateness and accuracy of various methods for analyzing SCED data, the interpretation of single-case effect sizes, and other concerns vital to the validity of SCED results has been ongoing for decades, and no clear consensus has been reached.

(Smith, 2012, p. 521)

Analysis of SCED results entails evaluation of both experimental and applied criteria (Kazdin, 2011). Evaluation of the experimental criteria refers to visual and/or statistical analysis of the data to determine if a there is a functional relationship between observed changes in the target behaviour (dependent variable) and the intervention (independent variable). In other words, to assess the reliability and level of evidence for the presence (or absence) of an intervention effect. Evaluation of the applied criteria refers to determining whether or not the intervention has had an important or clinically significant impact in the day-to-day life of the participant.

In the first section of this chapter we discuss visual analysis of the graphed data. Systematic approaches aimed at strengthening the reliability of conclusions drawn from visual inspection of the data are described, and factors influencing the reliability of visual analysis are also considered. Statistical techniques are discussed in the second section. The major types of analytic techniques are evaluated in terms of how well they deal with potentially confounding features in the data (e.g. autocorrelation, also known as serial dependence; see section below on autocorrelation) and how well they control for Type I and Type II error. Assessment and evaluation of applied criteria are discussed in the next section. Social validity and clinical significance are the two domains that need to be addressed in this context.

Visual analysis

Historically, the primary and preferred method of evaluating SCED data has been through visual analysis of the graphed data (Kazdin, 2011; Parsonson & Baer, 1986). Parsonson and Baer suggested that visual analysis of SCED data developed naturally from the practice of monitoring and graphing study results as they emerged during the SCED trial. This inspection highlighted relationships between the target behaviour and the experimental variables, so that "the graph served as a comprehensive yet simple means of recording, storing, representing, communicating, and above all, analysing behavioural data" (p. 157). Parsonson and Baer emphasise that "One of the central points of visual analysis is to leave with maximal clarity to each researcher and each member of the research audience whether the current experimental intervention has had an effect on the behaviour under study" (p. 22). According to Kazdin (2011), graphing SCED results is "part of the inferential process" (p. 285), based on visually inspecting the graphed data in order to reach "a judgement about the reliability or consistency of intervention effects" (p. 286).

Visual analysis emphasises clinical, rather than statistical, significance. Baer (1977) champions the use of visual analysis arguing that "a difference has to be seen to be affirmed" (p. 169). Large, clinically significant effects should be readily apparent in the graphed data, and detecting a functional relationship from visual inspection largely relies upon there being a large intervention effect (Sidman, 1960). Thus, if an intervention has truly had an effect on the participant's behaviour, this should be clearly obvious in the graphed data. Small intervention effects may be difficult to detect visually and even if they are statistically significant, may not be clinically meaningful (Baer, 1977; Parsonson & Baer, 1986). Baer et al. (1968) consider that if an intervention "does not produce large enough effects for practical value, then application [i.e. the intervention] has failed" (p. 96).

Visual analysis is still considered to be the primary method for analysing SCED data (Kazdin, 2011). Moreover, some investigators have reported that relatively few published studies (approximately 10%) use statistical analysis solely (Busk & Marasculio, 1992;

Parker et al., 2005). In a survey of 409 SCEDs from the special education and applied behaviour research literature, Smith (2012) reported that visual analysis (20.8%) was more frequently used than statistical analysis (13.9%); 7.3% of studies used both techniques but more than half did not report any analytic technique. By contrast, all 66 studies surveyed from the sport psychology literature used both visual and statistical analyses (Barker et al., 2013), and 64% of 89 studies surveyed from the neurorehabilitation literature used statistical analysis (Perdices & Tate, 2009).

Systematic procedures for visual analysis

A major criticism of visual analysis has been that it lacks formal rules and decision-making criteria, but several protocols to systematise the procedures have been proposed. Almost 40 years ago, Furlong and Wampold (1981) proposed a four-step system for conducting visual analyses. The steps consist of the following: first, examining the data for stability, trend, and level within-phase and across similar phases (e.g. all B phases); second, determining whether or not there is an intervention effect by examining changes across dissimilar phases (i.e. A versus B) in level and/or trend when intervention was introduced; third, determining the meaningfulness of the intervention effect by examining whether or not it was immediate or delayed, permanent or temporary, and clinically significant. The fourth step concerns generalisability which consists of replicating the study results in other individuals with similar characteristics to the participant/s in the original study as well as individuals with different relevant characteristics. This last step in the system, although important for external validity, is not generally considered to be a central aspect of visual analysis. Decisions are indexed as yes, no, or unsure, but specific quantitative operational criteria defining these three response categories are not provided. The authors admit that visual evaluation of trend is problematic and acknowledged that data with low variability are more reliable. They also suggest that determination of clinical significance needs to go beyond visual analysis.

According to Roane et al. (2011), level, stability (i.e. variability), and trend in the data are "The three critical elements of a single-case graph that allow prediction of future performance and should be the focus of visual inspection" (p. 134). All three were of primary importance in the system developed by Furlong and Wampold (1981) and, in essence, are the central foci of subsequently developed protocols.

Kratochwill et al. (2010) developed an influential protocol intended for use by trained raters as part of the WWC Single-Case Designs Technical Documentation (Kratochwill, Levin, Horner, & Swoboda; 2014; Kratochwill et al. 2013). After determining that the study either Meets Design Standards or Meets Design Standards with Reservations (see Chapter 1), data for the target behaviour and (other outcome variables) are visually inspected to see how well they meet evidence standards, and determine whether there is sufficient evidence to demonstrate a functional relationship between the target behaviour and the intervention. The presence of a functional relationship (i.e. that there is an intervention effect) is evaluated by using a four-step procedure:

- Step 1: evaluates the predictability (stability) of the baseline data
- Step 2: within-phase data are assessed for consistency
- Step 3: consists of making between-phase comparisons of adjacent phases (i.e. A-B, B-A) and similar phases (i.e. all A phases, all B phases, etc.)
- Step 4: consists of integrating all this information to determine if the intervention effect has been independently demonstrated at least three times

Visual analysis has greater accuracy if there is relative stability in the initial baseline phase, and also little, if any, trend and minimal overlap of data with subsequent phases (Franklin, Gorman, Beasley, & Allison, 1996; Parsonson & Baer, 1978). Six within-phase and between-phase features of the data are examined in Steps 1–3 to evaluate whether or not a functional relationship has been established: (i) level: the magnitude (usually the mean, although Lane and Gast (2014) recommend the median) or value of the data points; (ii) trend: the slope of a straight line of best fit for the data within a phase; (iii) variability: the range or standard deviation of data about the best-fitting straight line; (iv) immediacy of the effect: level change between the last three and first 3 data points respectively of adjacent phases; (v) overlap: proportion of data points overlapping with data from the previous phase; and (vi) consistency of data patterns across similar phases (Barlow et al., 2009; Fisher, Kelley, & Lomas, 2003; Gast & Spriggs, 2014; Kazdin, 1982; Kratochwill et al., 2010; 2013). Changes in the target behaviour in the hypothesised direction when the intervention is introduced demonstrate a functional relationship between the dependent and independent variables. Using hypothetical data, Kratochwill et al. (2010) illustrate in detail how to make, and when applicable quantify, this systematic evaluation of the data. Qualitative characteristics of the data that should be considered to decide whether or not there is an intervention effect are discussed, but specific or quantitative criteria for making a decision are not defined.

In Step 4, evidence for a functional relationship in those studies that meet design standards (with or without reservations) is then categorised as follows:

- Strong Evidence: at least three demonstrations of the intervention effect and no demonstration of no intervention effect
- Moderate Evidence: at least three demonstrations of the intervention effect with at least one demonstration of no intervention effect
- No Evidence: less than three demonstrations of the intervention effect

Effect size (ES) is then estimated if the data provide either Strong Evidence or Moderate Evidence for a functional relationship. Regression-based estimates of ES are recommended in preference to non-parametric or multi-level methods (see next section). It is also recommended that more than one ES index should be calculated and compared for consistency.

Gast and colleagues (Gast & Spriggs, 2014; Lane & Gast, 2014) codified a very detailed protocol for systematic visual analysis (Table 9.1), which was "designed as an assistive tool for novice researchers who will visually analyse data when using a SCED" (Lane & Gast, 2014, p. 449). In addition, Gast and Spriggs (2014; pp. 199–201) provide detailed summary and worksheets to record data as well as a worked-out example, using hypothetical data, illustrating how to conduct the analysis.

Issues with visual analysis

The reliability of visually guided judgements has been examined in terms of whether or not an intervention effect can be reliably detected by different individuals. It has been generally evaluated in terms of making global judgements about the presence or absence of an intervention effect, or rating the likelihood that

TABLE 9.1 Summary of systematic visual analysis procedure

Within-phase analysis

Step 1: label phases A, B, C, etc.

Step 2: Count data points per phase

	Specifics	Evaluation
Step 3: Descriptive statistics of data	Calculate: • mean, median, range, • stability envelope=+80% of data points within ± 25% of phase A median same stability envelope superimposed on phase B	Evaluates variability of baseline and intervention phase data
Step 4: Level change	4a – Relative Change: calculate medians for first and second half of data points in each phase	Use medians to determine if level in each phase shows *relative* improvement/ deterioration
	4b – Absolute Change: calculate difference between the first and last data point in each phase	Use obtained difference values to determine if level in each phase shows *absolute* improvement/ deterioration
Step 5: Trend line	Split-middle trend line plotted for each phase	Evaluate within-phase direction of trend
Step 6: Variability	• Superimpose stability envelope from Step 1 on trendline from Step 5 • Calculate percentage of data points within the stability envelope	Evaluate within-phase variability
Step 7: Integration of Steps	Compile the information from previous steps to evaluate trends in each phase	Evaluate trend direction, whether it is stable or variable or if there are multiple paths

Between-phase analysis

Step 1: Determine number of variables that changed between phases. Ideally the only change is the introduction/withdrawal of the intervention

Step 2: Identify trend direction across adjacent phases – upward (accelerating), downward (decelerating), or none (zero-celerating) and whether they are in the expected direction

Step 3: compare the decision from Step 6 of the within-condition analysis section to Step 2 above

Step 4: Evaluate – 4a: relative; 4b: absolute; 4c: median; and 4d: mean level change

Steps 5: 5a: calculate percentage of non-overlapping data (PND); 5b: calculate percent of overlapping data (POD) using method described by Scruggs, Mastropieri, and Casto (1987)

Source: adapted from Gast & Spriggs (2014); Lane & Gast (2014)

there is an intervention effect,[1] but not in the context of the reliability of systematic visual analysis of the graphed data. Inter-rater agreement for global judgements is generally around, or below, chance level (Brossart, Parker, Olson, & Mahadevan, 2006; Gibson & Ottenbacher, 1988; Harrington & Velicer, 2015). Ninci, Vannest, Willson, and Zhang (2015) recently conducted a meta-analysis to identify variables that may potentially affect inter-rater agreement. They identified 19 studies published between 1982 and 2013 that had investigated this issue. Inter-rater agreement was affected by design type (.81;[2] for multi-element designs;[3] .74 for A-B/reversal designs), rating scale used (.76 for dichotomous ratings; .69 for three-point scale) and whether or not definitions of the construct being rated were provided (.84 if provided; .74 if not provided). By contrast, inter-rater reliability was unaffected by whether or not contextual information about the data being evaluated was provided, the use of visual aids, or the rater's level of experience and expertise.

Inter-rater agreement is also influenced by features in the data and how they are presented. It is enhanced if variability is low, there is no trend, and large ESs are apparent in graphed data (Harrington & Velicer, 2015). Changes in variability between phases are, however, unrelated to inter-rater agreement, and changes in level and mean shift across phases are associated with consistency across raters (Gibson & Ottenbacher, 1988). Inter-rater disagreement tends to occur when there is significant slope, change in slope, or both in the data (Gibson & Ottenbacher, 1988; Harrington & Velicer, 2015). Morales, Domínguez, and Jurado (2001) found that for hypothetical A-B graphs, inter-rater agreement was better if the data were presented as Tukey box plots rather than bar graphs or the traditional line graphs.

Agreement between visual and statistical analysis

Agreement between visual and statistical analyses is variable and depends largely on the statistical technique used for comparison.

1   Raters' evaluation of the intervention effect are generally made in terms of: (i) a dichotomy: yes/no; (ii) a three-point scale: yes/no/uncertain; or (iii) a six-point scale: 0=strongly disagree, to 5=strongly agree.
2   Correlation coefficients refer to medians.
3   Multi-element designs described by Ninci et al. (2015) refer to functional analysis studies.

There is good agreement between visual analysis and t-tests (86%; Bobrovitz & Ottenbacher, 1998) or randomisation tests (80%: Park, Marascuilo, & Gaylord-Ross, 1990). By contrast, agreement between visual judgement and statistical analysis can be poor, even for raters with substantial experience in graphic analysis. Brossart et al. (2006) found that agreement between visual judgements regarding how convinced raters were that there was an intervention effect (rated on a 5-point scale, with 1=not convinced and 5=very convinced) and ESs (R^2) calculated using five different statistical techniques,[4] were at or below chance level, with correlations between the two ranging between .39 and .57. Others have reported similar findings (e.g. Harrington & Velicer, 2015; Jones, Weinrott, & Vaught, 1978). Parsonson and Baer (2015) question the relevance of comparing visual analysis to statistical tests, given that no single 'gold standard' statistical test exists for SCEDs and the different techniques may produce different results. They conclude that "The fact that these methods often generate different conclusions about the same data is an almost useless fact, unless we know which conclusion is somehow the better one" (p. 37).

Agreement between visual judgement (whether or not there is an intervention effect) and statistical analysis (whether or not time-series analysis yields a significant p-value) is relatively better (.73) when autocorrelation in the data is low, and poorer (.50) when it is high (Jones et al., 1978). It has been claimed that visual analysis is insensitive to small intervention effects and is conservative compared with statistical analysis and likely to have a low Type I error rate (Baer, 1977; Kazdin, 1982; Parsonson & Baer, 1986). However, detection of intervention effects by visual judgement has been shown to have a high Type I error rate, particularly if there is high variability in the data, while Type II error rate remains relatively low (usually < 10%) irrespective of degree of autocorrelation or variability in the data (Matyas & Greenwood, 1990).

---

4   Statistical tests used in the study: (a) binomial test on extended Phase A baseline (White & Haring, 1980); (b) Last Treatment Day (White, Rusch, Kazdin & Hartmann, 1989); (c) Gorsuch's trend ES (Faith, Allison & Gorman, 1996; Gorsuch, 1983); (d) Center's mean plus trend difference (Center, Skiba & Casey, 1985–1986); and (e) Allison's mean plus trend difference (Allison & Gorman, 1993; Faith et al., 1996). Some of these will be discussed in the statistical analysis section below.

Statistical analysis[5]

Parsonson and Baer (2015) note that visual analysis is criticised for being subjective, but argue that selecting a suitable statistical test involves many judgements about complex theoretical premises and assumptions, and the process might not be as objective as supposed. Nonetheless, Kazdin (2011), acknowledges that statistical analysis is valuable when: (i) there are unstable baselines and/or variability is large and might confound visual inspection; (ii) evaluating new interventions where the treatment effect is not well understood; (iii) interventions produce small but important changes in the target behaviour which might not be readily detected by visual analysis; and (iv) enhancing replicability in data evaluation. Statistical techniques to evaluate SCED data have proliferated over recent decades. There is still, however, no agreed-upon criteria for statistical analysis of SCED data (Kratochwill et al., 2013; Smith, 2012), and different techniques applied to the same data can yield different results (e.g. Brossart et al., 2006). Moreover, data cyclicity, trends, and auto-correlation also differentially influence the validity of statistical tests (Allison, 1992; Campbell, 2004; Harrington & Velicer, 2015; Jones et al., 1978; Matyas & Greenwood, 1990; Parker, Vannest, & Davis, 2011a; Velicer & Molenaar, 2013).

Autocorrelation

Autocorrelation, or serial dependency, refers to the lack of independence between one score in a time series and a subsequent score in the series. In the context of SCEDs, the score for the target behaviour at time 1 is likely to be correlated with the score at time 2 and possibly the score at subsequent times because they are measures of the target behaviour for the same individual. There are several methods to calculate autocorrelation and reduce bias in these estimates (see Huitema & McKean, 1991; Solanas, Manolov, & Sierra, 2010). Calculation of the statistical significance of autocorrelation estimates can also take into account the number of observations in the data. The most

5 In the discussion of specific analytic methods that follows, we have taken the position that the intervention will have the effect of increasing the score that reflects the level of the target behaviour so that the scores in phase A will be lower than in phase B. The same logic and procedures apply if the intervention is intended to decrease the scores that reflect the level of the target behaviour, in which case scores in A will be higher than in B.

frequently-used method to calculate lag-1 autocorrelation, known as the conventional estimator, is the Pearson Product–Moment Correlation coefficient between a series consisting of the scores in a given phase (i.e. $S_1, S_2, S_3 \ldots S_i \ldots S_n$) and a series of the same scores commencing at the second observation (i.e. $S_2, S_3, S_4 \ldots S_i \ldots S_n$). A lag-2 coefficient reflects the correlation between an observation and the second subsequent observation, and so forth. Generally, it is lag-1 autocorrelation and its impact that is evaluated in SCEDs

There is persuasive evidence that autocorrelation, rather than being rare or insignificant (Huitema, 1985; Huitema & McKean, 1998), is highly prevalent and significant (up to 83%; ranging between .10 and >.90) in both baseline and intervention phases (Busk & Marascuilo, 1988; Jones et al., 1978; Robey, Schultz, Crawford, & Sinner, 1999; Shadish & Sullivan, 2011). The effects of autocorrelation are discussed in the sections below describing specific analytic techniques.

Effect sizes

Cohen is credited with introducing the concept of ES to psychological research. A wide range of ES measures to evaluate intervention effectiveness in between-groups research have been available over the last 60 years (Huberty, 2002). They were originally developed to provide a measure of the degree to which the observed between-groups differences deviated from the expectations postulated in the null hypothesis and are independent of sample size (Cohen, 1994). An ES quantifies the size of a difference between two groups and provides a point estimate of treatment effect; that is, how well an intervention works.

Most of the techniques discussed below yield ES indices and with some, p-values can also be obtained. How ESs are to be interpreted in SCEDs is, however, a vexed question. Cohen (1988) suggested guidelines for interpreting the magnitude of d (see below): small=.20; medium=.50; large=.80, and R^2: small=.01; medium=.09; large=.25 for continuous predictors, and small=.01; medium=.059; large=1.37 for categorical predictors. Guidelines for interpreting the magnitude of other ES indices with potential application to SCED data have also been developed over the years (e.g. Bakeman, 2005; Draper, 2016; Kraemer, Morgan, Leech, Gliner, Vaske, & Harmon 2003; Rea & Parker, 1992). All these guidelines were, however, formulated to interpret results of group studies. Their applicability to SCED data has been questioned due to the lack of correspondence with the ESs typically found in these kinds of data, and lack of agreement about how they should be interpreted (Kratochwill et al., 2010, 2013; Parker et al., 2005; Shadish, Rindskopf, & Hedges, 2008). For instance, based on surveys of the speech and language literature, Robey and colleagues (Robey et al., 1999; Robey & Beeson, 2005, cited in Beeson & Robey, 2006) have proposed guidelines for interpreting ESs for Cohen's *d* (see below) that not only differ from those originally proposed by Cohen, but vary according to the target behaviour being treated (small=2.6, medium=3.9, large=5.8 for acquired alexia and agraphia; small=6.0, medium= 12.0, large=18.0 for syntactic production; small=4.0, medium=7.0, large=10.1 for lexical retrieval).

Specific techniques

Techniques for analysing SCED data are described in the following sections. Our selection focuses on techniques that are better known and commonly used, but is far from exhaustive. Univariate ANOVA methods for analysing SCED data have been proposed (see Gentile, Roden, & Klein, 1972; Shine & Bower, 1971). We have not, however, included ANOVA (or t-tests), because their use has been questioned, given that SCED data do not meet the required assumptions (Kratochwill et al., 1974) and Type I error rate for ANOVA is unacceptable (Toothaker, Banz, Noble, Camp, & Davis, 1983).

Manolov, Gast, Perdices, and Evans (2014) and Manolov, Moeyaert, and Evans (2015) describe a more comprehensive set of analytic techniques, as well as a listing of websites offering free statistical packages, stand-alone programs, and calculators to implement these techniques. The paper by Manolov, Moeyaert, and Evans in particular, provides detailed, step-by-step descriptions for using R-code applications to perform the analytic techniques and guidelines for interpreting results of the analyses.

Standardised mean difference ESs

Cohen's d: (Cohen, 1988)

Cohen's d is a standardised ES index developed for between-group research, and it expresses the difference between means (ES) in standard deviation units. It can be used to analyse SCED data, under the assumption that the data are serially independent. It is calculated with the following formula:

$$d = \frac{\bar{x}_B - \bar{x}_A}{\sigma_{pooled}}$$

where

$\bar{x}_A = mean\ of\ A\ phase$

$\bar{x}_B = mean\ of\ B\ phase,$

$\sigma_{pooled} = pooled\ standard\ deviation\ of\ A$

$and\ B, and\ can\ be\ calculated\ with\ the$

$formula: \sigma_{pooled} = \sqrt{(\sigma_A^2 + \sigma_B^2)/2}$

Busk and Serlin (1992) propose a variant that uses the standard deviation of the baseline phase, rather than the pooled standard deviation of phases A and B to calculate what is essentially Cohen's d. However, using σ_{pooled} means that Cohen's d then takes into account variability in the intervention phase. In that case, if there is also trend in the intervention data, it will be confounded with variability and Cohen's d should not be used (Manolov et al., 2015); the Busk and Serlin method should be considered instead. In addition, Cohen's d is applicable only if there is no improving (or declining) trend in the baseline.

Cohen's d is comparable to White's d. The latter is exclusively used as an ES index for the Last Treatment Day method (White et al., 1989), and is calculated from differences between scores for the target behaviour on the last day of treatment, predicted from regression of data in the baseline and intervention phases. Cohen's d yields smaller magnitude ES estimates and is less affected by increasing autocorrelation than White's d and regression-based methods such as Allison's Mean plus Trend difference (ALLISON-MT: Allison & Gorman, 1993; see below). Cohen's d also tends to produce greater estimates of ES if there is trend in the phase B data than if there is a change in level due to the intervention effect. Notwithstanding, Cohen's d performs better in detecting the intervention effect in short data series (i.e. 5–10 data points in each phase) than White's d or the ALLISON-MT method (Manolov & Solanas, 2008a).

Cohen's d can be converted to an R^2 ES index[6] using the formula $R^2 = d^2/d^2 + 4$, thus providing a common index for comparison with other analytic methods. It has been criticised because it only takes level into account and is insensitive to trends in the intervention phase or change in trend between the baseline and intervention that might indicate intervention effectiveness (Faith et al., 1996).

d for single case designs (Shadish et al. 2014)

This statistic was specifically developed as the SCED counterpart of Cohen's d. It has two fundamental assumptions: that there is no trend in the data and that target behaviour scores are normally distributed. The procedure evaluates intervention effects across participants (a minimum of three participants are required to estimate d and its standard error) and takes into account: the number of participants; number of data points per participant; both within-participant and between-participants variability; first-lag autocorrelation; and, when applied to multi-phase withdrawal designs, the number of A-B pairs in the design. The procedure can be used to analyse A-B designs replicated on three participants, withdrawal designs with at least three A-B pairs, and MBDs with at least three tiers. It can also be used to calculate statistical power and as an ES index in meta-analyses. Estimation of the standard error of d means that a z-score (i.e. $z = d/standard\ error$) can be used to calculate a p-value. Marso and Shadish (2015) have developed SPSS™ macros (and a manual on how to use them) to calculate d for both AB and MBDs (available at http://faculty.ucmerced.edu/wshadish/software/software-meta-ana lysis-single- case-design/ddhps-version-march-7-2015).

Non-overlap methods

Non-overlap methods are predicated on the concept that the effectiveness of an intervention is reflected in the degree to which data in the intervention phase do not overlap with data in the baseline phase. All non-overlap methods have five major advantages: (i) relative ease of computation, requiring for the most part only basic arithmetical skills; (ii) non-parametric approach requiring minimal assumptions about the data distribution (e.g. serial independence of data or normal

---

6   R^2 is the most commonly used ES index in the social and behavioural sciences (Kirk, 1996).

distribution); (iii) do not require interval or ratio scale data; (iv) intuitive correspondence with visual analysis; and (v) can be used with all SCED types. Many non-overlap methods are described in the literature (see Table 9.2), and several authors have published studies comparing methods head-to-head (Parker et al., 2011a; Rakap, Snyder, & Pasia, 2014; Wolery, Busick, Reichow, & Barton, 2010).

Most non-overlap methods are insensitive to trend (Parker, Vannest, Davis, & Sauber, 2011b) and have other significant limitations. For example, Percentage of Non-overlap Data (PND) (Scruggs et al., 1987), the first developed, and still frequently used, non-overlap method (Parker, Hagan-Burke, & Vannest, 2007; Schlosser, Lee, & Wendt, 2008) works well with small data sets (5 data points per phase), and is less affected by autocorrelation than some regression-based techniques (Manolov & Solanas, 2009). It is, however, prone to Type II error (Lenz, 2013), and is not suitable if: (i) there are outlying data points in the baseline; (ii) the intervention has detrimental effect; (iii) trend in the intervention phase is a continuation of trend in baseline; (iv) if there is an orthogonal change in trend at phase change such that the intervention reverses a deteriorating trend in baseline; or (v) if there is significant variability in the baseline (Allison & Gorman, 1993; Parker et al., 2007). For these reasons, some have

TABLE 9.2 Non-overlap methods

Method	Source
Split-middle trend line (SMTL)	White & Haring (1980)
DC and CDC variants of SMTL	Fisher et al. (2003)
Percentage of non-overlap data (PND)	Scruggs et al. (1987)
Percentage of non-overlapping corrected data (PNCD)	Manolov and Solanas (2009)
Percentage of data exceeding the median (PEM)	Ma (2006)
Percentage of data exceeding a median trend (PEM-T)	Wolery et al. (2010)
Pairwise data overlap (PDO)	Parker & Vannest (2007) [cited in Rakap et al., 2014)]
Pairwise data overlap squared (PDO^2)	Wolery, Busick, Reichow, & Barton (2008) [cited in Wolery et al. (2010)]
Percentage of all non-overlapping data (PAND)	Parker et al. (2007)
Nonoverlap of all pairs (NAP)	Parker & Vannest (2009)
Improvement rate difference (IRD)	Parket, Vannest & Brown (2009)
Tau-U	Parker et al. (2011b)

questioned the utility of PND and recommend that it not be used (Kratochwill et al., 2010; Parker & Vannest, 2009).

Below we describe the Split-Middle Trend Line (SMTL) which is arguably the prototype non-overlap method, and the only one, apart from the Percentage of data Exceeding a Median Trend (PEM-T) (Wolery et al., 2010) and Tau-U (Parker et al., 2011b), that takes into account baseline trend. We also describe two other methods, the Improvement Rate Difference (IRD) (Parker et al., 2009) and Tau-U that best address the limitations of non-overlap techniques.

Split-Middle Trend Line (White & Haring, 1980)

The SMTL is a quasi-statistical technique for quantitatively analysing graphed data. It is easy to compute (see procedure in Figure 9.1) and its rationale is straightforward. The number of data points in phase A is divided in half, such that half are above, and half are below the trend line, which is then extended into the intervention phase (B). The index of intervention effectiveness is the proportion of data points in that fall above the line. If there is no intervention effect, it is expected that same proportion of data points will fall above and below the line in both phases (Gingerich & Feyerherm, 1979). SMTL is also referred to as the Celeration Trend Line technique. The latter is calculated the same way as the SMTL, but means instead of medians are used to derive the trend line (White, 1977).

SMTL assumes a linear trend in the intervention phase, otherwise it might be relatively insensitive to real but modest treatment effects. It takes into account the effects of an 'improving' trend in the baseline as part of overlap, which is a major limitation of other overlap techniques, except Tau-U. However, Type I error rate tends to increase if there is a trend in the baseline but not in the intervention phase (Fisher et al. 2003). If the baseline has few data points and high variability, the trend line might be unreliable, and if the intervention phase is long, it might project above the upper limit of the y-axis (Scruggs & Mastropieri, 2001). The method can be used with small data sets (8–10 data points) but may not be reliable if there are changes in both level and trend when the intervention is introduced (Gingerich & Feyerherm, 1979). The binomial distribution[7] can be

7   Calculator for the binomial test is available at www.danielsoper.com/sta tcalc/calculator.aspx?id=69

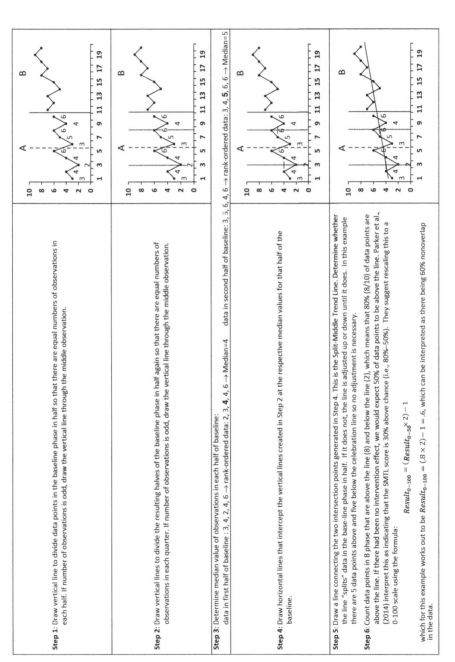

Step 1: Draw vertical line to divide data points in the baseline phase in half so that there are equal numbers of observations in each half. If number of observations is odd, draw the vertical line through the middle observation.

Step 2: Draw vertical lines to divide the resulting halves of the baseline phase in half again so that there are equal numbers of observations in each quarter. If number of observations is odd, draw the vertical line through the middle observation.

Step 3: Determine median value of observations in each half of baseline:
data in first half of baseline : 3, 4, 2, 4, 6 → rank-ordered data: 2, 3, **4**, 4, 6 → Median=4   data in second half of baseline: 3, 5, 6, 4, 6 → rank-ordered data: 3, 4, **5**, 6, 6 → Median=5

Step 4: Draw horizontal lines that intercept the vertical lines created in Step 2 at the respective median values for that half of the baseline.

Step 5: Draw a line connecting the two intersection points generated in Step 4. This is the Split-Middle Trend Line. Determine whether the line "splits" data in the base-line phase in half. If it does not, the line is adjusted up or down until it does. In this example there are 5 data points above and five below the celebration line so no adjustment is necessary.

Step 6: Count data points in B phase that are above the line (2), which means that 80% (8/10) of data points are above the line. If there had been no intervention effect, we would expect 50% of data points to be above the line. Parker et al., (2014) interpret this as indicating that the SMTL score is 30% above chance (i.e., 80%–50%). They suggest rescaling this to a 0-100 scale using the formula:

$$Result_{0-100} = (Result_{0-50} \times 2) - 1$$

which for this example works out to be $Result_{0-100} = (.8 \times 2) - 1 = .6$, which can be interpreted as there being 60% nonoverlap in the data.

FIGURE 9.1 Procedure for calculating SMTL

used to calculate the probability that the observed number of data points will fall above the line if there is no intervention effect (Kazdin, 1982), using the following formula:

$$P(x) = \frac{(N!)(p^x)(q^{N-x})}{(x!)(N-x)!}$$

where

$P(x)$ = probability that x data points fall above the line

N = number of data points in phase B

$N!$ = factorial of N

$x!$ = factorial of x

$(N - x)!$ = factorial of $N - x$

p = probability that a data point will fall above the line if there is no intervention effect (assumed to be chance, that is 0.5)

q = probability that data point will fall below the line, which if there is no intervention effect (also assumed to be chance, that is 0.5)

However, the rate of Type I errors with the binomial test becomes unacceptably high with increasing autocorrelation (Crosbie, 1987). Comparing the proportion of data points above and below the line in each phase with Fisher's exact probability test[8] is considered more appropriate (Parker, Vannest, & Davis, 2014). An approximate z-score for a binomial distribution[9] can also be calculated (Parker & Brossart, 2003). The z-score can then be transformed in to an R^2 index with the formula:

$$R^2 = \frac{z^2}{n} \quad \text{where } n \text{ is the number of data points in phase B}$$

8   Calculator for Fisher's exact probability available at www.danielsoper.com/statcalc/calculator.aspx?id=29
9   Calculator for approximate z-score of binomial probability available at http://vassarstats.net/binomialX.html

Fisher et al. (2003) developed a conservative refinement of SMTL, called the dual criteria (DC) method and an even more conservative refinement called the conservative dual-criteria (CDC) method. The logic underlying both methods is similar to that of SMTL. The DC method involves calculating the SMTL and the mean of the data in the baseline. A horizontal line is then drawn at the mean and extended into the intervention phase along with the SMTL, such that both trend and level of baseline data are taken into account. The index of intervention effectiveness is the proportion of data points in the intervention that fall above both lines. For the CDC method, the standard deviation of the baseline data is also calculated. The SMTL and the horizontal line at the mean are then shifted upward by 0.25 of the standard deviation. The index of intervention effectiveness is, again, the proportion of data points in the intervention that fall above both lines. For intervention phases containing 5, 10, or 20 data points, 5, 8, and 14 points above both lines respectively indicate a reliable intervention effect using either the DC or CDC method. The CDC method is relatively unaffected by autocorrelation. Both methods, reduce Type I error rate (CDC more than DC) with small data sets (5 data points/phase) for autocorrelation levels of up to .5 compared with the SMTL and interrupted time-series analysis (Fisher et al., 2003). Swoboda, Kratochwill, and Levin (2010) illustrated the application of the CDC method to A-B, A-B-A-B, and MBDs with worked examples and exercises.

Improvement Rate Difference[10] (Parker et al. 2009)

The rationale of IRD is based on that of the odds-ratio method. Because it has a known sampling distribution, confidence intervals can be calculated and IRD can be used in meta-analytic studies. In this context, it supersedes Percentage of All Non-overlapping Data (PAND) (Parker et al. 2007). IRD compares the improvement rates in the baseline and intervention phases, which is defined in terms of the data overlap between the two phases. The minimum number of data points that need to be removed, either from the baseline or intervention phase, in order to eliminate overlap is determined. These numbers are subtracted from the total number of data points in their respective phase. The results for each phase are then divided by the total number of data points in that phase to yield improvement rates in the baseline (IR_b) and

10 Calculator to compute IRD is available at www.singlecaseresearch.org/ calculators (Vannest, Parker, Gonen, & Adiguzel, 2016).

intervention (IR_i) phases and IRD= IR_i – IR_b. IRD scores range between 0 and 1, with the authors reporting a score ≤ .5 indicating small/questionable effect, .5 to .7 moderate effect and >.7 large effect. IRD can reliably detect medium-size effects in short data sets (Parker et al., 2014). It correlates strongly with PND (.83) and the Kruskal–Wallis test (.86), but has better agreement with visual judgements (.71–.82) than PND (.61–.72) or PEM (.55–.67) (Parker et al. 2009).

Tau-U (Parker et al., 2011b)

Tau-U is analogous to Kendall's Rank Correlation Coefficient and the Mann–Whitney U tests. Like Non-overlap of All Pairs (NAP), it is based on comparison of overlap in all data pairs, but in addition to percentage of non-overlap, also takes into account the percentage of overlap in the data. Like SMTL, Tau-U is the only other non-overlap method that combines non-overlap and trend to control for effects of 'improving' trend (whether linear, curvilinear, or mixed) in the baseline. It is fairly impervious to confounding effects of autocorrelation (Parker et al., 2011b) and reliably detects medium-size effects in short data sets (Parker et al., 2014). Vannest and Ninci (2015, p. 408) suggest the following guide for interpreting ESs generated by Tau-U: "A 0.20 improvement may be considered a small change, 0.2 to 0.60 a moderate change, 0.60 to 0.80 a large change and above 0.80 a large to very large change, depending on the context." Moreover, it has good statistical power and a known sampling distribution (same as that of Kendall's Rank Correlation Coefficient), hence p-values and confidence intervals can be calculated, and Tau-U can be used in meta-analytic studies. The online calculator[11] available for TAU-U can check for trend in the baseline, adjust for it when necessary, and compute contrasts between individual phase pairs (i.e. A vs B), as well as omnibus statistics.

Regression-based methods

Regression methods based on General Linear Models have, in general, sufficient power for small data series, control well for positive baseline trend (improvement or deterioration), are sensitive to improvement in level change trends, and tend to discriminate better

---

11 Calculator to compute Tau-U is available at www.singlecaseresearch.org/calculators (Vannest et al., 2016).

among data patterns than non-overlap methods (Parker et al., 2014). The four single-level methods described below account reasonably well for autocorrelation (Gorsuch, 1983; Huitema, 2011; Huitema & McKean, 2000), and estimate ESs related to changes in level and slope in terms of R^2 (and its p-value) which can be converted to standardised mean difference indices such as Cohen's d. The main drawback of regression-based methods is that SCED data usually challenge the required parametric assumptions: normal distribution of data, homogeneity of variance (across phases), linear relationship between variables, independence (i.e. no autocorrelation), and at least interval-level measurement.

Single-level regression methods[12]

Gorsuch's trend ES – GORSUCH (Gorsuch, 1983): GORSUCH is an Ordinary Least Squares regression analysis method that tests mean differences between phases, and is analogous to ANCOVA where the overall data trend is used as a covariate. Overall data tend is removed (semi-partialled out dependent scores only) in order not to obfuscate intervention effects, and the analysis is performed on the 'detrended' scores or residuals after they are regressed on time.

Center's Mean plus Trend difference – CENTER-MT (Center et al., 1985–1986): a piece-wise regression method that takes into account changes in mean level between phases and, like *GORSUCH*, also controls for overall data trend. In this instance, however, data trend is partialled out of both predictors and the raw data. If, on visual inspection, trend in the baseline is stronger than in the intervention phase, the trend parameter can be taken out of the model, which then calculates an ES for change in mean level only.

Allison's Mean plus Trend Difference – ALLISON-MT (Allison & Gorman, 1993). ALLISON-MT takes into account trend and changes in mean level between phases, like GORSUCH and CENTER-MT. Unlike these techniques, ALLISON-MT controls for baseline trend only, rather than overall trend of all the data. The rationale for this is that trend in the intervention phase might reflect intervention effect and removing it over-corrects the data. Trend is semi-partialled out of dependent scores only and, like GORSUCH, the analysis is performed on the 'detrended' residuals. Comparative studies using

---

12 Parker and Brossart (2003) provide an appendix describing how to parametrise GORSUCH, CENTER-MT, and ALLISON-MT.

hypothetical data have shown that these three methods yield ES indices of different magnitude for the same data (see Table 9.3; Brossart et al., 2006; Parker & Brossart, 2003). Indeed, Brossart et al. concluded that "Despite the use of the standard R^2 ES, results obtained from the five[13] statistical techniques varied so much that guidelines would have to be constructed separately for each" (p. 554). Controlling for autocorrelation increased slightly the magnitude of ES (expressed as eta squared: η^2) calculated with GORSUCH, and decreased the magnitude of ESs calculated with CENTER-MT and ALLISON-MT.

Recent refinements and discussions of single-level, regression-based models can be found in Maggin, Swaminathan, Rogers, O'Keeffe, Sugai, and Horner (2011) and Swaminathan, Rogers, Horner, Sugai, and Smolkowski (2014).

Multi-level models

Also known as hierarchical linear models, multi-level models (MLMs) are mathematically sophisticated methods suitable for analysing data from several participants simultaneously and identify similarities and differences between participants (Rindskopf & Ferron, 2014). MLM can be used to determine the magnitude of intervention effect for each participant, determine an overall intervention effect across participants, and evaluate how these might change over time (e.g. in different A-B pairs in WRDs or different tiers in MBDs). The method can also be used to explore factors that might account for variability across participants. They are also well suited for meta-analytic studies. MLM have the advantage over single-level models such as those described above in that a number of error structures can be built into the model to account for autocorrelation (Baek, Moeyaert, Petit-Bois, Beretvas, Van den Noortgate, Ferron, 2014). In two-level models (e.g. Van den Noortgate & Onghena, 2003a; 2003b) observations (i.e. measures of the target behaviour) are nested within participants, and in three-level models (e.g. Moeyaert, Ugille, Ferron, Beretvas, & Van den Noortgate, 2013; Van den Noortgate & Onghena, 2008) observations are nested within participants and participants are nested within studies. A detailed (and rather mathematical) discussion on how SCED data can

13 The Binomial test (White & Haring, 1980) and the Last Treatment Day test (White et al., 1989) were also examined in this study but are not included in the table.

TABLE 9.3 Effect sizes for three regression methods

Test	Range of ES (R^2)	
	Effective intervention [1]	Ineffective intervention
GORSUCH	.03	-ive
CENTER-MT	.53	.36
ALLISON-MT	.87	.65

Source: data reported in Brossart et al. (2006)

be modelled in MLM can be found in several sources (e.g. Moeyaert, Ugille, Ferron, Beretvas, & Van den Noortgate, 2013; 2014; Moeyaert, Ferron, Beretvas, & Van den Noortgate, 2014; Shadish, Nagler Kyse, & Rindskopf, 2013). Onghena, Michiels, Jamshidi, Moeyaert and van den Noortgate (2018) provide detailed illustrations on how to apply MLMs with worked examples using published neurorehabilitation data.

Time series

C-statistic (Tryon, 1982)

The C-statistic is a simplified time-series analysis specifically developed to evaluate intervention effects in small data sets, and makes few assumptions about the characteristics of the data. The method evaluates variability in serial data relative to changes in slope from one phase to the next and identifies if a there is a departure from random variation across phases (Tryon, 1982). The C-statistic is calculated with the formula:

$$c = 1 - \frac{\sum (X_i - X_{i-1})^2}{2 \times \sum (X_i - \bar{X})^2}$$

where

N = number of data points in the phase

$\bar{X} = mean\ of\ phase\ data$

$X_i = the\ ith\ data\ point\ in\ the\ phase$

$X_{i-1} = the\ data\ point\ preceding\ the\ ith\ data\ point$

A *p*-value can be derived for C by dividing it by its standard error (Sc), which is calculated with the formula:

$$S_c = \sqrt{\frac{N+2}{(N-1)(N+1)}}$$

The ratio of C to its standard error has a distribution that does not significantly deviate from normality when used with data sets with as few as eight observations, hence, a *p*-value can be determined from a *z*-score table. C is calculated for the baseline and if it is not significant, it suggests that there is no baseline trend. Baseline and intervention data are then concatenated, and C is calculated for the combined data set. If the new C is significant, it indicates that there is a trend in the combined data, attributable to the intervention. If there is trend in the baseline data Tryon (1982) suggests two de-trending 'adjustments', one of which is not applicable if the number of data points in both phases is not equal; the other is not effective if baseline trend is non-linear. The main advantages of C are that it is easy to calculate and is relatively unaffected by autocorrelation. Its main limitation is that it tends to produce Type II errors if slopes of trends in the baseline and treatment data are comparable, but are at different levels.

Auto-Regressive Integrated Moving Average (Box & Jenkins, 1970; Gottman & Glass, 1978)

Auto-Regressive Integrated Moving Average (ARIMA) involves estimation of three parameters to generate a model: autoregressive (*p*), which controls for effects of correlation with preceding scores; integrated (*d*) controls for data trends; and moving average (*q*) which controls for effects of preceding random shocks (i.e. extraneous events). Model estimation is crucial and selecting the three central parameters can be a complicated process, but a *p* =1, *d* =0, and *q* =0 model works well with data sets of at least 40 data points (Harrop & Velicer, 1985). ARIMA yields a t-statistic and its associated probability for intervention effect and can be performed with SPSS™ and SAS™. Unbiased estimates of the changes in level and trend across phases can also be calculated (Glass, Willson, & Gottman, 2008). ARIMA's main strengths are that it controls for autocorrelation (thus minimising Type I error which is elevated by autocorrelation), and it can test for abrupt changes in level separately from changes in slope, and determine if these changes are attributable to normal fluctuation or the effect of intervention. Its main drawback is that it is not appropriate for small data sets. Shadish and Sullivan (2011) reported that the median number of data points in a sample of 809 SCEDs was 20, and up to 90% had fewer than 50. However, consensus is that at least 50–100 data points per phase are needed (Hartmann, Gottman, Jones, Gardner, Kazdin & Vaught, 1980). Type II error rate is unduly elevated in the analysis of data sets with fewer than 50 observations (Tabachnick & Fidell, 2007) and Type I error becomes unacceptably high in small data sets (5 per phase) when auto-correlation exceeds .5 (Fisher et al., 2003).

Randomisation tests

Randomisation tests for SCEDs were popularised by Edgington (1964). Edgington (1980; 1987) proposed two basic randomisation strategies. One is to randomly sequence the order of baseline and intervention phases. The other consists of randomly selecting the point in time when a given phase commences. The randomisation process generates a series of 'permutations' of the data set, say n per-mutations. An appropriate statistical test is then selected and calcu-lated for all the possible permutations of the data. The probability of the statistic for the permutation schedule that was *actually selected* at random is determined by the total number of permutations; that is, $1/n$. Randomisation provides statistical control of two significant threats to internal validity: history and maturation. Moreover, some consider that randomisation makes SCEDs truly 'experimental' (Barlow et al., 2009) and greatly enhances their scientific validity (Ferron & Levin, 2014; Kratochwill & Levin, 2010; 2014). Rando-misation tests are not, however, commonly utilised in SCEDs (Shadish & Sullivan, 2011).

Randomisation strategies have been criticised because at least 20 permutations are necessary (i.e. $1/20 = 0.05$) before randomisation provides sufficient statistical power (see Arnau & Bono, 1998). It has been shown, however, that if phases contain more than 5 data points, ESs (measured as difference in treatment means) are > 1, and if autocorrelation is not negative, randomisation tests can be implemented with statistical power exceeding .80 (Ferron & Onghena, 1996). Another major concern is that randomising phase sequence might generate permutations that are not con-sistent with clinical constraints or the rationale of the study. Simi-larly, randomising the point in time when the intervention phase commences may be counter-intuitive in a clinical setting when response guided intervention (e.g. introduce the intervention after baseline has stabilised) is more appropriate. Strategies for addressing these issues have been proposed (e.g. Ferron & Ware, 1994; Ferron & Onghena, 1996; Kratochwill & Levin, 2014; Onghena & Edgington, 2005) and a range of randomisation techniques and randomisation tests have been specifically developed for A-B and A-B-A-B designs (Manolov & Solanas, 2008b; Marascuilo & Busk, 1988; Onghena, 1992), MBDs (Wampold & Worsham, 1986) and ATDs (Onghena & Edgington, 1994). Bulté and Onghena (2013) have developed the RcmdrPlugin.SCDA, which includes a computer package for designing randomised A-B, A-B-A, A-B-A-B, and ATDs and analysing the results of these studies. The package also includes programs for performing visual analysis and meta-analytic studies.

Evaluation of applied criteria

The primary aim of a SCED is to determine if there is a functional relationship between an intervention and observed changes in the target behaviour. In a broader sense, the aim is (or should be) to also determine if the intervention has had a practical effect for the participant (Baer et al., 1968). Visual and/or statistical analyses do not necessarily convey information about the practical value of the intervention, or what benefit, if any, it has conferred to the participant. The latter requires evaluation of applied criteria (Kazdin; 1999; 2011). That is, evaluation of the intervention's clinical significance, its social validity, and its social impact. Even though the effect of an intervention might be statistically significant, it does not necessarily mean that the treatment will have an important or meaningful impact on the participant's day-to-day life; that is, be *clinically* significant (Kazdin, 2001; 2008).

Moreover, it is not completely clear exactly how large an intervention ES must be before we can be confident that the intervention is likely to produce meaningful improvement for the participant (although the larger the ES, the more likely it is to be clinically significant). Furthermore, the ES might reflect improvement on a measure that is not directly related to day-to-day living. There is scant evidence that a change in score or an ES of a given magnitude automatically translates into a clinically significant or meaningful and important effect in the participant's day-to-day life (Kazdin, 2001).

Evaluation of clinical significance has tended to emphasize symptomatology as the defining characteristic (Kazdin, 2011). The construct of clinical significance, however, is multi-dimensional and includes not only changes to the target behaviour but also social aspects such as the individual's ability to meet the demands of his or her psychosocial role, to function in day-to-day life, their quality of life, and their subjective perception of their circumstances (Gladis, Gosch, Dishuk, & Crits-Christoph, 1999; Kazdin, 1999). Clinical significance is generally evaluated from three main perspectives: (i) normative comparisons; (ii) departure from dysfunctional level; and (iii) social validation.

Normative comparisons

Normative comparisons involve determining if after being treated, the individual becomes indistinguishable from an appropriate normative reference group (Kendall, Marr-Garcia, Nath, & Sheldrick, 1999). Ideally, the comparison group is demographically similar to the study participant, but 'normal' in terms of performance on the target behaviour. The main obstacle here is finding an appropriate normative group. Apart from demographic variables, there should be other important variables in the make-up of a suitable reference group for participants in neurorehabilitation. Many of these individuals might have been living with significant chronic disability for years. Their cognitive and physical impairments might have significantly restricted their ability to work and the range of their social participation. They might live in high-level supported accommodation. They might have significant co-morbidities and/or require intensive and ongoing medical treatment. The list goes on; and it would be very difficult to compile a reference group that encompassed all of these dimensions. Of equal concern is the fact that even if a suitable reference group is identified, it is rather unlikely that there will be normative data directly relevant to the target behaviours that are the focus of neurorehabilitation interventions. Normative comparisons are also used in social validation.

Departure from a dysfunctional level

Clinical significance can also be evaluated in terms of a departure from a dysfunctional level. In this instance, the twofold criterion proposed by Jacobson and colleagues to determine the impact of psychotherapy is used (e.g. Jacobson, Follette, & Revenstorf, 1984). The focus of their approach was to determine whether or not the individual had moved from the dysfunctional to the functional range as a consequence of the intervention. First, the magnitude of pre-post treatment differences on the outcome variable (i.e. target behaviour in the context of SCEDs) used to measure the therapeutic effect has to be sufficiently large so that it could not be attributed to measurement error. This is determined by calculating the Reliable Change Index, specifically developed for the purpose. Second, the post-treatment score on the outcome measure has to be within the functional or normal range for that measure.[14] If both conditions are met, the person treated is deemed to have recovered (Jacobson, Roberts, Berns, & McGlinchey, 1999).

Another approach to evaluating clinical significance is also derived from the psychotherapy field. This involves determining if the intervention produces changes in the individual's diagnostic status. If, after treatment, the individual does not meet diagnostic criteria for the condition that was treated, that individual is deemed to have recovered (Kazdin, 2011). The applicability of this approach and of the Reliable Change Index in evaluating changes in the target behaviour is, however, limited. Calculation of the Reliable Change Index requires not only normative data, but also reliability and test–retest coefficients[15] which are unlikely to be available for many target behaviours that are the focus of neurorehabilitation in SCEDs. Moreover, it is quite unlikely that there will be specific diagnostic criteria that are directly applicable to the target behaviours being treated.

Social validation

Social validation encompasses three broad dimensions which to some extent overlap with the constructs comprising clinical significance: (i)

14 Post-treatment measures of the outcome variable were considered to be in the functional or 'normal' range if: (a) the score was ≥ 2 standard deviations *above* the mean of the dysfunctional group; (b) the score surpassed two standard deviations *below* the mean of the normal group; and (c) the score was statistically more likely to belong in the functional than in the dysfunctional distribution. Cut-off (a) was the most conservative and (b) the most permissive, and (c) was recommended if there was overlap of the functional and dysfunctional score distributions.

15 Various statistical methods for determining clinically significant change have been derived, based on the Jacobson method (e.g. Hageman & Arrindell, 1999) and hierarchical linear modelling (e.g. Speer & Greenbaum, 1995).

the relevance of intervention goals to everyday life; (ii) the acceptability of intervention procedures to the participant and the community at large; and (iii) the impact and importance of intervention outcomes to the participant's life. The two primary approaches used for social validation are the *social comparison* method and *subjective evaluation*. Like normative comparisons to evaluate clinical significance, the *social comparison* method involves comparing the behaviour of the study participant with that of a normal, non-impaired group; and has comparable shortcomings. *Subjective evaluation* relies on the opinions and ratings of informed others about the importance of the intervention and is described in Chapter 2. These informants can be clinicians, family members, carers, and significant others who are familiar with the participant. The participant's own perception of the impact of the treatment may also be sought. Although standardised rating scales and questionnaires might be used to gather this information, the validity of results is always an issue.

The impact of an intervention can also be evaluated in terms of its *social impact*, although this is not frequently done in SCED research (Kazdin, 2011). This primarily involves examining benefits to the community and to the individual, ensuing from the effect of the intervention. Many of the measures that can be used to evaluate social impact also index clinical significance. Costs and financial benefits are frequently considered. The cost-effectiveness of the intervention, and the financial benefit this might represent for the rehabilitation facility can be evaluated. If, for example, the participant has attained a better level of independence, this might mean that the costs of ongoing care might be reduced. The participant might have resumed some level of employment, which means increased productivity for their employer. If the intervention has significantly reduced the participant's aggressive behaviour, relationships with family, friends, clinic staff, and residents might be more harmonious. In essence, however, what makes the intervention clinically and socially significant and how this will be manifest day-to-day is not totally clear and is very likely to differ among individuals.

At a fundamental level, the measures and criteria used to evaluate clinical significance and social validity need to map onto the clinical concerns, value system, goals, and life situation of the person being treated. The overarching concern, however, is whether or not indices of clinical significance and social validity accurately capture and reflect what is importance or meaningful in the individual's life. As Kazdin (2001) points out, "Clinically significant change can be measured in many ways, but it is still not entirely clear what any of the ways means in the lives of clients" (p. 455). In other words, what makes an intervention clinically significant for a given individual is not clear, nor is it clear how this is going to manifest in their day-to-day lives. Nonetheless, attempts to evaluate this aspect of SCED results cannot be neglected.

Concluding remarks

Evaluating SCED results is complex. To establish whether or not an intervention has been effective, one needs to first decide how this might be manifest in the data. Relative to the baseline phase, scores in the intervention phase can show differences in level, trend, and variability, or various combinations of these. Which changes indicate that the intervention has been effective? If an intervention reduces the frequency of memory failures it can be, undeniably, counted as a success. Yet, if overall frequency (i.e. level) is unchanged but variability of their occurrence over time is greatly reduced, would this qualify as an intervention being effective? To resolve these sorts of questions, the goal of the intervention needs to be formulated within a framework that aims to achieve a clinically significant outcome for the participant.

One needs to know how to analyse the data. Visual analysis of the data can provide evidence that captures and integrates disparate and complex features of the data in a clinically meaningful way. Evaluation of SCED results is not, however, an either/or process: visual or statistical analysis. They supplement each other and need to be utilised in conjunction. As Parker, Cryer, and Byrns (2006) have pointed out "No present statistical technique can concurrently consider data variability, trend magnitude and direction, mean levels and shifts, embedded cycles (e.g., weekly), and precipitous changes in performance at the point of intervention [and autocorrelation]" (p. 419). Regression-based analysis and, arguably, MLM methods in particular, come closest to achieving this aim. The choice of statistical method needs to be informed by the data characteristics, and the dimension/s of the target behaviour that provide evidence of intervention effectiveness in the context of the clinical formulation. Manolov and Solanas (2018) have developed thoughtful and comprehensive guidelines to help with these decisions.

10

PRACTICAL APPLICATION OF SINGLE-CASE METHODS IN THE NEUROREHABILITATION SETTING

Hints for the researcher and clinician

This chapter integrates information from previous chapters to show how single-case methods can be implemented. We present a practical, ten-step procedure for implementing a SCED in the neurorehabilitation setting, which is particularly applicable to clinical practice, but also useful in research. The chapter concludes with a model of clinical practice that incorporates a range of practice options, including single-case methodology.

Ten steps for implementing a single-case experiment

In this section of the chapter, we present a structured procedure to implement a single-case experiment. Throughout the section, we illustrate how the ten steps can be implemented by using the example of Ben, one of two participants described in the SCED study reported by Feeney and Ylvisaker (2008). The target behaviour of the case example involves challenging behaviours, but the ten-step framework can be applied to any target behaviour, including cognitive, communicative, emotional, functional, or motor-sensory domains.

Implementing an intervention can be divided into two main stages: the planning stage and the conduct stage, both of which are conducted in collaboration with the participant. If the planning stage can proceed carefully, systematically and thoroughly, then this provides optimal conditions for the conduct stage.

Stage 1: The planning stage

The order of the first two steps (the participant and the literature) will depend on circumstance. If the SCED is implemented in response to a referral in the clinical setting, the logical place to start is with the participant. If the SCED is implemented as a consequence of research interest in a particular topic, the literature may be the better starting point. Having refined the topic, the researcher then seeks to identify participants meeting selection criteria.

Step 1: The participant

Many different types of information need to be gathered about the participant. This will include medical information, a psychosocial history, evaluation of current level of functioning, and an articulation of the presenting problem. All of this knowledge, together with more detailed information about the target behaviour (see Step 3), will be used in the case formulation described in Step 4.

Pertinent *medical information* is essential to obtain in neurorehabilitation, especially in terms of the participant's presenting neurological condition (type, onset, severity, course, impairments), as well as any pre-existing conditions and comorbidities. A targeted *psychosocial history* provides critical contextual information about the participant and his/her social environment, along with his/her plans, hopes, aspirations, personal preferences, and values. Supplementary interview with an informant, such as a family or staff member, is vital if the participant has cognitive impairments (particularly in memory, executive function, self-awareness) that may compromise accuracy of information. In some circumstances, it may be necessary to obtain detailed information about the functioning of members of the family or the family unit because this may be relevant to and impinge upon the target behaviour.

Current *level of function* needs to be documented in a standardised way. One approach is to administer a rating scale that captures the overall level of functioning (e.g. World Health Organization – Disability Assessment Schedule 2.0 (Garin et al., 2010)). Other situations may indicate specific neuropsychological, language or functional assessment. This is then supplemented by detailed and comprehensive evaluation of the particular domain of function to be treated using direct observation and/or performance-based measures wherever possible.

The *presenting clinical or research problem* needs to be articulated and evaluated. Some standardised instruments are helpful, but often they are not sufficiently specific to the target behaviour. The practitioner may need to develop a tailor-made measure that captures the presenting issue or problem in order to delineate its dimensions. This is described in more detail in Step 3.

ILLUSTRATION: STEP 1: THE PARTICIPANT

In Ben's case, from the Feeney and Ylvisaker (2008) study, he was aged 5 years when he sustained traumatic brain (and other organ) injuries when his bicycle was hit by a car one year previously.

- *Medically*, Ben's past history was unremarkable, and he did not have any developmental or other problems. He sustained an extremely severe brain injury with bilateral focal frontal injury, as well as damage to the meso-limbic regions. Ben was hospitalised for two weeks in acute care, and thereafter for four months in an inpatient rehabilitation facility. He was discharged home to his family, but had continuing impairments that impacted on his functioning.
- *Psychosocially*, before the accident, Ben lived with his parents and three older siblings. Educationally, there were no academic problems and he had established many friendships. After the injury, Ben's parents divorced, and he lived with his mother and siblings, and had little contact with his father. He returned to his preinjury school and repeated the kindergarten first grade.
- *Current level of function.* According to his teacher, Ben did not experience motor deficits. Academically, his skills were similar to preinjury levels, but he exhibited challenging behaviours, including physical aggression and episodes of screaming in class. Ben was socially immature, bullied other students who were frightened by him, and he became socially isolated.

The *presenting problem* was Ben's challenging behaviour and its adverse impact on his schoolwork, which was further analysed (see Steps 3 and 4).

Step 2: The literature

Prior to developing an intervention, recommended practice is that the literature is searched to identify interventions with the best evidence of effectiveness (Sackett, Straus, Richardson, Rosenberg, &

Haynes, 2000). This makes sense, because an appropriate intervention to treat a particular target behaviour may already have been trialled and would be recommended for clinical practice if (i) the study was methodologically sound and (ii) the intervention had proved successful and was appropriate for the target behaviour.

Many hundreds of systematic reviews are available that synthesise the evidence for interventions in multiple problem areas in various neurological conditions. A search of PsycBITE, for example, an evidence-based database of nonpharmacological interventions to treat the psychological consequences of acquired neurological conditions (accessed 20 September 2017) identified 789 systematic reviews. This represents a huge amount of evidence that synthesises results from thousands of clinical trials.

Of course, literature review may not yield fruitful results. In this situation, the investigator may find it helpful to repeat the search using another but broadly similar clinical population. If the search results are still unproductive, then the investigator may need to adapt an already existing intervention or even develop an intervention de novo (see Step 5).

ILLUSTRATION: STEP 2: THE LITERATURE

- Regarding suitable interventions for Ben, one of the authors had previously conducted a systematic review of the literature on challenging behaviours after traumatic brain injury (Ylvisaker et al., 2007). The review highlighted the increasing use of positive behaviour intervention supports in comparison with the traditional contingency management approach to treating challenging behaviours.
- In Ben's case, the authors were interested in building on their previous work and replicating the multi-component intervention (using *inter alia* positive behaviour supports) which they had developed and used in previous single-case experiments.

Step 3: Identify, define, and measure the target behaviour

The target behaviour/s need to be (i) identified, (ii) operationally defined in precise, specific and quantifiable terms, and (iii) details about the method of measurement determined. Chapter 3 covers these and other issues pertinent to the target behaviour.

Identifying the target behaviour

How does one go about identifying the target behaviour? Although referring agents, staff, families, and the participant may have a general idea about the domain of behaviour in question, this is not sufficient for the purpose of implementing an intervention in a single-case study. Moreover, on occasion the behaviour that drives the referral, may not, when further examined, be the behaviour of relevance. In other cases, participants may present with multiple problems, and initially it may not be clear which behaviour should be targeted for intervention.

Careful observation, documentation, and discussion with relevant persons (one of whom will be the participant, even if he/she experiences significant cognitive impairment) is necessary. Depending on the domain, the procedure will involve assessment (usually) with standardised instruments or direct observation of overt behaviour.

In many cases, behavioural observations can take place in the settings in which the to-be-targeted behaviour occurs. Observations can be made in a number of ways, and the ABC (antecedents, behaviour, consequences) approach is frequently used, particularly in the context of challenging behaviours. Other domains addressed by SCEDs in neurorehabilitation (e.g. cognitive, communicative, emotional, functional, motor-sensory) may not be suitable for a structured behavioural observation, and Chapter 3 describes alternatives. The principle to emphasise here is the importance of undertaking a systematic evaluation of the target behaviour and the context in which it occurs, because this will inform the intervention.

If an ABC assessment is made, documentation should include at least the following:

- the behaviour (what occurred)
- the time (when it occurred)
- frequency (how often it occurred)
- duration (how long it lasted)
- intensity/severity/magnitude
- consistency of the behaviour over time

In addition to a record of the observed behaviour, it is necessary to record other information:

- contextual factors (e.g. the setting, presence of other people)
- antecedents (what was happening just before the behaviour occurred)
- consequences (what happened after the behaviour occurred)

- factors that might have exacerbated/attenuated the behaviour while it was occurring

The data produced from the above areas are particularly important, because they may provide insights into factors that serve to maintain the target behaviour (see Step 4), which will inform case formulation and guide selection of the intervention. In cases where direct observation is not practical or possible (e.g. 'private events' such as mood or pain), interview with the participant and using his/her self-ratings is indicated. The practitioner may wish to supplement subjective self-report with proxy measures that are related to the construct of interest and are observable (e.g. for depression, to document the number of activities completed). The practitioner may not be able to directly observe behaviours occurring in some settings and in this case she/he will need to rely upon other people (including the participant) to record the behaviour or report details of its occurrence.

Defining the target behaviour

Having identified the target behaviour, it then needs to be operationally defined. What do we mean by this? Take, for example, 'losing balance'. Although the general domain is clear (i.e. it is *not* memory, or challenging behaviour, or communication), more information is required to define 'losing balance'. Is a self-adjusted stagger classified as losing balance, or a trip, or is it necessary for the person to fall to the ground? The objectivity, clarity and completeness of the operational definition of the target behaviour has important implications for reliable measurement (see Step 8).

Measuring the target behaviour

After identifying and defining the target behaviour, the next step is to determine how to measure it. The single-case study measures the target behaviour continuously during every phase, both prior to commencing the intervention (A phase), and while ever the intervention is in place (B-phase). The requirement in single-case methodology for measures to be taken repeatedly and frequently can be a challenge because it will preclude the use of lengthy test batteries, as well as instruments that are subject to practice effects.

In addition to their length and possible practice effects, standardised instruments are often too general to capture the target behaviour. This can make them an inefficient and imprecise way to track the target behaviour. Measures need to be direct and proximal to the behaviour that is to be targeted by the intervention. Nonetheless, sometimes standardised instruments *do* make suitable measures of the target behaviour if they are amenable to repeated administration and contain items directly relevant to the target behaviour. Of course, standardised instruments and assessment batteries can be administered before and after implementing the intervention (just as in a between-groups design) or intermittently throughout the study and may provide valuable information about the response generalisation effects of the intervention to other behaviours, both those closely related to the target behaviour, as well as more distal aspects of function (e.g. quality of life).

But it is usually the case that measures of the target behaviour are developed for the study at hand. The more objective the measure, the better. In some situations, self-report measures are crucial for tracking the target behaviour (e.g. mood, pain, insomnia) but because of their subjective and unverifiable nature they should be supplemented with other measures wherever possible. Measures of the target behaviour often comprise frequency counts of the target behaviour, its duration, intensity, and so forth (see the SCED studies summarised in the Appendix, which document a wide variety of target behaviours used in neurorehabilitation and their measurement). The downside of tailor-made measures is the lack of external evaluation of, in particular, their reliability. Thus, any measure requiring human judgement needs to have a reliability evaluation, and this is covered in Step 8.

In the course of determining the measure that will be used for the target behaviour, the practitioner will need to consider the following:

- What mode will be used to measure the target behaviour: self-report, informant report, direct observation, performance-based response, machine recording?
- Where, when, and how often will the measures/observations take place?
- Who will measure the target behaviours and is training required?
- Will coding of responses be required, can another person independent of the observer do it, and is training required?
- Are there ways that the measures can be recorded so that they can be rated at a later time with the rater being blind to phase, as well as to be used for determining inter-observer agreement?

For example, by using manual recording sheets, audio or videotape recordings.

- Can equipment be used to measure the target behaviour to enhance objectivity? For example, computers, weighing scales, pedometers, audio/video records.
- In addition to the target behaviours, are there any other aspects that need to be measured? For example, generalisation measures sampled throughout all phases, social validity measures made at the conclusion of the intervention.

ILLUSTRATION: STEP 3: IDENTIFY, DEFINE, AND MEASURE THE TARGET BEHAVIOUR

Ben's two target behaviours were specified as follows:

Domain	Target behaviour definition	Measure
Aggression	"attempted or completed physical aggression (e.g. hitting, pushing) or verbal aggression (e.g. threats). The aggressive behaviors of the participants were operationally defined by the consultant who then trained classroom staff in data collection" (p. 118)	– Frequency counts of observed incidents of aggressive acts (as defined) – 20 disruptiveness items from the Aberrant Behavior Checklist rated on four-point intensity scale. Completed by staff after each aggressive act
Schoolwork	"the number of activities, problems, questions, or assignments completed", based on hard copies of Ben's work that the staff provided	– Percentage of work completed

- Staff were trained to mastery in accurately recording the (i) frequency and (ii) intensity of the aggression target behaviour. Their ratings were compared against those of the consultant, and the study did not commence until two consecutive ratings exceeded the a priori specified threshold (90% agreement).
- In addition to the target behaviours, two measures of social validity were made: staff judgements about the effectiveness of the intervention for (i) the student, and (ii) the staff, using the Intervention Effectiveness Evaluation Scale.

Step 4: Case formulation/functional behavioural analysis

Case formulation can occur in a descriptive way to integrate the information collected in the assessments conducted in Step 1 (contextual information) and Step 3 (e.g. ABC approach). This will provide hypotheses about factors that serve to maintain the behaviour, which will inform selection of the intervention (see Step 4 below). At its most sophisticated level (and particularly applicable to the domain of challenging behaviours), case formulation will be based on a functional or structural experimental analysis of behaviour in which environmental conditions serving to maintain the target behaviour will be verified via an experiment (see Chapter 3).

ILLUSTRATION: STEP 4: CASE FORMULATION

In Ben's case, the following steps were taken to arrive at a case formulation:

- In an initial step, the consultant met with classroom staff to obtain a descriptive functional behavioural assessment to identify situations and consequences associated with the target behaviours.
- The staff then completed the 16-item Motivational Assessment Scale (MAS) to identify factors that served to maintain Ben's challenging behaviours: attention, tangible reinforcement, escape/avoidance, sensory stimulation.
- Finally, the consultant scored the MAS and corroborated the results with direct observation of Ben, using the ABC approach, over several school days.
- The results "indicated that aggression and other disruptive behaviours typically served the primary function of avoiding assigned work, especially in situations that required organization or that were cognitively challenging" (Feeney & Ylvisaker, 2008, p. 119).
- These data informed the intervention (see Step 5) which had "the goal of making challenging behaviours unnecessary and inefficient" (p. 119)

Step 5: The intervention

The intervention (see also Chapter 4) will be informed from two principal sources: the literature review, as conducted in Step 2, and the case formulation, as completed in Step 4.

In any given situation, the practitioner is likely to encounter one of three scenarios from the literature review:

1. an intervention is available and can be implemented without adaptation
2. an intervention is available, but for any of a number of reasons, it needs to be adapted for the purpose at hand
3. no suitable intervention is available, and so the practitioner has to develop one de novo

All of the above scenarios are compatible with an evidence-based approach when using single-case experimental methods. Indeed, single-case methodology will provide evidence for the effectiveness of the intervention (cf. practice-based evidence), albeit only for that particular individual unless the study is replicated.

In the happy event of scenario 1 (a suitable intervention is identified), the next steps are to read the report to (i) evaluate its scientific quality and (ii) consider the evidence for its effectiveness. This is important because if a study has significant methodological flaws, it will be at risk of bias and the results of the study and conclusions drawn may be misleading (see Chapter 2 for discussion of issues surrounding risk of bias and threats to validity). It also stands to reason that if (in a well-designed study) an intervention is shown *not* to be effective, the practitioner or researcher needs to have a very good reason for implementing it without adaptation.

The more challenging event of scenario 2 (an intervention is available but needs to be adapted), may occur for many reasons. In particular, an intervention developed for the general or other clinical populations may need to be adapted to accommodate the configuration of the participant's cognitive and non-cognitive impairments, functional and emotional status, and other personal and environmental factors.

In the disappointing event of scenario 3 (no suitable intervention is available), the practitioner will need to develop one de novo. It goes without saying that an intervention that has not been evaluated previously should be implemented in the context of a single-case experiment (or evaluated in an RCT).

In all scenarios, a procedural manual should be compiled, treatment protocols developed, practitioners trained in the procedures, and ongoing monitoring/supervision provided. Having treatment protocols assists in ensuring that a treatment is implemented as intended (see Step 9). At this point, many decisions need to be made:

- What number, duration and regularity of intervention sessions is required?

- Who will implement the intervention?
- Do practitioners need training?
- What form will supervision/mentoring take?
- How will the intervention be delivered?
- What are the factors that will maximise participant adherence and how will they be built into the intervention plan?

ILLUSTRATION: STEP 5: THE INTERVENTION

The intervention used with Ben was a combination treatment, "derived from the functional behavioural assessment and elements based on theory and experience with children with TBI [traumatic brain injury]" (Feeney & Ylvisaker, 2008, p. 119). It drew upon contextually relevant cognitive (executive function) and behavioural strategies, along with positive-behaviour supports.

- The components of the intervention were as follows:

  - Daily routine: negotiations about the minimum amount of work to be completed
  - Behavioural momentum: tasks sequenced in such a way that easy tasks with high success rates were used before difficult work was introduced
  - Reduction of errors: staff provided modelling and assistance
  - Escape communication: Ben was taught positive communication alternatives (e.g., "I need a break")
  - Adult communication style: staff were trained in specific techniques
  - Graphic advance organisers: Ben was provided with photographic cues because of his executive impairments in organisation
  - Goal–plan–do–review routine: brief questions posed by staff for sequencing of activities
  - Consequence procedures: procedures for staff to follow in the event of target behaviour occurrence

- Staff were trained with a 30-min orientation and training in each component, followed by training to mastery for components in the use of photographic prompts and escape communication strategies

---

Step 6: The design

The design of the study will be dictated by multiple factors, including the type of target behaviour/s, number of participants/settings involved, the nature of the intervention, as well as the level of functioning of the participant. Chapters 5 to 8 described four prototypical designs and their variants used in single-case interventions. There are other, and more complex, designs (e.g. nested designs – see Chapter 1), but these require expertise to design and implement with scientific rigour.

Compared with the relatively small number of designs used in between-groups research, the newcomer to the field of single-case methodology can be overwhelmed with the variety of designs available, and knowing which type of design to choose can be a daunting task. To this end, we have developed a decision tree (Figure 10.1) and the answers to questions will guide selection of the appropriate design to evaluate the intervention.

- An initial question that the investigator needs to answer is whether the intervention can be meaningfully withdrawn. By this we mean, that it is possible to, literally, take away the intervention, such that its effect on the target behaviour will only be manifest when the intervention is being delivered. Withdrawable interventions usually (but not always – see example of Feeney & Ylvisaker, 2008, below) involve aids, equipment, or substances. It is clear that such interventions can be taken away so that there are no long-lasting 'carry-over' effects of the intervention to the subsequent A phases. Non-withdrawable interventions include those that teach a skill (e.g. communication competence, improved gait mobility, behavioural self-regulation). Once learned, such skills generally cannot be unlearned. Accordingly, if the answer to the question (can the intervention can be meaningfully withdrawn?) is yes, then consider a WRD (e.g. A-B-A-B; see Chapter 5). An ATD (see Chapter 7) could also be considered, if the aim is to compare two interventions (one of which could be a no-treatment control condition). MBD (Chapter 6) and CCD (Chapter 8) are also suitable, and are parti-cularly relevant for non-withdrawable treatments.
- Deciding between a WRD or ATD will depend on a number of factors. Of most relevance in the WRD is the issue of the ethics of withdrawing an intervention which is proving successful. If this is a problem, then consider using an MBD, which can be applied to both withdrawable and non-withdrawable interventions.
- The ATD can appear to be an attractive option because of its efficiency in comparing multiple interventions simultaneously (as opposed to sequentially in the A-B-A-B WRD), but there are challenges in its application. It will require fairly rapid (e.g. daily) alternation of multiple conditions (e.g. intervention 1 and inter-vention 2), and this may be a limiting factor in its practical

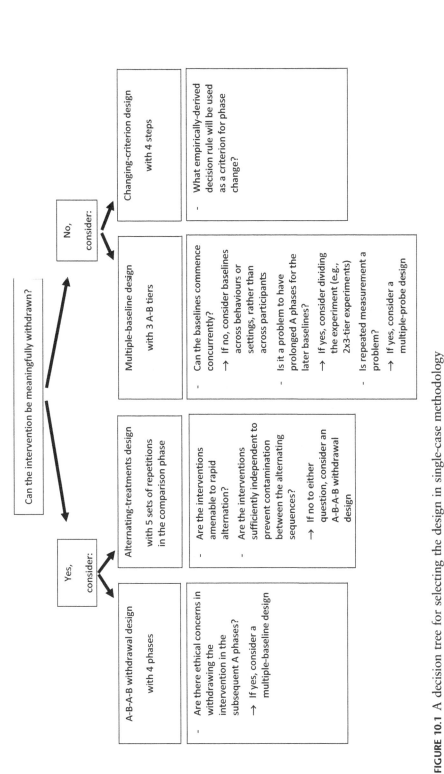

FIGURE 10.1 A decision tree for selecting the design in single-case methodology

application. Additionally, the conditions of the intervention need to be sufficiently independent that carry-over effects are minimised, and the target behaviour needs to be responsive.

• If the intervention *cannot* be meaningfully withdrawn, consider an MBD or CCD. If using an MBD, a series of decisions need to be made (see Chapter 6 for a discussion of options in the MBD):

  a Will the different baselines (tiers) be across behaviours, settings or participants?

  b If the different baselines are across participants, will the baselines be concurrent (i.e. data collection for all participants commences at the same point in time)? There are important consequences of using a concurrent versus non-concurrent design.

  c If the different baselines are across behaviours or settings, interdependence of behaviours/setting needs to be minimised to reduce the risk of behavioural covariation.

  d Because the MBD is sequential in nature, it (like the A-B-A-B WRD and CCD) can result in a lengthy study. This has particular ramifications for the later baselines (tiers), and the practitioner could consider using a multiple-probe study.

• If the desired level of the target behaviour is difficult or slow to achieve, a CCD may be useful, so that behaviours can be shaped. The main decisions to be made in a CCD is the criterion that will be used to change phase.

All the foregoing designs will require decisions to be made about the length of phases and when to change phases (see Chapter 1). Recommended practice is that phase change occurs after stabilisation of responses. But a rule of thumb is that each phase should have at least three data points (but a minimum of five is better) to ensure sufficient sampling of behaviours. Sometimes, this is necessarily curtailed in the initial baseline phase if the intervention needs to commence immediately because of concerns for the safety of the participant or other people.

The recommended number of phases required to demonstrate the experimental effect should be used (see Chapter 1 for more detail), because the greater the number of intra-subject replications, the more convincing the evidence of a functional relationship between the dependent and independent variables. Current standards recommend a four-phase WRD (which allows for three opportunities to demonstrate the experimental effect); a six-phase, three-tier MBD; five sets of alternating sequences in the comparison phase of an ATD; and a four-step CCD (Horner et al., 2005; Kratochwill et al., 2010; 2013; Tate et al., 2013a; 2015).

ILLUSTRATION: STEP 6: THE DESIGN

Feeney and Ylvisaker (2008) argued that a withdrawal A-B-A-B design would be the most appropriate way to evaluate the effect of the intervention for Ben. They hypothesised that when the supports underpinning the intervention were withdrawn, the target behaviours would return to baseline levels.

- The authors reported that the criterion for phase change (B–A), was that the target behaviours occurred no more than two times per day for five consecutive days.
- Following a five-day baseline, the intervention was implemented across nine days in the first B phase, followed by a three-day second A phase, with the intervention reinstated for a further four days in the second B phase.

Step 7: Other considerations

Three other issues should be considered in the planning stage: randomisation, blinding, and consent to conduct the study. The randomised, double-blind, placebo-controlled trial is considered the gold standard of between-groups intervention research because it incorporates strategies to minimise risk of bias, thus making study results more credible. Undoubtedly two of the strongest strategies to minimise risk of bias are randomisation and blinding. To date, these strategies have not been widely incorporated into the single-case paradigm.

Randomisation

This can be used in the prototypical designs. In single-case research randomisation procedures differ to those used in between-groups designs in which participants are randomly allocated to different conditions. It is obvious that in single-case studies, where the sample comprises a single individual, this is not possible. The main way that randomisation works in single-case studies is by randomising (i) phase order (or in alternating-treatments designs, alternation sequence) and/or (ii) the onset of the phases (Edgington, 1980; 1987).

Other features of the design can also be randomised (see Ferron & Levin, 2014; Kratochwill & Levin, 2010; 2014), but in terms of minimising threats to internal validity randomising order and/or onset of the interventions are the most important.

Blinding (or masking) in a SCED

This refers to the person (whether participant, practitioner or assessor) being blind to phase. Although blinding of the participant and practitioner are difficult to achieve with most behavioural interventions commonly used in the neurorehabilitation setting, use of technologically driven interventions may provide the opportunity for blinding the practitioner (see Chapter 2). Blinding of the assessor is easier to achieve if a permanent product record of the target behaviour can be made. In this case, an independent person re-orders the sessions so that they are not chronological, and the assessor then evaluates the data not knowing whether they come from the baseline or intervention phase. If blinding the assessor is not possible (e.g. observations of the target behaviour are made in real time), then it is advised that the assessor is independent of the practitioner, which addresses possible bias due to investigator reactivity.

Consent

This can be considered from two perspectives: participant consent to treatment and approval from a formally constituted ethics committee to conduct the study. Recommended practice is that the participant should provide informed and written consent to participate in any single-case intervention (Mechling et al., 2014; Tate et al., 2016b). In the case where a person is unable to provide informed consent (e.g. due to cognitive impairment), they should assent to the intervention, and written consent be provided by their appointed guardian. Ethics approval from a formally constituted ethics committee is almost a universal requirement for research.

Stage 2: Conduct after the study starts

Once the study starts the investigator needs to pay ongoing attention to two features in particular: (i) measurement of the target behaviour and (ii) implementation of the intervention. It is necessary to monitor data quality and procedural fidelity, and take remedial action, when and if necessary.

Step 8: Data fidelity

As discussed in Chapter 2, instrumentation, testing and participant and investigator reactivity can pose threats to internal validity compromising the reliability of data being collected. Close monitoring of the data collection process is necessary to maintain high standards of accuracy. These include ensuring that observations are being made how, when, where, and as frequently as planned. 'Observer drift' needs to be avoided, so that the behaviour as recorded continues to meet operational definitions as initially established. If equipment is used, it is important to ensure that it continues to function as intended and is regularly recalibrated so that data can be accurately recorded throughout the duration of the study.

It is necessary but not sufficient to have procedures in place to maximise data fidelity; evidence for data fidelity also needs to be established empirically. This is done by conducting an inter-rater/observer agreement study. It is particularly important in situations where human observers are used, but not so critical if the target behaviour is measured with equipment free from human influence (Tate et al., 2015). In situations where the target behaviour is measured via self-report it is not possible to establish inter-rater reliability and for this reason it is advantageous to have other measures in addition to self-report.

The following steps are recommended for an inter-rater agreement study:

1. A permanent product record of the target behaviour (e.g. video, audio, written response) allows for two raters to independently evaluate the data records after the event, and also the opportunity to verify decisions.
2. The rules of thumb for establishing inter-rater/observer agreement are described in Chapter 3 and are repeated here:

   - at least 20% of data points are selected from each condition (e.g. baseline condition, intervention condition). It strengthens the methodology if the data are randomly selected which can be done if a permanent product record is available
   - two raters independently evaluate the data (for occurrence, frequency, intensity, or other quality of the target behaviour as being measured) separately for each condition (baseline; intervention)

- inter-rater agreement is calculated by the following simple formula:

$$\frac{number\ of\ agreements}{(number\ of\ agreements) + (number\ of\ disagreements)} \times 100$$

- a high level of agreement, at least 80%, is required

ILLUSTRATION: STEP 8: DATA FIDELITY

Feeney and Ylvisaker (2008) put procedures in place to maximise data fidelity and also evaluated inter-rater agreement.

- First, as noted in Step 3, staff were trained to mastery in recording the frequency and intensity of the aggression target behaviours. Staff recordings were compared with those of the consultant and the study did not commence until there were two consecutive occasions where agreement was at least 90%
- An inter-rater agreement study was conducted. Two observers were present and made ratings at the beginning of the study and after every fifth session (corresponding to 20%). More than 80% and 85% agreement occurred throughout all conditions for ratings of frequency and intensity respectively.

Step 9: Procedural fidelity

Procedural fidelity, which is discussed in Chapter 4, is closely related to the intervention (see Step 5). It stands to reason that if one wants to know whether an intervention is effective, then it is necessary to know exactly what occurred. Was the intervention implemented as intended and described in the manual or was the intervention somehow inadvertently modified during the study (e.g. some procedures were omitted/not followed, or extra components were added)? Having a study with high treatment adherence enhances both internal and external validity.

Moreover, authorities in the fields of clinical psychology and special education have emphasised that it is not only the active intervention that needs to be evaluated for adherence to protocol, but also the baseline conditions. This addresses threats to internal validity posed by diffusion of treatment effect (see Chapter 2). Ensuring adherence to protocol in both the baseline and intervention conditions is referred to as procedural fidelity. The advantage of establishing procedural fidelity is that it not only allows the researcher to comment on treatment adherence, but also on treatment differentiation (i.e. that procedures/ techniques specific to a condition/intervention are confined to that condition/intervention and do not occur in other conditions/interventions; see Chapter 4).

Periodic checks should be made to ensure that the practitioner continues to adhere to the requirements for implementing the conditions of the study. For empirical demonstration of procedural fidelity, the rules of thumb are described in Chapter 4 and are repeated here:

- Compile a protocol of required components in both the baseline and intervention conditions
- Select at least 20% of sessions in each of the baseline and intervention conditions
- A person who is independent of the practitioner (and not in a personal relationship with the participant) evaluates each of the selected sessions to determine whether each component of the protocol did or did not occur
- Treatment adherence is calculated by the following simple formula:

$$\frac{\begin{array}{c} number\ of\ times\ an\ agreement\ is\ recorded\ between \\ the\ rater's\ observation\ and\ the\ protocol \end{array}}{(number\ of\ agreements) + (number\ of\ disagreements)} \times 100$$

- High fidelity is suggested by at least 80% agreement between the rater and protocol in each of the baseline and intervention conditions

---

ILLUSTRATION: STEP 9: PROCEDURAL FIDELITY

Feeney and Ylvisaker (2008) put procedures in place to maximise procedural fidelity, although they did not formally evaluate adherence:

- Prior to commencing the experiment, the staff were oriented and trained in each component of the intervention in a 30-min session. They then practiced and were required to reach mastery for two of the components (photographic cues and escape communication strategies)
- Specification of procedures to be followed in the baseline conditions minimised the risk of diffusion of treatment effect and enhanced treatment differentiation. At the beginning of each day of the baseline (A) phases (and "intermittently throughout the day"), Ben was given reminders about his work schedule and assignments. Reminders were often consequent upon off-task, inappropriate or oppositional behaviours. None of the supports trialled in the B phases were used during baseline phases.
- During the intervention (B) phases, "periodic checks of procedural mastery" were conducted, and the consultant met with staff from time to time to evaluate progress of the intervention.

Step 10: Data evaluation

A wide variety of analytic techniques is available to evaluate data from single-case studies, using both visual analysis and statistical procedures (see Chapter 9). Traditionally, single-case data are presented graphically, and visual inspection is used to determine whether there are differences between phases. The reasoning is along the lines that if differences are not visually apparent, then they are probably not clinically meaningful and socially important. Statistical analysis has gained prominence over recent years and it is generally recommended to use both visual and statistical analysis as complementary methods of data evaluation (e.g. Parker & Brossart, 2003; Kratochwill et al., 2014).

ILLUSTRATION: STEP 10: DATA EVALUATION

Feeney and Ylvisaker (2008) made descriptive comments about the results of the intervention, supplemented with graphical representation of the daily recordings throughout the 22 days of the experiment. They did not, however, conduct formal analysis of the results using statistical procedures. Visual inspection of the data suggest that Ben showed a dramatic response.

- The frequency of the aggressive target behaviour decreased from between 8 and 13 occurrences per day during the first A phase, to less than two per day when the B phase was implemented (apart from the first day of the B phase). The target behaviours increased to pre-intervention levels when the second A phase was introduced, and immediately decreased with the reinstatement of the B phase.
- A similar pattern occurred for the intensity of the aggressive target behaviour which decreased from a mean of 2.5/4 in the first baseline to 1.7/4 in the first B phase
- Similarly, completion of schoolwork improved, increasing from approximately 30% in the first baseline to more than 90% during the intervention.

In summary, the above ten-step procedure facilitates the implementation of a single-case study, both in clinical practice, as well as the research setting. Of course, we could have added an eleventh step. Having carefully conducted a SCED, the investigator needs to consider whether the work should be published. A reporting guideline, specifically developed for SCEDs in the behavioural sciences (Tate et al., 2016a; 2016b; see Chapter 2) is available to assist authors to write reports with clarity and completeness. As we noted in Chapter 2, the neurorehabilitation field needs more good quality SCEDs and we encourage investigators to publish their work.

The study by Feeney and Ylvisaker (2008), used as an example throughout, was implemented in the everyday context of a school setting. Even so, the study was rigorously designed and implemented, giving the reader confidence that the risk of bias was minimised. Although elements such as randomisation and blinding of assessors to phase of the study would have strengthened internal validity, nonetheless the study scored reasonably well on the Internal Validity (5/14) and External Validity and Interpretation (11/16) subscales of the RoBiNT Scale (Tate et al., 2013a; 2015). Parenthetically, it must be kept in mind that RoBiNT Scale, which uses stringent criteria in keeping with standards of evidence proposed by Kratochwill et al.

(2010; 2013), was published subsequent to the Feeney and Ylvisaker report and so the authors are at disadvantage in being evaluated on a scale that was not available at the time of their study. Their study was carefully planned and conducted in accordance with accepted criteria at the time.

A model for neurorehabilitation practice in the clinical setting

One might reasonably ask whether it is feasible to use single-case methods in the general neurorehabilitation setting, where patients/clients often have multiple areas of impairments all of which are treated concurrently by therapists from different disciplines. In addition, there are often many pressures to implement an intervention immediately upon referral. Sometimes pressures are external, for example, payors may set limits on the number of therapy sessions available, or institutions may dictate the length of admission. Other times pressures are clinically driven, when, for instance, a patient poses a threat to the safety of him/herself or others. Examples commonly encountered in neurorehabilitation include swallowing problems, risk of falls, physical violence. Of course, one could always implement a B-A-B-A-B design (if the intervention was withdrawable) in the above situations, and hence commence the intervention immediately, but when safety issues are involved the withdrawal design raises ethical concerns.

Because it is not always possible to implement single-case experiments in the clinical environment, Tate and colleagues developed a framework, the Model for Assessing Treatment Effect (MATE; Tate, Aird, & Taylor, 2012; Tate et al., 2013b), that incorporates all scenarios encountered in clinical practice. We describe the MATE here because it provides the clinician and researcher with a range of options to implement an intervention that might be considered in situations where it is not feasible to conduct a textbook-quality, single-case experiment. The structure of the MATE also serves the purpose of a conduit to allow clinical practice, within the practical constraints described above, to be elevated to a more scientifically rigorous level.

The seven levels of the MATE are shown in Table 10.1. The most scientifically rigorous way to implement an intervention is at Level 6 of the MATE: a single-case experiment with controlled implementation of the intervention and sufficient sampling of the target behaviour in each phase, operationally defined for the MATE as at least three measurement occasions per phase. But circumstances may dictate implementation at a lower MATE level. In our opinion, Level 5

TABLE 10.1 Levels of the Model for Assessing Treatment Effect (MATE)

MATE Level and definition	Distinctive features
Level 0: No intervention is implemented	Typical scenarios include patients who are admitted for assessment only, or those with very low levels of functioning who are not ready to engage in an active therapy programme.
Level 1: An intervention is implemented, but without a formal pre-intervention evaluation.	A common reason that formal pre-intervention assessment is not conducted is due to urgency of dealing with behaviours that present a risk to the safety of the patient or other people, with previously noted examples including swallowing problems, risk of falls, presence of challenging behaviours.
Level 2: An intervention is implemented following a formal pre-intervention evaluation.	By a formal pre-intervention assessment we refer to the administration of standardised instruments (tests, rating scales, questionnaires, interviews), structured observations with a quantitative record, or measures of a specific target behaviour. Some case descriptions that contain pre-intervention data are eligible for classification at Level 2.
Level 3: An intervention is implemented following a formal pre-intervention evaluation, including specific measure/s of the behaviour targeted for intervention.	Occasions of measurement of the target behaviour need to be made repeatedly and frequently during the intervention phase. Some B-phase training studies are characteristic of a Level 3 intervention.
Level 4: A formal evaluation is conducted before and after an intervention is implemented, including at least three measures of a specific target behaviour taken at some point.	The so-called "pre-post" designs, in which assessment occurs both before and after an intervention enables the clinician to document whether there has been a change in particular behaviours. This approach may be classified at Level 4, if the specific behaviour that is targeted for intervention is also measured on a minimum of three occasions.
Level 5: Single-case methods are used	There are at least two phases (baseline and intervention) during which measures of the target behaviour are taken repeatedly, even though the intervention may not be implemented in a scientifically controlled manner (e.g. some A–B designs) or other features of the design are less than optimal (e.g. fewer than 3 data points in any phase).
Level 6: A single-case experiment	There are three or more phases, during which measures of the target behaviour are taken on at least three occasions per phase. (See Chapters 6–9 for descriptions of prototypical single-case experiments.)

(an A-B design) or Level 4 (a pre-post design, which includes measurement of target behaviour/s) represent a minimum standard of clinical practice, in that the practitioner needs to at least evaluate the effect of the intervention at its conclusion. Levels 4 or 5 should be feasible to conduct in virtually all cases.

The MATE provides clear direction about what is required to progress from one level to the next. To further assist this process Tate et al. (2012) developed a decision tree consisting of a series of questions with yes/no responses (see Figure 10.2). Each question that is answered in the affirmative allows progression to the next step in the model; if it is answered in the negative then that is the level of the model which applies. The questions can be answered retrospectively to evaluate what was done, or prospectively to plan how an intervention will be delivered. Thus, a practitioner or researcher can use the MATE decision tree to reflect upon how an intervention was implemented with a particular patient/client and to determine where improvements could occur for subsequent patients/clients.

Concluding remarks

Single-case methods are certainly not new in the scientific literature, however their application in neurorehabilitation practice is, with some exceptions, neither routine nor common. This chapter has described a ten-step procedure to facilitate the planning and implementation of a single-case study. We also presented the MATE as a framework that incorporates all scenarios encountered in a clinical neurorehabilitation setting and identifies levels of scientific rigour of implementing interventions.

The traditional approach to clinical practice is usually characterised by the following sequential steps: initial assessment and case formulation, setting of goals, implementing an (ideally, evidence-based) intervention, and, following completion of the intervention, determining whether goals have been achieved. Single-case methodology also does this, but additionally includes two unique features: (i) repeated and frequent measurement of the behaviour targeted by the intervention throughout the rehabilitation programme, both before the intervention is implemented and while it is in progress, and (ii) implementing the intervention in a scientifically controlled way.

The advantage of the first feature (repeated and frequent measurement) is that systematic and continuous monitoring and

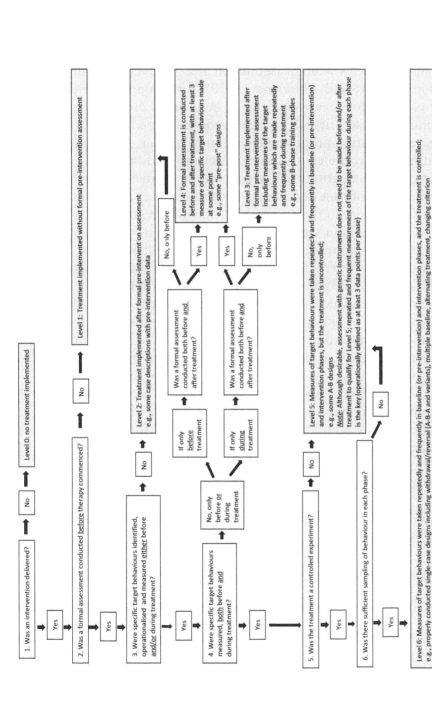

FIGURE 10.2 Decision tree for the MATE

Source: Tate, Aird, and Taylor (2012); reprinted with permission

measurement of the behaviour targeted for intervention means that an intervention that is not working, or not working optimally, can be recognised and adapted. And this can occur without necessarily compromising the scientific rigour of the intervention implementation. Stewart and Alderman (2010), for example, treated a 39-year-old man for severe challenging behaviours after traumatic brain injury. The severity of his aggression interfered significantly with his rehabilitation programme, and in particular, developing a personal hygiene routine. An intervention, using differential reinforcement of incompatible behaviour was instigated for 26 sessions, but results of time-series analyses showed that there was no significant decrement in the aggressive behaviour from the baseline phase. The intervention was changed to differential reinforcement of low rates of responding, over 29 sessions, but that too proved ineffective. A third intervention was trialled, using situational time out with sustained prompting, and there was an immediate and dramatic response, which was sustained over 44 sessions.

The advantage of the second feature (implementing the intervention in a scientifically controlled way) is that single-case methods have the capacity to provide definitive evidence regarding the success (or otherwise) of Intervention X to treat Behaviour Y, allowing cause-effect functional relations to be established. Because the traditional clinical approach does not implement the intervention in a scientifically controlled manner, the capacity to draw valid inferences or conclusions about the effectiveness of the intervention per se is weakened. We encourage all practitioners to incorporate the steps outlined in this chapter as representing good clinical practice. In one sense, every patient/client in the neurorehabilitation setting is a single case, and single-case methods are the very embodiment of the scientist-practitioner model.

APPENDIX

Summary components of selected neurorehabilitation studies

TABLE A.1 Summary components of selected neurorehabilitation studies

Domain	First author (year)	Neurological condition	Target behaviour area	Measure/s of main target behaviour/s with continuous data collection	Intervention and dosage for active intervention/s (as available in the report)	Design
Basic and instrumental activities of daily living	Beattie (2004)	Dementia	Food consumption	1. Leaving table: number of occasions 2. Leaving table: duration (stopwatch) 3. Food eaten: weight 4. Food eaten: proportion accepted 5. Fluid consumption: proportion accepted	Systematic behavioural intervention package (to increase food consumption and reinforce 'sitting-at-table behaviour') Dosage: 20 mins/day for 10 wks	A-B-A-B x 3 pts
	Davis (1994)	TBI	Leisure activities (e.g. playing cards, socialising)	Percentage of observations where engaged in leisure activities, using momentary time sampling	Interdependent group contingency Dosage: 10 wks	CCD (baseline + 3 steps) and withdrawal phase x 6 pts
	Engelman (2002)	Dementia	Dressing independence	1. Dressing independence: 4-point clinician rating scale 2. Dressing time: mins	System of least prompts Dosage: 37 x 10–12-min sessions, 1–4 times/week for 6 mths	A-B x 3 pts

Klarborg (2012)	Meningitis; Stroke	Driving speed, defined as more than 5 km/hr above the speed limit	Percentage of time driving above the speed limit	Technology equipment fitted to car: Intelligent Speed Adaptation. Dosage: equipment in situ and operational for 12 wks	A-B-A x 2 pts
McEwen (2010)	Stroke	Activities of daily living tasks (various across pts: e.g. cutting, buttoning, transferring to chair, walking faster, gardening)	Skill performance on Performance Quality Rating Scale: 10-point observation (range: can't do skill at all – does skill very well)	CO-OP (Cognitive Orientation to daily Occupational Performance) treatment approach. Dosage: ~10 sessions, 1–2 times/week	Multiple-probe x behaviours x 3 pts
McGraw-Hunter (2006)	TBI	Stovetop cooking	Percentage of steps completed from a 25-step task analysis	Video self-modelling with feedback. Dosage: 3–4 sessions, during which pts watched 2–3-min video then engaged in cooking	Multiple-probe x pts (n=4)
Perilli (2013)	Dementia	Making telephone calls	1. Number of phone calls made 2. Duration of phone calls	Computer-aided telephone system. Dosage: 20–50 x 10 min sessions, 1–2/day	N-C MBD x pts (n=5)
Skinner (2000)	Schizophrenia	Reading for leisure	Number of pages read continuously (as operationally defined)	Contingency program (obtaining a soft drink). Dosage: daily sessions for ~ 6 wks	CCD (baseline + 8 steps)

(Continued)

TABLE A.1 *(Continued)*

Domain	First author (year)	Neurological condition	Target behaviour area	Measure/s of main target behaviour/s with continuous data collection	Intervention and dosage for active intervention/s (as available in the report)	Design
	Tate (2018)	TBI	Leisure and meaningful activity	Various across pts: generally, the number of activities completed	PEPA (Program for Engagement, Activities and Participation), based on a therapeutic recreation model. Dosage: 15 x 60 min sessions, once/week + 2 x 60 min booster sessions	MBD x pts (n=7)
Challenging behaviour	Dixon (2004)	TBI	Inappropriate verbalisations (various across pts: e.g. aggressive, suicidal, profane, sexual)	Number of targeted verbal utterances per session	Differential reinforcement of alternative vocalisations. Dosage: 3–11 sessions (across pts)	BAB (following a functional behavioural analysis) x 4 pts
	Feeney (2008)	TBI in students	School setting: Physical aggression (e.g. hitting, pushing), verbal aggression (e.g. threats)	1. Number of targeted behaviours 2. Intensity of targeted behaviours: 4-point scale of 20 aggressive-type items from the Aberrant Behavior Checklist 3. Percentage of work completed	Multi-component interventions, comprising context-sensitive, cognitive-behavioural supports. Dosage: throughout the school day x 2 wks	A-B-A-B x 2 pts

Feeney (2010)	TBI in students	School setting: physical aggression (e.g. hitting, pushing), verbal aggression (e.g. threats)	1. Number of targeted behaviours 2. Intensity of targeted behaviours: 4-point scale of 20 aggressive-type items from the Aberrant Behavior Checklist 3. Percentage of work completed	Multi-component intervention with cognitive-behavioural intervention using context-sensitive, self-regulatory scripts Dosage: throughout the three classes (English, Math, Science) x 5 wks (tier 1)	MBD x settings x 2 pts
Freeman (2009)	TBI	Self-injurious behaviours (e.g. eye and face gouging, head banging, biting self)	Number of targeted behaviours	Behavioural program including verbal (and if needed, physical) cues, verbal praise, tokens, with aversive conditioning (noxious stimuli) Dosage: 22 weeks; continuous observation	A-B
Guercio (2012)	TBI	Problem gambling	Number of lotto tickets/poker chips 'purchased'	Cognitive-behavioural intervention package Dosage: 8 x 1 hr sessions, once/wk	MBD x pts (n=3)
Hufford (2012)	TBI	Agitation and poor adherence to therapy procedures	Score on the Agitated Behavior Scale	Behavioural contracting for treatment adherence Dosage: continuous (all nursing shifts) for 4 days	A-B

(Continued)

TABLE A.1 (Continued)

Domain	First author (year)	Neurological condition	Target behaviour area	Measure/s of main target behaviour/s with continuous data collection	Intervention and dosage for active intervention/s (as available in the report)	Design
	Lane-Brown (2010)	TBI	Apathy, specifically difficulty sustaining activities	Sustaining activity, measured by time (mins) per day spent on goals	Motivational interviewing and external compensation (reminder alerts from personal digital assistant, PDA) Dosage: 20 sessions (tier 1) x 1-hr, once/wk	MBD x behaviours
	Locke (2010)	Dementia	Disruptive vocalisations, defined as all sounds emitted by pt, except involuntary noises, e.g. coughing	Percentage of 10 sec intervals without vocalisation	Music under 4 conditions: - baseline - ambient music - music with headphones - headphone without music Dosage: 55 (comparison and best treatment phases) x 20-min sessions, once/day	ATD
	Stewart (2010)	TBI	Verbal and physical aggression towards self, objects and other people	Number of aggressive outbursts during morning hygiene programme	Operant interventions Three active interventions: Differential reinforcement of: B: incompatible behaviour (DRI) C: low rates of responding (DLR) D: situational time out and sustained verbal prompting Dosage: ~180 sessions (across all conditions), once/day	B-C-D-B-D

	Tasky (2008)	TBI	On-task behaviour; defined as physical contact with one or more objects in a manner that could result in task completion	Percentage of intervals on-task, using momentary time-sampling	Use of choice (vs assignment in A phase) Dosage: 10–12 sessions (across pts) x 60-min, 5 days/wk	A-B-A'-B x 3 pts
	Valle Padilla (2013)	Dementia	Wandering/escape behaviour, defined as approaching the exit door within range of the alarm sensor (~2m)	Number of occasions approached exit door	Three active interventions: B: environmental C: cognitive-behaviour (including differential reinforcement of incompatible behaviour) BC: combined Dosage: 15 observation periods (across conditions) x 4 hours, 5 days/wk	A-B-A-C-A-B-BC-B (B-BC-B sequence to check effect of joint intervention)
Communication, language and speech	Andrews-Salvia (2003)	Dementia	Discourse (conversational) skills	Number of on-topic facts in the first 2.5 mins of conversation	Topic prompts provided by the practitioner and memory book of personally-relevant facts used as a memory aid for the pts Dosage: 6 sessions (per tier) x 8–23 mins, 3 times/wk	MBD x behaviours x 4 pts

(Continued)

TABLE A.1 (*Continued*)

Domain	First author (year)	Neurological condition	Target behaviour area	Measure/s of main target behaviour/s with continuous data collection	Intervention and dosage for active intervention/s (as available in the report)	Design
	Douglas (2014)	TBI	Communication-specific coping	Score on the clinician-rated Discourse Coping Scale, rated using 10-cm visual analogue scale from video-recordings	Communication-specific coping intervention, incorporating strategies and principles from cognitive-behaviour therapy and context-sensitive social communication therapy. Dosage: 12 x 1 hr sessions, twice/wk	A-B+Fup
	Francis (2001)	TBI	Agnosic alexia (reading disorder due to visual object/letter recognition impairment)	Study 4: Number of irregular words read	A series of hierarchical interventions addressing: Study 1. letter identities Study 2. letter to phoneme assignment Study 3. consonant clusters Study 4. Irregular words with two active interventions: - traditional - new interventions. Dosage: variable across studies: Study 1: 9 mths; Study 3: 1 session; Study 4: 12 sessions	Study 4: ATD
	Hickey (2004)	Stroke	Broca's aphasia, specifically making comprehensible utterances in conversation	Percentage of comprehensible and incomprehensible utterances in 10 mins	Conversation partner training: Five-step multi-modal training programme. Dosage: 5–6 x 10 min sessions, 1–3 times/wk	Multiple-probe design x pts (n=2)

Kiran (2008)	Stroke	Conduction/Broca's aphasia, specifically anomia	Percentage of correctly named coloured photographs of objects	Semantic feature intervention. Dosage: ~20 x 2-hr sessions, twice/wk	Multiple-probe x behaviours x 5 pts
LaFrance (2007)	Stroke	Verbal communication (e.g. attempts to verbalise, automatic speech) and non-verbal communication (e.g. smiling, head nods)	Rate: number of verbal and non-verbal behaviours observed per min	Animal-assisted therapy programme. B: dog handler alone. C: dog handler and dog. Dosage: 7 x 2–3-min (duration of the walk) sessions, once/wk	A-B-C-A
Lancioni (2010)	Profound disability after acquired brain injury	Basic communication strategies via text messages	Number of messages sent and received	Teaching steps to learn the messaging technology (including use of micro-switches). Dosage: ~86 x 30-min sessions, repeated throughout the day as required	Multiple-probe x pts (n=2)
Leon (2005)	Stroke	Aprosodia (disturbance of the emotional tone/intent of speech)	Percentage of correctly read sentences with the requested emotional tone of voice	Two active interventions. B: Imitative vs C: cognitive-linguistic. Dosage: 20 x 1-hr sessions for each intervention, over 1 mth	A-B-A-C x 3 pts

(Continued)

TABLE A.1 (*Continued*)

Domain	First author (year)	Neurological condition	Target behaviour area	Measure/s of main target behaviour/s with continuous data collection	Intervention and dosage for active intervention/s (as available in the report)	Design
	Raymer (2007)	Stroke	Broca's aphasia (6/8 pts), specifically noun and verb retrieval	Number of correct responses in picture naming	Semantic–phonological question intervention Dosage: 10 sessions per tier, 2–4 times/wk	MBD x behaviours x 8 pts
	Rose (2008)	Stroke	Broca's aphasia, specifically verb retrieval	Number of correct responses to naming actions from line drawings	Three conditions: - semantic - gesture - combined semantic and gesture Dosage: 18 x 1-hr sessions, 3 times/wk	ATD x 3 pts
	Savage (2013)	Semantic dementia	Naming accuracy	Percentage of coloured photographs of objects correctly named	Word training program to rebuild the semantic (vocabulary) store Dosage: home-based: 30–60 mins, once/day, for 3–6 weeks per tier	MBD x behaviours x 4 pts
	Tate (2013b)	TBI	Expressive language output	Number of words produced in response to stimuli	Response elaboration training principles Dosage: 11 (tier 1) x 1-hr sessions, twice/wk	MBD x behaviours

	Wambaugh (2000)	Stroke	Apraxia of speech, specifically rate and rhythm of speech	1. Percentage of words produced without sound errors 2. Percentage of total consonants produced correctly, in the correct position within the target word	Repeated practice with metronome and hand tapping Dosage: ~17 x 1-hr sessions, 3 times/wk	MBD x behaviours
	Wright (2008)	Stroke	Conduction aphasia, specifically anomia	Percentage of pictures (line drawings) correctly named	Writing intervention, adapted from Copy and Recall Treatment (CART) Dosage: 10 (tier 1) x 1-hr sessions, 2–3 times/wk	Multiple probe x behaviours x 2 pts
Memory, learning and other cognitive	Bailey (2002)	Stroke	Unilateral spatial neglect	1. Score on the Start Cancellation Task 2. Ratio score on the Baking Tray Task 3. Displacement (cm) from the midline on the Line Bisection Task	Scanning and cuing techniques (5 pts) Contralateral limb activation (2 pts) Dosage: minimum of 10 x 1-hr sessions on alternate weekdays	A-B-A x 5 pts (scanning and cuing) x 2 pts (limb activation)

(Continued)

Appendix

TABLE A.1 (*Continued*)

Domain	First author (year)	Neurological condition	Target behaviour area	Measure/s of main target behaviour/s with continuous data collection	Intervention and dosage for active intervention/s (as available in the report)	Design
	Baldwin (2015)	TBI	Remembering to do tasks	Percentage of forgotten events	Step-by-step instructional program to learn Google Calendar Dosage: 1-wk training prior to intervention which lasted for 6 wks	A-B
	Besharati (2015)	Stroke	Anosognosia (unawareness) for hemiplegia	Score on the Feinberg Awareness Scale	Self-observation by video-replay (a video clip of the Berti et al. interview) Dosage: view ~2–3 min video + interview questions, over 2–3 sessions	Multiple-probe x behaviours x 2 pts
	Bickerton (2006)	Carbon monoxide poisoning	Action disorganisation affecting ability to carry out routine everyday tasks	1. Number of correct steps completed in correct sequence 2. Number of errors (perseverations and additions) 3. Number of cues/prompts given by practitioner	Verbal strategies to complete tasks (learning and reciting a specially developed script re content and sequence of steps to be followed) Dosage: 13 sessions over a 7-month period, with up to 10 repetitions of task per session	A-B+F'up
	Boman (2010)	Stroke	Memory: Remembering to do tasks	Number of activities omitted	Electronic memory aid with individualised spoken reminders Dosage: aid in situ in pt's home for 9 wks	MBD x behaviours x 5 pts

Ehlhardt (2005)	TBI	Learning to use email	1. Number of steps completed and correctly sequenced 2. Number of steps completed (irrespective of sequence) 3. Number of sessions to attain mastery (100% correct completion of steps without prompt)	TEACH-M 7-step, 4-phase instructional package Dosage: daily, over 7–15 days across pts	Multiple-probe x pts (n=4)
Evans (1998)	Stroke	Executive action implementation, defined as delayed initiation of tasks	Latency: mins before action commences	External cueing system (NeuroPage) Dosage: continuous use during a 3-mth period (1st B phase)	A-B-A-B
Fiksdal (2012)	Dementia	Learning memory facts	Percentage of correct responses of personally relevant memory facts	Memory priming with spaced retrieval Dosage: 25–35-min sessions, 3–5 days/wk, over 3–5 weeks	Multiple-probe x behaviours (with embedded A-B-C+m +F'up)

(Continued)

TABLE A.1 (*Continued*)

Domain	First author (year)	Neurological condition	Target behaviour area	Measure/s of main target behaviour/s with continuous data collection	Intervention and dosage for active intervention/s (as available in the report)	Design
	Francis (2002)	Encephalitis	Prosopagnosia (inability to recognise faces in the visual modality) and person-specific semantic disorder	1. Number of faces with correct semantic information 2. Number of faces correctly named	Study 1 compared 3 interventions: - mnemonic (Lorayne) method - simplified visual imagery - rehearsal Dosage: 7 x 2 hr sessions over a fortnight	ATD
	Jamieson (2017)	Cerebral haemorrhage (x 2 pts), anoxic seizures	Reducing memory failures	Percentage of memory tasks successfully completed as recorded in the daily memory log and verified by text message to investigator	Smart-watch as a memory aid Dosage: 14 days of wearing the smart-watch, with weekly sessions with practitioner	A-B-A x 3 pts
	Kawahira (2009)	Cortico-basal degeneration	Limb kinetic apraxia (inability to execute familiar, skilled movements that is not due to motor-sensory impairment)	1. Rate: number of finger taps on Finger Tapping Test within 30 secs 2. Score on Simple Test for Evaluating Hand Function	Facilitation exercises Dosage: 20–30-min sessions, 5 days/wk, over 1 week per phase	Mixed design

Lancioni (2009)	Vegetative state and pervasive motor disability	Learning to activate micro-switches	Number of responses (using hand closure, 1 pt, or eye blinking, 2 pts) in response to stimuli (familiar voices, stories, visual images, lights, songs and musical items)	Assistive technology using micro-switches to detect signs of learning. Dosage: 133–180 x 5-min sessions, 5–10 times/day	Reversal design: A-B-A-B-C-B x 3 pts
Mechling (2006)	Profound intellectual disability in students	Learning to activate micro-switches	Number of stimulus activations during each 3-min intervention	Assistive technology to learn micro-switch activation. Compared three reinforcement conditions: - adapted toys and devices - cause-and-effect commercial software - instructor-created video. Dosage: 12 x 3-min sessions per condition; 1 session/day, 2–3 times/wk	ATD x 3 pts

(Continued)

TABLE A.1 (*Continued*)

Domain	First author (year)	Neurological condition	Target behaviour area	Measure/s of main target behaviour/s with continuous data collection	Intervention and dosage for active intervention/s (as available in the report)	Design
	Nikles (2014)	Traumatic brain injury in children	Attention, executive function and behaviour self-regulation	1. Score on the Connors's 3 Rating Scales 2. Score on the Behaviour Rating Inventory of Executive Function 3. Score on the Eyberg Child Behaviour Inventory	Stimulant medication (dex-amphetamine/methylphenidate) vs placebo Dosage: individually tailored for each child (data provided in report), usually twice/day, over 3 weeks	Medical N-of-1 trial x 7 pts
	Smith (2007)	Stroke	Unilateral spatial neglect (failure to attend to one side of space)	1. Score on the Bells Test 2. Score on the Behavioural Inattention Test	Virtual reality Dosage: 6 x 1 hr sessions, once/wk	A-B-A x 4 pts
	Tunnard (2014)	Stroke	Unilateral spatial neglect (failure to attend to one side of space)	1. Percentage of omissions on the Star Cancellation task 2. Percentage of omissions on the Line Crossing task 3. Deviation, in mm, from the midpoint on the Line Bisection task:	Five active interventions: B: music C: anchoring D: vibratory stimulation (using MotivAider®) E: limb activation F: anchoring+MotivAider Dosage: 5 sessions on consecutive days per condition	A-B-A-C-A-D-A-E-A-F

Mood and emotional function				
Arco (2008)	TBI	Obsessive urges, comprising compulsive counting and urges to void his bladder	Percentage of counting and voiding behaviours per hour, using partial interval recording	Cognitive-behaviour therapy package (including self-monitoring, stress-coping strategies, social reinforcement) Dosage: 7 x 1-hr sessions, over 10 weeks	CCD for voiding (baseline + 3 steps)
Jones (2015)	Brain tumour	Depression, anxiety, illness cognitions	Scores on Depression subtest of Depression, Anxiety and Stress Scales, Generalised Anxiety Disorder Scale-7 and Illness Cognitions Questionnaire for the respective target behaviours	Telephone-based psychotherapy with set treatment modules Dosage: 10 sessions, once/wk	MBD x pts (n=4)
Kneebone (2006)	TBI and Downs syndrome	Phobic levels of anxiety (screaming, screeching, occasional hitting whenever physiotherapists touched pt.'s feet during therapy sessions)	Percentage of time in 10 min segments distress occurred (defined as screeching/grizzling)	Exposure therapy (flooding and extinction) Dosage: single session, 90 mins	B-phase

(Continued)

TABLE A.1 (*Continued*)

Domain	First author (year)	Neurological condition	Target behaviour area	Measure/s of main target behaviour/s with continuous data collection	Intervention and dosage for active intervention/s (as available in the report)	Design
	Lundervold (2013)	Parkinson's disease	Dyskinesia (involuntary movements) and social anxiety	1. Subjective Units of Distress: self-rating on a 10-cm visual analogue scale 2. Score on the Clinical Anxiety Scale 3. Score on the Geriatric Depression Scale 4. Direct observation with the Behavioral Relaxation Scale	Behavioural relaxation training Dosage: 4 x 15min sessions, every 2–4 wks	A-B+F'up
	Mohlman (2010)	Parkinson's disease	Anxiety, described as "excessive uncontrollable worry"	Self-ratings of mood: scale of 0–8	Cognitive behaviour therapy and attention process training Dosage: 10 x 90–120-min sessions, once/wk	A-B
	Svanberg (2014)	Korsakoff syndrome	Mood and identity	Self-report on Likert scales of mood, confidence, self-efficacy, usefulness to others, identity, memory	SenseCam (wearable camera that takes hundreds of pictures/day, that are then downloaded to form a pictorial diary). Five activities (e.g. visit to art gallery) were recorded prospectively and viewed. Dosage: 8 weeks with daily review of the activity recorded that week	A-B-A

	Study	Condition	Target	Measures	Intervention	Design
	Rasquin (2009)	Stroke	Depression	Daily self-ratings of positive mood on a vertical 10-cm visual analogue scale	Cognitive behaviour therapy Dosage: 8 x 1-hr sessions, once/wk	A-B+F'up x 5 pts
Motor and sensory	Broach (2001)	Multiple sclerosis	Fatigue and motor activity	1. Number of stair-steps climbed 2. Number of miles using upper extremity ergometer 3. Number of miles using stationary bicycle 4. Score on the self-report Fatigue Questionnaire	Aquatic therapy programme Dosage: ~40 (tier 1) x 45-min sessions, 3 times/wk	Multiple-probe x pts (n=4)
	Broeren (2007)	Stroke	Upper extremity function	Kinematics recorded by computer: 1. Velocity (m/s) 2. Time needed to reach (in secs) 3. Hand path ratio	Virtual reality with haptics (tactile stylus) Dosage: 5 x 45-min sessions, 3 times/wk, over 5 weeks	A-B+F'up x 5 pts

(Continued)

TABLE A.1 (*Continued*)

Domain	First author (year)	Neurological condition	Target behaviour area	Measure/s of main target behaviour/s with continuous data collection	Intervention and dosage for active intervention/s (as available in the report)	Design
	Guercio (2001)	TBI	Ataxic tremor in performing letter-board communication	1. Score on Behavioral Relaxation Scale: percentage of relaxed behaviours 2. Extensor/flexor EMG levels while using communication board: measured in microvolts 3. Clinical rating of tremor severity: range 0–10	Two active interventions: B: Behavioural relaxation training C: biofeedback, with decreasing thresholds of biofeedback in phases BC_1 to BC_3 Dosage: 20 sessions	A-B-BC_1-BC_2-BC_3-A
	Kaminsky (2007)	Parkinson's disease	Akinetic gait (shuffling steps with reduced step length and occasions of cessation of movement {"freezing"})	1. Number of 'freezing' episodes 2. Number of occasions of loss of balance	Virtual cueing spectacles Dosage: planned use in home and community for 10 days	A-B-A
	Kreuzer (2012)	Traumatic brain injury	Tinnitus	Tinnitus Questionnaire	Repetitive transcranial magnetic stimulation Dosage: 5 treatment courses over ~3-yr period (Final course: 1000 stimuli @ 1 Hz over right dorsolateral prefrontal cortex, and then over left primary auditory cortex)	A-B

| McCrimmon (2015) | Stroke | Gait speed and foot drop | 1. Fast gait speed (meters/sec) 2. Dorsiflexion active range of movement, measured with a goniometer 3. 6-min walk test: distance covered in meters 4. Score on the Fugl-Meyer Assessment, Leg Motor | Functional electrical stimulation Dosage: 12 x 1-hr sessions, 3 times/wk, over 4 weeks | A-B+m x 9 pts |
| Ouellet (2007) | TBI | Insomnia | Total wake time (defined as time to sleep onset, time spent awake after sleep onset, time between last awakening and rising from bed), measured in mins from client's recorded data in sleep diary | Cognitive-behaviour therapy Dosage: 8 x 1-hr sessions, once/wk | MBD x pts (n=11) |

(Continued)

TABLE A.1 (*Continued*)

Domain	First author (year)	Neurological condition	Target behaviour area	Measure/s of main target behaviour/s with continuous data collection	Intervention and dosage for active intervention/s (as available in the report)	Design
	Park (2012)	Stroke	Upper extremity motor function	1. Box and Block Test: Number of blocks moved 2. Percentage of activities of daily living tasks (e.g. vacuuming a room) performed	Constraint-induced movement therapy Two active interventions: B: forced use (mitten on unaffected hand) C: forced use + home exercise program Dosage: 5 hrs/day (mitten; B), 100-min exercise sessions (C), over 14 sessions per condition	A-B-A'-C x 3 pts
	Slijper (2014)	Stroke	Upper extremity motor function	Score on Fugl-Meyer Assessment, motor scales A-D	Computer games of graduated difficulty level Dosage: 5 week intervention; total time on computers – range 267–4,727 mins; number of days – range 19–35	A-B+F'up x 11 pts

Notes: TBI=traumatic brain injury; MBD=multiple-baseline design; N-C MBD=nonconcurrent MBD; CCD=changing-criterion design; m=maintenance; F'up=follow-up; pts=participants

REFERENCES

Adams KH, Klinge V, Keiser TW (1973). The extinction of a self-injurious behaviour in an epileptic child. *Behavior Research and Therapy*, *11*(*3*) 351–356.

Allison DB (1992). When cyclicity is a concern: A caveat regarding phase change criteria in single-case designs. *Comprehensive Mental Health Care*, *2*(*2*), 131–149.

Allison DB, Gorman BS (1993). Calculating effect sizes for meta-analysis: The case of the single case. *Behavior Research and Therapy*, *31*(*6*), 621–631.

Andrews-Salvia M, Roy N, Cameron RM (2003). Evaluating the effects of memory books for individuals with severe dementia. *Journal of Medical Speech Language Pathology*, *11*(*1*), 51–59.

Arco L (2008). Neurobehavioural treatment for obsessive–compulsive disorder in an adult with traumatic brain injury. *Neuropsychological Rehabilitation*, *18*(*1*), 109–124.

Arnau J, Bono R (1998). Short-time series analysis: C Statistic vs Edington Model. *Quality and Quantity*, *32*(*1*), 63–75.

Ayres K, Ledford JR (2014). Dependent measures and measurement systems. In DL Gast and JR Ledford (Eds.), *Single case research methodology: Applications in special education and behavioral sciences* (2nd edn, pp. 124–153). New York: Routledge.

Baek EU, Moeyaert M, Petit-Bois M, Beretvas SN, Van den Noortgate W, Ferron MJ (2014). The use of multilevel analysis for integrating single-case experimental design results within a study and across studies. *Neuropsychological Rehabilitation*, *24*(*3–4*), 590–606.

Baer DM (1977). Perhaps it would be better not to know everything. *Journal of Applied Behavior Analysis*, *10*(*1*), 167–172.

Baer DM, Wolf MM, Risley TR (1968). Some current dimensions of applied behavior analysis. *Journal of Applied Behavior Analysis*, 1(1), 91–97.

Bailey JS, Burch MR (2005). *Ethics for behaviour analysts*. Mahwah, NJ: Erlbaum.

Bailey MJ, Riddoch MJ, Crome P (2002). Treatment of visual neglect in elderly patients with stroke: A single-subject series using either a scanning and cueing strategy or a left-limb activation strategy. *Physical Therapy, 82* (8), 782–797.

Bakeman R (2005). Recommended effect size statistics for repeated measures designs. *Behavior Research Methods*, 37(3), 379–384.

Baldwin VN, Powell T (2015). Google Calendar: a single case experimental design study of a man with severe memory problems. *Neuropsychological Rehabilitation, 25(4)*, 617–636.

Barker JB, Mellalieu SD, McCarthy PJ, Jones MV, Moran A (2013). A review of single-case research in sport psychology 1997–2012: Research trends and future directions. *Journal of Applied Sport Psychology, 25(1)*, 4–32.

Barlow DH, Hayes SC (1979). Alternating treatment designs: One strategy for comparing the effects of two treatments in a single subject. *Journal of Applied Behavior Analysis*, 12(2), 199–210.

Barlow DH, Hersen M (1984). *Single case experimental designs: Strategies for studying behavior change* (2nd edn). Boston: Allyn and Bacon.

Barlow DH, Hersen M, Miss J (1973). Single-case experimental designs: Uses in applied clinical research. *Archives of General Psychiatry*, 29(3), 319–325.

Barlow DH, Nock M (2009). Why can't we be more idiographic in our research? *Perspectives on Psychological Science*, 4(1), 19–21.

Barlow DH, Nock MK, Hersen M (2009). *Single case experimental designs: Strategies for studying behavior change* (3rd edn). Boston, MA: Pearson.

Beattie ERA, Algase DL, Song J (2004). Keeping wandering nursing home residents at the table: Improving food intake using a behavioural communication intervention. *Aging and Mental Health*, 8(2), 109–116.

Beeson PM, Robey RR (2006). Evaluating single-subject treatment research: Lessons learned from the aphasia literature. *Neuropsychology Review, 16* (4), 161–169.

Bellg AJ, Borelli B, Resnick B, Hecht J, Minicucci DS, Ory M, Ogedegbe G, Orwig D, Ernst D, Czajkowski S (2004). Enhancing treatment fidelity in health behaviour change studies: Best practices and recommendations from the NIH Behavior Change Consortium. *Health Psychology*, 23(5), 443–451.

Besharati S, Kopelman M, Avesani R, Moro V, Fotopoulou AK (2015). Another perspective on anosognosia: Self-observation in video replay improves motor awareness. *Neuropsychological Rehabilitation*, 25(3), 319–352.

Betz AM, Fisher WW (2011). Functional analysis: History and methods. In WW Fisher, CC Piazza and HE Roane (Eds.), *Handbook of applied behavior analysis* (pp. 206–225). New York: Guildford.

Bickerton WL, Humphreys GW, Riddoch MJ (2006). The use of memorised verbal scripts in the rehabilitation of action disorganisation syndrome. *Neuropsychological Rehabilitation*, 16(2), 155–177.

Birnbauer JS, Peterson CP, Solnick JV (1974). The design and interpretation of studies of single subjects. *American Journal of Mental Deficiency, 79* (2), 191–203.

Bobrovitz CD, Ottenbacher KJ (1998). Comparison of visual inspection and statistical analysis of single-subject data in rehabilitation research. *American Journal of Physical Medicine and Rehabilitation, 77*(2), 94–102.

Boman I-L, Bartfai A, Borrell L, Tham K, Hemmingsson H (2010). Support in everyday activities with a home-based electronic memory aid for persons with memory impairments. *Disability and Rehabilitation: Assistive Technology, 5*(5), 339–350.

Borelli B (2011). The assessment, monitoring, and enhancement of treatment fidelity in public health clinical trials. *Journal of Public Health Dentistry, 71*(s1), S52–S63.

Borelli B, Sepinwall D, Ernst D, Bellg AJ, Czajkowski S, Breger R, . . . Orwig D (2005). A new tool to assess treatment fidelity and evaluation of treatment fidelity across 10 years of health behaviour research. *Journal of Consulting and Clinical Psychology, 73*(5), 852–860.

Boutron I, Moher D, Altman DG, Shulz KF, Ravaud P for the CONSORT Group (2008). Extending the CONSORT Statement to randomized trials of nonpharmacologic treatment: Explanation and Elaboration. *Annals of Internal Medicine, 148*(4), 295–309.

Box GEP, Jenkins GM (1970). *Time series analysis: Forecasting and control.* San Francisco: Holden Day.

Broach E, Dattilo J (2001). Effects of aquatic therapy on adults with multiple sclerosis. *Therapeutic Recreation Journal, 35*(2), 141–154.

Broca P (1861). Perte de la parole: Ramollissement chronique et destruction partielle du lobe antérieur gauche du cerveau [Sur le siège de la faculté du langage]. *Bulletins de la Société d'anthropologie, 2*, 235–238.

Broeren J, Rydmark M, Björkdahl A, Sunnerhagen KS (2007). Assessment and training in a 3-dimensional virtual environment with haptics: A report on 5 cases of motor rehabilitation in the chronic stage after stroke. *Neurorehabilitation and Neural Repair, 21*(2), 180–189.

Brookshire RH (1970). Control of "involuntary" crying behaviour emitted by a multiple sclerosis patient. *Journal of Communication Disorders, 3*(3), 171–176.

Brossart DF, Parker RI, Olson EA, Mahadevan L (2006). The relationship between visual analysis and five statistical analyses in a simple AB single-case research design. *Behavior Modification, 30*(5), 531–563.

Brotherton FA, Thomas LL, Wisotzek IE, Milan MA (1988). Social skills training in the rehabilitation of patients with traumatic closed head injury. *Archives of Physical Medicine and Rehabilitation, 69*(10), 827–832.

Bumbarger BK (2014). Understanding and promoting treatment integrity in prevention. In LMH Sanetti and TR Kratochwill (Eds.), *Treatment integrity: A foundation for evidence-based practice in applied psychology* (pp. 35–54). Washington, DC: American Psychological Association.

Bulté I, Onghena P (2013). The single-case data analysis package: Analysing single-case experiments with R software. *Journal of Modern Applied Statistical Methods*, 12(2), 450–478.

Busk PL, Marascuilo LA (1988). Autocorrelation in single-subject research: A counterargument to the myth of no autocorrelation. *Behavioral Assessment*, 10(3), 229–242.

Busk PL, Marascuilo LA (1992). Statistical analysis in single-case research: Issues, procedures, and recommendations, with applications to multiple behaviors. In TR Kratochwill and JR Levin (Eds.), *Single case research design and analysis: New directions for psychology and education* (pp. 159–185). Hillsdale, NJ: Erlbaum.

Busk PL, Serlin RC (1992). Meta-analysis for single case research. In TR Kratochwill and JR Levin (Eds.), *Single-case research design and analysis: methodological and statistical advances* (pp. 197–198). Hillsdale, NJ: Erlbaum.

Byiers BJ, Reichle J, Symons FJ (2012). Single-subject experimental designs for evidence-based practice. *American Journal of Speech-Language Pathology*, 21(4), 397–414.

Campbell JM (2004). Statistical comparison of four effect sizes for single-subject designs. *Behavior Modification*, 28(2), 234–246.

Carr JE (2005). Recommendations for reporting multiple-baseline designs across participants. *Behavioral Interventions* 20(3), 219–224.

Center BA, Skiba RJ, Casey A (1985–1986). A methodology for the quantitative synthesis of intra-subject design research. *Journal of Special Education*, 19(4), 387–400.

Christ TJ (2007). Experimental control and threats to internal validity of concurrent and nonconcurrent multiple-baseline designs. *Psychology in the Schools*, 44(5), 451–459.

Cicerone KD, Wood JC (1987). Planning disorder after closed head injury: A case study. *Archives of Physical Medicine and Rehabilitation*, 68(2), 111–115.

Cohen J (1988). *Statistical power analysis for the behavioural sciences* (2nd edn). Hillsdale, NJ: Erlbaum.

Cohen J (1994). The Earth is round (p<.5). *American Psychologist*, 49(12), 997–1003.

Cohen RE (1986). Behavioral treatment of incontinence in a profoundly neurologically impaired adult. *Archives of Physical Medicine and Rehabilitation*, 67(12), 883–884.

Connell PJ, Thompson CK (1986). Flexibility of single-subject experimental designs. Part III: using flexibility to design or modify experiments. *Journal of Speech and Hearing Disorders*, 51(3), 214–225.

Cooper JO, Herron TE, Heward WL (2007). *Applied behavior analysis* (2nd edn). Upper Saddle River: Prentice Hall.

Crosbie J (1987). The inability of the binomial test to control Type I error with single-subject data. *Behavioral Assessment*, 9(2), 141–150.

Davis PK, Chittum R (1994). A group-oriented contingency to increase leisure activities of adults with traumatic brain injury. *Journal of Applied Behavior Analysis*, 27(3), 553–554.

Des Jarlais DC, Lyes C, Crepaz N and the TREND Group (2004). Improving the reporting quality of nonrandomized evaluations of behavioural and public health interventions: The TREND Statement. *American Journal of Public Health*, 94(3), 361–366.

Didden R, Korzilius H, van Oorsouw W, Sturmey P (2006). Behavioral treatment of challenging behaviors in individuals with mid mental retardation: meta-analysis of single-subject research. *American Journal on Mental Retardation*, 111(4), 290–298.

Dijkers MP, Hart T, Tsaousides T, Whyte J, Zanca JM (2014). Treatment taxonomy for rehabilitation: Past, present, and prospects. *Archives of Physical Medicine and Rehabilitation*, 95(1 s1), S6–S16.

Dixon MR, Guercio J, Falcomata T, Horner MJ, Root S, Newell C, Zlomke K (2004). Exploring the utility of functional analysis methodology to assess and treat problematic verbal behaviour in persons with acquired brain injury. *Behavioral Interventions*, 19(2), 91–102.

Domholdt E (2005). *Rehabilitation research: Principles and applications.* (3rd edn). St Louis, MO: Elsevier Saunders.

Donaghy M (2011) Brain's diseases of the nervous system (12th edn). In CA Noggle and R Dean (Eds.) (2013). *The neuropsychology of cancer and oncology* (pp. 1–12). New York: Springer.

Douglas JM, Knox L, De Maio C, Bridge H (2014). Improving communication-specific coping after traumatic brain injury: evaluation of a new treatment using single-case experimental design. *Brain Impairment*, 15(3), 190–201.

Downs SH, Black N (1998). The feasibility of creating a checklist for the assessment of the methodological quality both of randomised and non-randomised studies of health care interventions. *Journal of Epidemiology and Community Health*, 52(6), 377–384.

Draper SW (2016). Effect size. Accessed 5 November 2017 from: www.psy.gla.ac.uk/~steve/best/effect.html

Ducharme JM, Ng O (2012). Errorless academic compliance training: A school-based application for young students with autism. *Behaviour Modification*, 36(5), 650–669.

Edgington ES (1964). Randomization tests. *Journal of Psychology*, 57(2), 445–449.

Edgington ES (1967). Statistical inference from N=1 experiments. *Journal of Psychology*, 65(2), 195–199.

Edgington ES (1980). Validity of randomization tests for one-subject experiments. *Journal of Educational Statistics*, 5(3), 235–251.

Edgington ES (1987). Randomized single-subject experiments and statistical tests. *Journal of Counseling Psychology*, 34(4), 437–442.

Ehlhardt LA, Sohlberg MM, Glang A, Albin R (2005). TEACH-M: A pilot study evaluating an instructional sequence for persons with impaired memory and executive functions. *Brain Injury*, 19(8), 569–583.

Ehlhardt LA, Sohlberg MM, Kennedy M, Coelho C, Ylvisaker M, Turkstra L, Yorkston K (2008). Evidence-based practice guidelines for instructing individuals with neurogenic memory impairments: What have we learned in the past 20 years? *Neuropsychological Rehabilitation, 18(3)*, 300–342.

Engelman KK, Mathews RM, Altus DE (2002). Restoring dressing independence in persons with Alzheimer's disease: a pilot study. *American Journal of Alzheimer's Disease and Other Dementias, 17(1)*, 37–43.

Evans JJ, Emslie H, Wilson BA (1998). External cueing systems in the rehabilitation of executive impairments of action. *Journal of the International Neuropsychological Society, 4(4)*, 399–408.

Faith MS, Allison DB, Gorman BS (1996). Meta-analysis of single-case research. In RD Franklin, DB Allison and BS Gorman (Eds.), *Design and analysis of single case research* (pp. 245–277). Mahwah, NJ: Erlbaum.

Feeney TJ (2010). Structured flexibility: The use of context-sensitive self-regulatory scripts to support young persons with acquired brain injury. *Journal of Head Trauma Rehabilitation, 25(6)*, 416–425.

Feeney TJ, Ylvisaker M (2008). Context-sensitive cognitive-behavioral supports for young children with TBI. *Journal of Positive Behavior Interventions, 10(2)*, 115–128.

Ferron JM, Levin JR (2014). Single-case permutation and randomization statistical tests: Present status, promising new directions. In TR Kratochwill, JR Levin (Eds.). *Single-case intervention research. Methodological and statistical advances.* pp. 153-183. Washington DC: American Psychological Association.

Ferron J, Onghena P (1996). The power of randomization tests for single-case phase designs. *Journal of Experimental Education, 64(3)*, 231–239.

Ferron J, Sentovich C (2002). Statistical power of randomization tests used in multiple-baseline designs. *Journal of Experimental Education, 20(2)*, 165–178.

Ferron J, Ware W (1994). Using randomization tests with responsive single-case designs. *Behavioral Research and Therapy, 32(7)*, 787–791.

Fiksdal BL, Houlihan D, Buchanan JA (2012). Improving recall in a person with dementia: investigating the effectiveness of memory priming and spaced retrieval in an older adult with dementia. *Clinical Case Studies, 11* (5), 393–405.

Fisher WW, Kelley ME, Lomas JE (2003). Visual aids and structured criteria for improving visual inspection and interpretation of single-case designs. *Journal of Applied Behavior Analysis, 36(3)*, 387–406.

Fotopoulou A, Rudd A, Holmes P, Kopelman M (2009). Self-observation reinstates motor awareness in anosognosia for hemiplegia. *Neuropsychologia, 47(5)*, 1256–1260.

Francis DR, Riddoch MJ, Humphreys GW (2001). Treating agnosic alexia complicated by additional impairments. *Neuropsychological Rehabilitation, 11(2)*, 113–145.

Francis DR, Riddoch MJ, Humphreys GW (2002). 'Who's that girl?' Prosopagnosia, person-based semantic disorder, and the reacquisition of face identification ability. *Neuropsychological Rehabilitation, 12(1)*, 1–26.

Franklin RD, Gorman BS, Beasley TM, Allison DB (1996). Graphical display and visual analysis. In RD Franklin, DB Allison, and BS Gorman

(Eds.), *Design and analysis of single-case research* (pp. 119–158). Mahwah, NJ: Erlbaum.

Freeman T, High WM (2009). Treatment of a patient with traumatic brain injury-related severe self-injurious behaviour. *Journal of Head Trauma Rehabilitation, 24(4)*, 292–296.

Freud S, Breuer J (1895/2004). *Studies in hysteria.* New York: Penguin.

Furlong MJ, Wampold BE (1981). Visual analysis of single-subject studies by school psychologists. *Psychology in the Schools, 18(1)*, 80–86.

Garin O, Ayuso-Mateos JL, Almansa J, Nieto M, Chatterji S, Vilagut G . . . Ferrer M (2010). Validation of the 'World Health Organization Disability Assessment Schedule, WHODAS-2' in patients with chronic diseases. *Health and Quality of Life Outcomes, 8*, 51–65.

Gast DL, Baekey DH (2014). Withdrawal and reversal designs. In DL Gast and JR Ledford (Eds.), *Single case research methodology: Applications in special education and behavioral sciences* (2nd edn, pp. 211–250). New York: Routledge.

Gast DL, Lloyd BP, Ledford JR (2014). Multiple baseline and multiple probe designs. In DL Gast and JR Ledford (Eds.), *Single case research methodology: Applications in special education and behavioral sciences* (2nd edn, pp. 251–296). New York:Routledge.

Gast DL, Spriggs AD (2014). Visual analysis of graphic data. DL Gast and JR Ledford (Eds.), *Single case research methodology: Applications in special education and behavioral sciences* (2nd edn, pp. 176–210). New York: Routledge.

Gentile JR, Roden AH, Klein RD (1972.) An analysis of variance model for the intra subject replication design. *Journal of Applied Behavior Analysis, 5(2)*, 193–198.

Gianutsos R, Gianutsos J (1979). Rehabilitating the verbal recall of brain-injured patients by mnemonic training: An experimental demonstration using single-case methodology. *Journal of Clinical Neuropsychology, 1(2)*, 117–135.

Gibson G, Ottenbacher K (1988). Characteristics influencing the visual analysis of single-subject data: An empirical analysis. *Journal of Applied Behavioral Science, 24(3)*, 298–314.

Giles GM, Morgan JH (1988). Training functional skills following herpes simplex encephalitis: A single case study. *Journal of Clinical and Experimental Neuropsychology, 11(2)*, 311–318.

Giles GM, Shore M (1989). A rapid method for teaching severely brain injured adults how to wash and dress. *Archives of Physical Medicine and Rehabilitation, 70(2)*, 156–158.

Gingerich WJ, Feyerherm WH (1979). The celeration line technique for assessing client change. *Journal of Social Service Research, 3(1)*, 99–113.

Gladis MM, Gosch EA, Dishuk NM, Crits-Christoph P (1999). Quality of life: Expanding the scope of clinical significance. *Journal of Consulting and Clinical Psychology, 67(3)*, 320–331.

Glass GV, Willson VL, Gottman JM (2008). *Design and analysis of time-series experiments.* Charlotte, NC: Information Age Publishing.

Glasziou P, Meats E, Heneghan C, Shepperd S (2008). What is missing from descriptions of treatment in trials and reviews? *BMJ*, *336(7659)*, 1472–1474.

Glisky EL, Schacter DL (1987). Acquisition of domain-specific knowledge in organic amnesia: Training for computer-related work. *Neuropsychologia*, *25(6)*, 893–906.

Goodkin R (1966). Case studies in behavioural research in rehabilitation. *Perceptual and Motor Skills*, *23(1)*, 171–182.

Gorsuch RL (1983). Three methods for analysing limited time series (N of 1) data. *Behavioral Assessment*, *5(2)*, 141–154.

Gottman JM, Glass GV (1978). Analysis of interrupted time series analysis. In TR Kratochwill (Ed.), *Single subject research. Strategies for evaluating change.* (pp. 197–235). New York: Academic Press.

Gouvier WMD, Cottam G, Webster JS, Beissel GF, Woffard JD (1984). Behavioral interventions with stroke patients for improving wheelchair navigation. *International Journal of Clinical Neuropsychology*, *6(3)*, 186–190.

Greenhalgh T (1997). How to read a paper: Getting your bearings (deciding what the paper is about). *BMJ*, *315(7102)*, 243–246.

Gresham FM (2014). Measuring and analysing treatment integrity data in research. In LMH Sanetti and TR Kratochwill (Eds.), *Treatment integrity: A foundation for evidence-based practice in applied psychology* (pp. 109–130). Washington, DC: American Psychological Association.

Guercio JM, Ferguon KE, McMorrow MJ (2001). Increasing functional communication through relaxation training and neuromuscular feedback. *Brain Injury*, *15(12)*, 1073–1082.

Guercio JM, Johnson T, Dixon MR (2012). Behavioral treatment for pathological gambling in persons with acquired brain injury. *Journal of Applied Behavior Analysis*, *45(3)*, 485–495.

Guyatt GH, Keller JL, Jaeschke R, Rosenbloom D, Adachi JD, Newhouse MT (1990). The N-of-1 randomised controlled trial: Clinical usefulness. Our three-year experience. *Annals of Internal Medicine*, *112(4)*, 293–299.

Guyatt G, Sackett D, Adachi J, Roberts R, Chong J, Rosenbloom D, Keller J (1988). A clinician's guide for conducting randomized trials in individual patients. *CMJA (Canadian Medical Association Journal)*, *139(6)*, 497–503.

Guyatt G, Sackett D, Taylor DW, Chong J, Roberts R, Pugsley S (1986). Determining optimal therapy – Randomized trials in individual patients. *New England Journal of Medicine*, *314(14)*, 889–892.

Hageman WJ, Arrindell WA (1999). Establishing clinically significant change: Increment of precision between individual and group level analysis. *Behaviour Research and Therapy*, *37(12)*, 1169–1193.

Hagopian LP, Fisher WW, Thompson RH, Owen-DeSchryver J, Iwata BA, Wacker DP (1997). Toward the development of structured criteria for interpretation of functional analysis data. *Journal of Applied Behavior Analysis*, *30(2)*, 313–326.

Hains HA, Baer DM (1989). Interaction effects in multielement designs: inevitable, desirable, and ignorable. *Journal of Applied Behavior Analysis*, *22(1)*, 57–69.

Hall RV (1971). *Managing behavior: Behavior modification, the measurement of behavior*. Lawrence, KS: H & H Enterprises.

Hammond D, Gast DL (2010). Descriptive analysis of single subject research designs: 1983–2007. *Education and Training in Autism and Developmental Disabilities*, 45(2), 187–202.

Hanley GP, Iwata BA, McCord BE (2003). Functional analysis of problem behaviour: A review. *Journal of Applied Behavior Analysis*, 36 (2), 147–185.

Harrington M, Velicer WF (2015). Comparing visual and statistical analysis in single-case studies using published studies. *Multivariate Behaviour Research*, 50(2), 162–183.

Harrop JW, Velicer WF, (1985). A comparison of three alternative methods of time series model identification. *Multivariate Behavioral Research*, 20 (1), 27–44.

Hart T (2009). Treatment definition in complex rehabilitation interventions. *Neuropsychological Rehabilitation*, 19(6), 824–840.

Hart T (2017). Challenges in the evaluation of neuropsychological rehabilitation effects. In BA Wilson, J Winegardner, C van Heugten, T Ownsworth (Eds.), *International handbook of neuropsychological rehabilitation* (pp. 559–568). London: Routledge.

Hart T, Tsauosides T, Zanca JM, Whyte J, Packel A, Ferrano M, Dijkers MP (2014). Toward a theory-driven classification of rehabilitation treatments. *Archives of Physical Medicine and Rehabilitation*, 95(1 s1), S33–S44.

Hart T, Whyte J, Dijkers M, Packel A, Turkstra L, Zanca J ... Van Stan J (2018). *Manual of Rehabilitation Treatment Specification*. version 6.2. http://mrri.org/innovations/manual-for-treatment-specification/ accessed 7 September 2018.

Hartmann DP, Gottman JM, Jones RR, Gardner W, Kazdin AE, Vaught R (1980). Interrupted time-series analysis and its application to behavioral data. *Journal of Applied Behavior Analysis*, 13(4), 543–559.

Hartmann DP, Hall RV (1976). The changing criterion design. *Journal of Applied Behavior Analysis*, 9(4), 527–532.

Harvey MT, May ME, Kennedy CH (2004). Nonconcurrent multiple-baseline designs and the evaluation of educational systems. *Journal of Behavioral Education*, 13(4), 267–276.

Hayes SC (1981). Single case experimental design and empirical clinical practice. *Journal of Consulting and Clinical Psychology*, 49(2), 193–211.

Helmick JW, Wipplinger M (1975). Effects of stimulus repetition on the naming behaviour of an aphasic adult: A clinical report. *Journal of Communication Disorders*, 8(1), 23–29.

Hersen M, Barlow DH (1976). *Single case experimental designs: Strategies for studying behaviour change*. New York: Pergamon.

Hickey EM, Bourgeois MS, Olswang LB (2004). Effects of training volunteers to converse with nursing home residents with aphasia. *Aphasiology*, 18(5–7), 625–637.

Higgins JPT, Altman DG, Gøtzsche PC, Jüni P, Moher D, Oxman AD, . . . Sterne JAC (2011). The Cochrane Collaboration's tool for assessing risk of bias in randomised trials. *BMJ, 343,* doi: 10.1136/bmj.d5928.

Hoffmann, TC, Glasziou, PP, Milne R, Perera R, Moher D, Altman DG . . . Michie S (2014). Better reporting of interventions: Template for intervention description and replication (TIEieR) checklist and guide. *BMJ, 348,* g1687. doi:10.1136/bmj.g1687.

Horner RD, Baer DM (1978). Multiple probe technique: A variation of the multiple baseline. *Journal of Applied Behavior Analysis, 11(1),* 189–196.

Horner RH, Carr EG, Halle J, McGee G, Odom S, Wolery M (2005). The use of single-subject research to identify evidence-based practice in special education. *Exceptional Children, 71(2),* 165–179.

Howick J, Chalmers I, Glasziou P, Greenhalgh T, Heneghan C, Liberati A . . . Thornton H (2011). Explanation of the 2011 Oxford Centre for Evidence-Based Medicine (OCEBM) Levels of Evidence (Background Document). Oxford Centre for Evidence-Based Medicine. Accessed 5 November 2017 from: www.cebm.net/index.aspx?0=5653

Huberty CJ (2002). A history of effect size indices. *Educational and Psychological Measurement, 62(2),* 227–240.

Hufford BJ, Williams MK, Malec JF, Cravotta D (2012). Use of behavioral contracting to increase adherence with rehabilitation treatments on an inpatient brain injury unit: A case report. *Brain Injury, 26(13–14),* 1743–1749.

Huitema BE (1985). Autocorrelation in applied behaviour analysis: A myth. *Behavioral Assessment, 7(2),* 107–118.

Huitema BE (2011). *The analysis of covariance and alternatives: Statistical methods for experiments, quasi-experiments, and single-case studies* (2nd edn). Hoboken, NJ: Wiley.

Huitema BE, McKean JW (1991). Autocorrelation estimation and inference with small samples. *Psychological Bulletin, 110(2),* 291–304.

Huitema BE, McKean JW (1998). Irrelevant autocorrelation in least-squares intervention models. *Psychological Methods, 3(1),* 104–116.

Huitema BE, McKean JW (2000). Design specification issues in time-series intervention models. *Educational and Psychological Measurement, 60(1),* 38–58.

Hurlburt RT, Knapp TJ (2010). Münsterberg in 1898, not Allport in 1937, introduced the terms 'idiographic' and 'nomothetic' to American psychology. *Theory & Psychology, 16(2),* 287–293.

Jacobson NS, Follette WC, Revenstorf D (1984.) Psychotherapy outcome research: Methods for reporting variability and evaluating clinical significance. *Behaviour Therapy, 15(4),* 336–352.

Jacobson NS, Roberts LJ, Berns SB, McGlinchey JB (1999). Methods for defining and determining the clinical significance of treatment effects: Description, application, and alternatives. *Journal of Consulting and Clinical Psychology, 67(3),* 300–307.

Jamieson M, Monastra M, Gilles G, Manolov R, Cullen B, . . . Evans J (2017). The use of a smartwatch as a prompting device for people with acquired brain injury: A single case experimental design study. *Neuropsychological Rehabilitation*. doi: 10.1080/09602011. 2017.1310658

Jenning EA, Lubinski RB (1981). Strategies for improving productive thinking in the language impaired adult. *Journal of Communication Disorders*, 14(4), 255–271.

Jones RR, Weinrott MR, Vaught RS (1978). Effects of serial dependence on the agreement between visual and statistical inference. *Journal of Applied Behavior Analysis*, 11(2), 277–283.

Jones S, Ownsworth T, Shum DHK (2015). Feasibility and utility of telephone-based psychological support for people with brain tumour: A single-case experimental study. *Frontiers in Oncology*, 5. doi:10.3389/fonc.2015.00071

Kahng SW, Ingvarsson ET, Quigg AM, Seckinger KE, Teichman HM (2011). Defining and measuring behavior. In WW Fisher, CC Piazza, and HE Roane (Eds.), *Handbook of applied behavior analysis* (pp. 113–131). New York: Guildford.

Kaminsky TA, Dudgeon BJ, Billingsley FF, Mitchell PH, Weghorst SJ (2007). Virtual cues and functional mobility of people with Parkinson's disease: A single-subject pilot study. *Journal of Rehabilitation Research and Development*, 44(3), 437–448.

Kawahira K, Noma T, Iiyama J, Etoh S, Ogata A, Shimodozono M (2009). Improvements in limb kinetic apraxia by repetition of a newly designed facilitation exercise in a patient with corticobasal degeneration. *International Journal of Rehabilitation Research*, 32(2), 178–183.

Kazdin AE (1980). Obstacles in using randomization tests in single-case experimentation. *Journal of Educational Statistics*, 5(3), 253–260.

Kazdin AE (1981). External validity and single-case experimentation: Issues and limitations (a response to J. S. Birnbrauer). *Analysis and Intervention in Developmental Disabilities*, 1(2), 133–143.

Kazdin AE (1982). *Single-case research designs: Methods for clinical and applied settings*. New York: Oxford University Press.

Kazdin AE (1983). Single-case research designs in clinical child psychiatry. *Journal of the American Academy of Child Psychiatry*, 22(5), 423–432.

Kazdin AE (1986). Comparative outcome studies of psychotherapy: Methodological issues and strategies. *Journal of Consulting and Clinical Psychology*, 54(1), 95–105.

Kazdin AE (1993). Evaluation in clinical practice: clinically sensitive and systematic methods of treatment delivery. *Behavior Therapy*, 24(1), 11–45.

Kazdin AE (1999). The meanings and measurement of clinical significance. *Journal of Consulting and Clinical Psychology*, 67(3), 332–339.

Kazdin AE (2001). Almost clinically significant (p < .10): Current measures may only approach clinical significance. *Clinical Psychology: Science and Practice*, 8(4), 455–462.

Kazdin AE (2008). Evidence-based treatment and practice: New opportunities to bridge clinical research and practice, enhance the knowledge base, and improve patient care. *American Psychologist*, 63(3), 146–159.

Kazdin AE (2011). *Single-case research designs: Methods for clinical and applied settings*. (2nd edn). New York: Oxford University Press.

Kazdin AE, Geesey S (1977). Simultaneous-treatment design comparisons of the effects of earning reinforcers for one's peers versus for oneself. *Behavior Therapy*, 8(4), 682–693.

Kazdin AE, Hartman DP (1978). The simultaneous-treatment design. *Behavior Therapy*, 9(5), 912–922.

Kazdin AE, Kopel SA (1975). On resolving ambiguities of the multiple-baseline design: Problems and recommendations. *Behavior Therapy*, 6(5), 601–608.

Kearns KP (1986). Flexibility of single-subject experimental designs. Part II: Design selection and arrangement of experimental phases. *Journal of Speech and Hearing Disorders*, 51(3), 204–213.

Keller JL, Guyatt GH, Roberts RS, Adachi JD, Rosenbloom D (1988). An N of 1 service: Applying the scientific method in clinical practice. *Scandinavian Journal of Gastroenterology* 23(Suppl 147), 22–29.

Kendall PC, Marr-Garcia A, Nath SR, Sheldrick RC (1999). Normative comparisons for the evaluation of clinical significance. *Journal of Consulting and Clinical Psychology*, 67(3), 285–299.

Kerley J (1982). Improved arm and hand function in head injury. *Physiotherapy*, 68(3),74–76.

Khan-Bourne N, Brown RG (2003). Cognitive behavior therapy for the treatment of depression in individuals with brain injury. *Neuropsychological Rehabilitation*, 13(1–2), 89–107.

King AH, Bosworth H (2014). Treatment fidelity in health sciences research. In LMH Sanetti and TR Kratochwill (Eds.), *Treatment integrity: A foundation for evidence-based practice in applied psychology* (pp. 15–33). Washington, DC: American Psychological Association.

Kiran S (2008). Typicality of inanimate category exemplars in aphasia treatment: Further evidence for semantic complexity. *Journal of Speech, Hearing and Language Research*, 51(6), 1550–1568.

Kirk RE (1996). Practical significance: A concept whose time has come. *Educational and Psychological Measurement*, 56(5), 746–759.

Klarborg B, Lahrmann H, Agerholm N, Tradisaukas N, Harms L (2012). Intelligent speed adaptation as an assistive device for drivers with acquired brain injury: A single-case field experiment. *Accident Analysis and Prevention*, 48, 57–62.

Klein LA, Houlihan D, Vincent JL, Panahon CJ (2017). Best practices in utilizing the changing criterion design. *Behavior Analysis Practice*, 10(1), 52–61.

Kneebone II, Al-Daftary S (2006). Flooding treatment of phobia to having her feet touched by physiotherapists, in a young woman with Down's syndrome and a traumatic brain injury. *Neuropsychological Rehabilitation*, 16(2), 230–236.

Kraemer HC, Morgan GA, Leech NL, Gliner JA, Vaske JJ, Harmon RJ (2003). Measures of clinical significance. *Journal of the American Academy of Child and Adolescent Psychiatry*, 42(12), 1524–1529.

Kratochwill TR (Ed.) (1978). *Single-subject research strategies for evaluating change*. New York: Academic Press.

Kratochwill TR, Alden K, Demuth D, Dawson D, Panicucci C, Arntson P, Mcmurray N, Hempstead J, Levin J (1974). A further consideration in the application of an analysis-of-variance model for the intrasubject replication design. *Journal of Applied Behavior Analysis, 73(4)*, 629–633.

Kratochwill TR, Hitchcock J, Horner RH, Levin JR, Odom SL, Rindskopf DM, Shadish WR (2010). Single-case designs technical documentation. Accessed 5 November 2017 from: http://ies.ed.gov/ncee/wwc/pdf/wwc_scd.pdf

Kratochwill TR, Hitchcock J, Horner RH, Levin JR, Odom SL, Rindskopf DM, Shadish WR (2013). Single-case intervention research design standards. *Remedial and Special Education, 34(1)*, 26–38.

Kratochwill TR, Levin JR (2010). Enhancing the scientific credibility of single-case intervention research: Randomization to the rescue. *Psychological Methods, 15(2)*, 124–144.

Kratochwill TR, Levin JR (2014). Enhancing the scientific credibility of single-case intervention research: Randomization to the rescue. In TR Kratochwill and JR Levin (Eds.) *Single-case intervention research: Methodological and statistical advances* (pp. 53–89). Washington, DC: American Psychological Association.

Kratochwill TR, Levin JR, Horner RH, Swoboda CM (2014.) Visual analysis of single-case intervention research: Conceptual and methodological issues. In TR Kratochwill and JR Levin (Eds.), *Single-case intervention research: Methodological and statistical advances* (pp. 91–125). Washington, DC: American Psychological Association.

Kravitz RL, Duan N (Eds.) and the DEcIDE Methods Center N-of-1 Guidance Panel (Duan N, Eslick I, Gabler NB, Kaplan HC, Kravitz RL, Larson EB ... Vohra S) (2014) *Design and implementation of N-of-1 Trials: A user's guide*. AHRQ Publication No. 13(14)-EHC122-EF. Rockville, MD: Agency for Healthcare Research and Quality; www.effectivehealthcare.ahrq.gov/N1-Trials.cfm

Kreuzer PM, Landgrebe M, Frank E, Langguth B (2012). Repetitive transcranial magnetic stimulation for the treatment of chronic tinnitus after traumatic brain injury: A case study. *Journal of Head Trauma Rehabilitation, 28(5)*, 386–389.

LaFrance C, Garcia LJ, Labreche J (2007). The effect of a therapy dog on the communication skills of an adult with aphasia. *Journal of Communication Disorders, 40(3)*, 215–224.

Lancioni GE, Singh NN, O'Reilly MF, Sigafoos J, Buonocunto F, Sacco V, . . . Megna G (2009). A technology-assisted learning setup as assessment supplement for three persons with a diagnosis of post-coma vegetative state and pervasive motor impairment. *Research in Developmental Disabilities, 30(5)*, 1034–1043.

Lancioni GE, Singh NN, O'Reilly MF, Sigafoos J, Signorino M, Oliva D . . . De Tommaso (2010). A special messaging technology for two persons with acquired brain injury and multiple disabilities. *Brain Injury*, 24(10), 1236–1243.

Lane JD, Gast DL (2014). Visual analysis in single case experimental design studies: Brief review and guidelines. *Neuropsychological Rehabilitation*, 24(3–4), 445–463.

Lane K, Wolery M, Reichow B, Rogers L (2007). Describing baseline conditions: Suggestions for study reports. *Journal of Behavioral Education*, 16(3), 224–234.

Lane-Brown A, Tate R (2010). Evaluation of an intervention for apathy after traumatic brain injury: A multiple-baseline, single-case experimental design. *Journal of Head Trauma Rehabilitation*, 25(6), 459–469.

Ledford JR, Gast DL (2014). Combination and other designs. In DL Gast and JR Ledford (Eds.), *Single case research methodology: Applications in special education and behavioral sciences* (2nd edn, pp. 346–376). New York: Routledge.

Ledford JR, Wolery M, Gast DL (2014). Controversial and critical issues in single-case research. In DL Gast and JR Ledford (Eds.), *Single case research methodology: Applications in special education and behavioral sciences* (2nd edn, pp. 377–396). New York:Routledge.

Leitenberg H (1973). The use of single-case methodology in psychotherapy research. *Journal of Abnormal Psychology*, 82(1), 87–101.

Lenz AS (2013). Calculating effect size in single-case research: A comparison of nonoverlap methods. *Measurement and Evaluation in Counseling and Development*, 46(1), 64–73.

Leon SA, Rosenbek JC, Crucian GP, Hieber B, Holiway B, Rodriguez AD . . . Gonzalez-Rothi L (2005). Active treatments for aprosodia secondary to right hemisphere stroke. *Journal of Rehabilitation Research and Development*, 42(1), 93–102.

Liberati A, Altman DG, Tetzlaff J, Mulrow C, Getzsche PC, Ioannidis JPA, . . . Moher D (2009). The PRISMA statement for reporting systematic reviews and meta-analyses of studies that evaluate health care interventions: Explanation and elaboration. *PLoS Medicine*, 6(7), 1–28.

Locke JM, Mudford OC (2010). Using music to decrease disruptive vocalizations in a man with dementia. *Behavioral Interventions*, 25(3), 253–260.

Logan LR, Hickman RR, Harris SR, Heriza CB (2008). Single-subject research design: Recommendations for levels of evidence and quality rating. *Developmental Medicine and Child Neurology*, 50(2), 99–103.

Lundervold DA, Pahwa R, Lyons KE (2013). Behavioral relaxation training for Parkinson's disease related dyskinesia and comorbid social anxiety. *International Journal of Behavioral Consultation and Therapy*, 7(4), 1–5.

Ma HH (2006). An alternative method for quantitative synthesis of single-subject researches: Percentage of data points exceeding the median. *Behavior Modification*, 30(5), 598–617.

McCrimmon CM, King CE, Wang PT, Cramer SC, Nenadic Z, Do AH (2015). Brain-controlled functional electrical stimulation therapy for gait rehabilitation after stroke: A safety study. *Journal of NeuroEngineering and Rehabilitation, 12*, 57. doi:10.1186/s12984-015-0050-4

McDougall D (2005). The range-bound changing criterion design. *Behavioral Interventions, 20*(2), 129–137.

McDougall D, Hawkins J, Brady M, Jenkins A (2006). Recent innovations in the changing criterion design: Implications for research and practice in special education. *Journal of Special Education, 40*(1), 2–15.

McEwen SE, Polatajko HJ, Huijbregts MPJ, Ryan JD (2010). Inter-task transfer of meaningful functional skills following a cognitive-based treatment: Results of three multiple-baseline design experiments in adults with chronic stroke. *Neuropsychological Rehabilitation, 20*(4), 541–561.

McGivern JE, Walter MJ (2014). Legal and ethical issues related to treatment integrity in psychology and education. In LMH Sanetti and TR Kratochwill (Eds.), *Treatment Integrity: A foundation for evidence-based practice in applied psychology* (pp. 229–254). Washington, DC: American Psychological Association.

McGraw-Hunter M, Faw GD, Davis PK (2006). The use of video self-modelling and feedback to teach cooking skills to individuals with traumatic brain injury: A pilot study. *Brain Injury, 20*(10), 1061–1068.

McReynolds LV, Kearns KP (1983). *Single-subject experimental designs in communicative disorders*. Baltimore: University Park Press.

Maggin DM, Briesch AM, Chafouleas SM (2013). An application of the What Works Clearinghouse Standards for evaluating single-subject research: Synthesis of the self-management literature base. *Remedial and Special Education, 34*(1), 44–58.

Maggin DM, Briesch AM, Chafouleas SM, Ferguson TD, Clark C (2014). A comparison of rubrics for identifying empirically supported practices with single-case research. *Journal of Behavioural Education, 23*(7), 287–311.

Maggin DM, Chafouleas SM, Goddard KM, Johnson AH (2011). A systematic evaluation of token economies as a classroom management tool for students with challenging behavior. *Journal of School Psychology, 49* (5), 529–554.

Maggin DM, Swaminathan H, Rogers HJ, O'Keeffe BV, Sugai G, Horner R (2011). A generalized least squares regression approach for computing effect sizes in single-case research: Application examples. *Journal of School Psychology, 49*(3), 301–321.

Maher CG, Sherrington C, Herbert RD, Moseley AM, Elkins M (2003). Reliability of the PEDro scale for rating quality of RCTs. *Physical Therapy, 83*(8), 713–721.

Manolov R, Gast DL, Perdices M, Evans JJ (2014). Single-case experimental designs: Reflections on conduct and analysis. *Neuropsychological Rehabilitation, 24*(3–4), 634–660.

Manolov R, Moeyaert M, Evans JJ (2015). Resources and guidelines for analysing SCED data. Accessed 5 November 2017 from: www.ub.edu/gcai/soft/Software_resources_for_applied_researchers_April2015.pdf

Manolov R, Solanas A (2008a.). Comparing N = 1 effect size indices in presence of autocorrelation. *Behavior Modification*, *32*(6), 860–875.

Manolov R, Solanas A (2008b). Randomization tests for ABAB designs: Comparing data-division specific and common distributions. *Psicothema*, *20*(2), 297–303.

Manolov R, Solanas A (2009). Percentage of nonoverlapping corrected data. *Behavior Research Methods*, *41*(4), 1262–1271.

Manolov R, Solanas A (2018). Analytical options for single-case experimental designs: Review and application to brain impairment. *Brain Impairment*, *19*(s1), 18–32.

Marascuilo L, Busk P (1988). Combining statistics for multiple-baseline AB and replicated ABAB designs across subjects. *Behavioral Assessment*, *10* (*1*), 1–28.

Marso D, Shadish WR (2015). Software for meta-analysis of single-case designs: DHPS macro. Accessed 5 November 2017 from: http://faculty.ucmerced.edu/wshadish/software/software-meta-analysis-single-case-de sign/ddhps-version-march-7-2015

Matyas TA, Greenwood KM (1990). Visual analysis of single-case time series: Effects of variability, serial dependence, and magnitude of intervention effects. *Journal of Applied Behavior Analysis*, *23*(3), 341–351.

Mechling LC (2006). Comparison of the effects of three approaches on the frequency of stimulus activations, via a single switch, by students with profound intellectual disabilities. *Journal of Special Education*, *40*(2), 94–102.

Mechling LC, Gast DL, Lane JD (2014). Ethical principles and practices in research. In DL Gast and JR Ledford (Eds.), *Single case research methodology: Applications in special education and behavioural sciences* (2nd edn, pp. 31–49). New York: Routledge.

Mitchell GK, Hardy JR, Nikles CJ, Carmont S-AS, Senior HE, Schluter PJ, . . . Currow DC (2015). The effect of methylphenidate on fatigue in advanced cancer: An aggregated N-of-1 trial. *Journal of Pain and Symptom Management*, *50*(3), 289–296.

Moeyaert M, Ferron J, Beretvas SN, Van den Noortgate W (2014). From a single-level analysis to a multilevel analysis of single-case experimental designs. *Journal of School Psychology*, *52*(2), 191–211.

Moeyaert M, Ugille M, Ferron J, Beretvas SN, Van den Noortgate W (2013). Modelling external events in the three-level analysis of multiple-baseline across participants designs: A simulation study. *Behavior Research Methods*, *45*(2), 547–559.

Moeyaert M, Ugille M, Ferron J, Beretvas SN, Van den Noortgate W (2014). Three-level analysis of single-case experimental data: Empirical validation. *Journal of Experimental Education*, *82*(1), 1–21.

Moher D, Hopewell S, Schulz KF, Montori V, Gøzsche PC, Devereaux PJ, . . . Altman DG (2010). CONSORT 2010 Explanation and elaboration: Updated guidelines for reporting parallel group randomised trials. *Journal of Clinical Epidemiology*, *63*(8), e1–e37.

Mohlman J, Reel DH, Chazin D, Ong D, Georgescu B, Tiu J, Dobkin RD (2010). A novel approach to treating anxiety and enhancing executive skills in an older adult with Parkinson's disease. *Clinical Case Studies, 9* (*1*), 74–90.

Moncher FJ, Prinz RL (1991). Treatment fidelity in outcome studies. *Clinical Psychology Review, 11*(3), 247–266.

Morales M, Domínguez MJ, Jurado T (2001). The influence of graphic techniques in the evaluation of effectiveness of treatment in time-series design. *Quality and Quantity: International Journal of Methodology, 35* (3), 277–289.

Morris RJ (1985). *Behavior modification with exceptional children: Principles and practices*. Glenview, IL: Scott, Foresman.

Nikles CJ, McKinlay L, Mitchell GK, Carmont S-AS, Senior HE, Waugh M-CA, . . . Lloyd OT (2014). Aggregated n-of-1 trials of central nervous system stimulants versus placebo for paediatric traumatic brain injury – A pilot study. *Trials, 15*, 54.

Nikles CJ, Mitchell G (Eds.) (2015a). *The essential guide to N-of-1 trials in health*. Dordrecht: Springer.

Nikles CJ, Mitchell G (2015b). Introduction In CJ Nikles and G Mitchell (eds). *The essential guide to N-of-1 trials in health* (pp. 1–7). Dordrecht: Springer.

Nikles CJ, Mitchell G, Del Mar CB, Clavarino A, McNairn N (2006). An n-of-1 trial service in clinical practice: Testing the effectiveness of stimulants for attention-deficit/hyperactivity disorder. *Pediatrics, 117*(6), 2041–2046.

Ninci J, Vannest KJ, Willson V, Zang N (2015). Interrater agreement between visual analysts of single-case data: A meta-analysis. *Behavior Modification, 39*(4), 510–541.

Noggle CA, Dean R, Barisa M (2013) *Neuropsychological rehabilitation (contemporary neuropsychology)*. New York: Springer.

OCEBM (2011). *The Oxford 2011 levels of evidence*. Accessed 5 November 2017 from: www.cebm.net/index.aspx?o=5653

O'Neil GW (1982). Behavior therapy for urinary frequency in a patient with neurogenic bladder: A case report. *General Hospital Psychiatry, 4*(1), 15–18.

Onghena P (1992). Randomization tests for extensions and variations of ABAB single-case experimental designs: A rejoinder. *Behavioral Assessment, 14*(2), 153–171.

Onghena P, Edgington ES (1994). Randomization tests for restricted alternating treatment designs. *Behaviour Research and Therapy, 32*(7), 783–786.

Onghena P, Edgington ES (2005). Customization of pain treatments single-case design and analysis. *Clinical Journal of Pain, 21*(1), 56–68.

Onghena P, Michiels B, Jamshidi L, Moeyaert M, van den Noortgate W (2018). One by one: accumulating evidence by using meta-analytical procedure for single-case experiments. *Brain Impairment, 19*(1), 53–58.

Ouellet M-C, Morin CM (2007). Efficacy of cognitive-behavioral therapy for insomnia associated with traumatic brain injury: A single-case experimental design. *Archives of Physical Medicine and Rehabilitation, 88* (12), 1581–1592.

Ownsworth T, Gracey F (2017). Cognitive behavioural therapy for people with brain injury. In: BA Wilson, T Winegardner, CM van Heugten, T Ownsworth (Eds.), *Neuropsychological Rehabilitation. The international handbook.* (pp. 313–326) London: Routledge.

Park HS, Marascuilo LA, Gaylord-Ross R (1990). Visual inspection and statistical analysis in single-case designs. *Journal of Experimental Education, 58(4),* 311–320.

Park H-Y, Yoo E-Y, Park SH, Park J-H, Kang D-H, Chung B-I, Jung M-Y (2012). Effects of forced use combined with scheduled home exercise program on upper extremity functioning in individuals with hemiparesis. *NeuroRehabilitation, 31(2),* 185–195.

Parker RI, Brossart DF (2003). Evaluating single-case research data: A comparison of seven statistical methods. *Behavior Therapy, 34(2),* 189–211.

Parker RI, Brossart DF, Vannest KJ, Long JR, Garcia De-Alba R, Baugh FG, Sullivan JR (2005). Effect sizes in single case research: How large is large? *School Psychology Review, 34(1),* 116–132.

Parker RI, Cryer J, Byrns G (2006). Controlling baseline trend in single-case research. *School Psychology Quarterly, 21(4),* 418–444.

Parker RI, Hagan-Burke S, Vannest KJ (2007). Percentage of all non-overlapping data (PAND): An alternative to PND. *Journal of Special Education, 40(2),* 194–204.

Parker RI, Vannest KJ (2007). Pairwise data overlap for single case research. Unpublished manuscript [Cited in Rakap, Snyder & Pasia, 2014]

Parker RI, Vannest KJ (2009). An improved effect size for single-case research: Nonoverlap of all pairs. *Behavior Therapy 40(4),* 357–367.

Parker RI, Vannest KJ, Brown L (2009). The improvement rate difference for single-case research. *Exceptional Children, 75(2),* 135–150.

Parker RI, Vannest KJ, Davis JL (2011a). Effect size in single-case research: A review of nine nonoverlap techniques. *Behavior Modification, 35(4),* 303–322.

Parker RI, Vannest KJ, Davis JL (2014). Non-overlap analysis for single-case research. In TR Kratochwill and JR Levin (Eds.), *Single-case research design and analysis: Methodological and statistical advances* (pp. 125–151). Hillsdale, NJ: Erlbaum.

Parker RI, Vannest KJ, Davis JL, Sauber SB (2011b). Combining non-overlap and trend for single-case research: Tau-U. *Behavior Therapy, 35(4),* 202–322.

Parrish JM, Cataldo MF, Kolko DJ, Neef NA, Egel AL (1986). Experimental analysis of response covariation among compliant and inappropriate behaviors. *Journal of Applied Behavior Analysis, 19(3),* 241–254.

Parsonson BS, Baer DM (1978). The analysis and presentation of graphic data. In TR Kratochwill (Ed.), *Single-subject research: Strategies for evaluating change* (pp. 101–165). New York: Academic Press.

Parsonson BS, Baer DM (1986). The graphic analysis of data. In A Poling and RW Fuqua (Eds.), *Research methods in applied behaviour analysis* (pp. 157–186). New York: Plenum Press.

Parsonson BS, Baer DM (2015). The visual analysis of data, and current research into the stimuli controlling it. In TR Kratochwill and JR Levine (Eds.), *Single-case research design and analysis: New directions for psychology and education* (pp. 15–39). New York: Routledge.

Perdices M, Schultz R, Tate R, McDonald S, Togher L, Savage S, . . . Smith K (2006). The evidence base of neuropsychological rehabilitation in acquired brain impairment (ABI): How good is the research? *Brain Impairment, 7*(2), 119–132.

Perdices M, Tate RL (2009). Single-subject designs as a tool for evidence-based clinical practice: Are they unrecognised and undervalued? *Neuropsychological Rehabilitation, 19*(6), 904–927.

Perepletchikova F (2014). Assessment of treatment integrity in psychotherapy research. In LMH Sanetti and TR Kratochwill (Eds.), *Treatment integrity: A foundation for evidence-based practice in applied psychology* (pp. 131–157). Washington, DC: American Psychological Association.

Perepletchikova F, Kazdin AE (2005). Treatment integrity and therapeutic change: Issues and research recommendations. *Clinical Psychology: Science and Practice, 12(4)*, 365–383.

Perepletchikova F, Treat TA, Kazdin AE (2005). Treatment integrity in psychotherapy research: analysis of the studies and examination of the associated factors. *Journal of Consulting and Clinical Psychology, 75(6)*, 829–841.

Perilli V, Lancioni GE, Laporta D, Paparella D, Caffó AO, Singh NN, . . . Oliva D (2013). A computer-aided telephone system to enable five persons with Alzheimer's disease to make phone calls independently. *Research in Developmental Disabilities, 34*(6), 1191–1997.

Peterson L, Homer AL, Wonderlick SA (1982). The integrity of independent variables in behaviour analysis. *Journal of Applied Behavior Analysis, 15 (4)*, 477–492.

Plavnic JB, Ferreri SJ (2013). Single-case experimental designs in educational research: A methodology for causal analyses. *Educational Psychology Review, 25*(4), 549–569.

Rakap S, Snyder P, Pasia C (2014). Comparison of nonoverlap methods for identifying treatment effect in single-subject experimental research. *Behavioral Disorders, 39*(3), 128–145.

Rasquin SMC, van de Sande P, Praamstra AJ, van Heugten CM (2009). Cognitive-behavioural intervention for depression after stroke: Five single case studies on effects and feasibility. *Neuropsychological Rehabilitation, 19*(2), 208–222.

Raymer AM, Ciampitti M, Holliway B, Singletary F, Blonder LX, Ketterson T, . . . Gonzalez-Rothi L (2007). Semantic–phonologic treatment for noun and verb retrieval impairments in aphasia. *Neuropsychological Rehabilitation, 17*(2), 244–270.

Rea LM, Parker RA (1992). *Designing and conducting survey research*. San Francisco: Jossey-Boss.

Reichow B, Volkmar FR, Cicchetti DV (2008). Development of the evaluative method for evaluating and determining evidence-based practices in autism. *Journal of Autism and Developmental Disorders, 38(7)*, 1311–1319.

Rindskopf DM, Ferron JM (2014). Using multilevel models to analyse single-case design data. In TR Kratochwill and JR Levin (Eds.), *Single-case intervention research: Methodological and statistical advances* (pp. 221–246). Washington, DC: American Psychological Association.

Roane HS, Ringdahl JE, Kelley ME, Glover AC (2011). Single-case experimental designs. In WW Fisher, CC Piazza, and HE Roane (Eds.), *Handbook of applied behavior analysis* (pp. 132–147). New York: Guildford.

Robertson I, Gray J, McKenzie S (1988). Microcomputer-based cognitive rehabilitation of visual neglect: Three multiple-baseline single-case studies. *Brain Injury, 2(2)*, 151–163.

Robey RR, Beeson PM (2005). Aphasia treatment: Examining the evidence. Presentation at the American Speech-Language-Hearing Association Annual Convention. San Diego, CA.

Robey RR, Schultz MC, Crawford AB, Sinner CA (1999). Single-subject clinical outcome research: Designs, data, effect sizes and analyses. *Aphasiology, 13(6)*, 445–473.

Robinson OC (2011). The idiographic/nomothetic dichotomy: Tracing historical origins of contemporary confusions. *History and Philosophy of Psychology, 13(2)*, 32–39.

Rose M, Sussmilch G (2008). The effects of semantic and gesture treatments on verb retrieval and verb use in aphasia. *Aphasiology, 22(708)*, 691–706.

Russo DC, Cataldo MF, Cushing PJ (1981). Compliance training and behavioral covariation in the treatment of multiple behavior problems. *Journal of Applied Behavior Analysis, 14(3)*, 209–222.

Sackett DL (1979). Bias in analytic research. *Chronic Diseases, 32(1–2)*, 51–63.

Sackett DL, Straus SE, Richardson WS, Rosenberg W, Haynes RB (2000). *Evidence-based medicine: How to practice and teach EBM* (2nd edn). Edinburgh: Churchill Livingstone.

Sanetti LMH, Kratochwill TR (2009). Toward developing a science of treatment integrity. *School Psychology Review, 38(4)*, 445–459.

Savage SA, Ballard KJ, Piguet O, Hodges JR (2013). Bringing words back to mind-improving word production in semantic dementia. *Cortex, 49(7)*, 1823–1832.

Schloss PJ, Thompson CK, Gajar AH, Schloss CN (1985). Influence of self-monitoring on heterosexual conversational behaviors of head trauma youth. *Applied Research in Mental Retardation, 6(3)*, 269–282.

Schlosser RW, Braun U (1994). Efficacy of AAC interventions: Methodologic issues in evaluating behaviour change, generalization, and effects. *AAC Augmentative and Alternative Communication, 10(4)*, 207–223.

Schlosser RW, Lee DL, Wendt O (2008). Application of the percentage of non-overlapping data (PND) in systematic reviews and meta-analyses: A systematic review of reporting characteristics. *Evidence-Based Communication Assessment and Intervention, 2(3),* 163–187.

Schneider PL, Crouter SE, Lukajic O, Bassett DR (2003). Accuracy and reliability of 10 pedometers for measuring steps over a 400-m walk. *Medicine and Science in Sports and Exercise, 35(10),* 1779–1784.

Scruggs TE, Mastropieri MA (2001). How to summarize single-participant research: Ideas and applications. *Exceptionality: A Special Education Journal, 9(4),* 227–244.

Scruggs TE, Mastropieri MA, Casto G (1987). The quantitative synthesis of single-subject research: Methodology and validation. *Remedial and Special Education, 8(2),* 24–33.

Seekins T, Fawcett SB, Mathews RM (1987). Effects of self-help guides on three consumer advocacy skills: using personal experiences to influence public policy. *Rehabilitation Psychology, 32(1),* 29–38.

Shadish WR, Cook TD, Campbell DT (2002). *Experimental and quasi-experimental designs for generalized causal inference.* Belmont, CA: Wadsworth.

Shadish WR, Hedges LV, Pustejovsky JE, Boyajian JG, Sullivan KJ, Andrade A, Barrientos JL (2014). A d-statistic for single-case designs that is equivalent to the usual between-groups d-statistic. *Neuropsychological Rehabilitation, 24(3–4),* 528–553.

Shadish WR, Nagler Kyse EN, Rindskopf DM (2013). Analyzing data from single-case designs using multilevel models: New applications and some agenda items for future research. *Psychological Methods, 18(3),* 385–405.

Shadish WR, Rindskopf DM, Hedges LV (2008). The state of the science in the meta-analysis of single-case experimental designs. *Evidence-Based Communication Assessment and Intervention, 2(3),* 188–196.

Shadish WR, Sullivan KJ (2011). Characteristics of single-case designs used to assess intervention effects in 2008. *Behavior Research Methods, 43(4),* 971–980.

Shamseer L, Sampson M, Bukutu C, Schmid CH, Nikles J, Tate R, . . . and the CENT group (2015). CONSORT extension for reporting N-of-1 trials (CENT) 2015: Explanation and elaboration. *BMJ, 350,* h doi: 10.1136/bmj.h1793.

Shea BJ, Barnaby CR, Wells G, Thurku M, Hamel C, Moran J, . . . Kristjansson E (2017). AMSTAR 2: A critical appraisal tool for systematic reviews that include randomized or non-randomised studies of healthcare interventions, or both. *BMJ, 358,* j4008.

Shea BJ, Grimshaw JM, Wells GA, Boers M, Andersson N, Hamel C, . . . Bouter LM (2007). Development of AMSTAR: A measurement tool to assess the methodological quality of systematic reviews. *BMC Medical Research Methodology, 7(10),* doi:10.1186/1471-2288-7-10.

Shine LC, Bower SM (1971). A one-way analysis of variance for single subject designs. *Educational and Psychological Measurement, 31(1),* 105–113.

Sidman M (1960). *Tactics of scientific research: Evaluating experimental data in psychology*. New York: Basic Books.

Simera I, Moher D, Hoey J, Schulz K, Altman D (2010). A catalogue of reporting guidelines for health research. *European Journal of Clinical Investigation*, 40(1), 35–53.

Skinner CH, Skinner AL, Armstrong KJ (2000). Analysis of a client-staff developed program designed to enhance reading persistence in an adult diagnosed with schizophrenia. *Psychiatric Rehabilitation Journal*, 24(1), 52–57.

Slijper A, Svensson KE, Backlund P, Engström H, Sunnerhagen KS (2014). Computer game-based upper extremity training in the home environment in stroke persons: A single subject design. *Journal of NeuroEngineering and Rehabilitation*, 11(1), 35, doi: 10.1186/1743-0003-11-35.

Slim K, Nini E, Forestier D, Kwiatowski F, Panis Y, Chipponi J (2003). Methodological Index for Non-randomized Studies (MINORS): Development and validation of a new instrument. *Australian and New Zealand Journal of Surgery*, 73(9), 712–716.

Smith J, Herbert D, Reid D (2007). Exploring the effects of virtual reality on unilateral neglect caused by stroke: Four case studies. *Technology and Disability*, 19(1), 29–40.

Smith JD (2012). Single-case experimental designs: a systematic review of published research and current standards. *Psychological Methods*, 17(4), 510–550.

Sohlberg MM, Mateer CA (1987). Effectiveness of an attention-training program. *Journal of Clinical and Experimental Neuropsychology*, 9(2), 117–130.

Sohlberg MM, Sprunk H, Metzelaar K (1988). Efficacy of an external cuing system in an individual with severe frontal lobe damage. *Cognitive Rehabilitation*, 6(4), 36–41.

Sohlberg MM, Turkstra LS (2011). *Optimizing cognitive rehabilitation: Effective instructional methods*. New York: Guildford.

Solanas A, Manolov R, Sierra V (2010). Lag-one autocorrelation in short series: Estimation and hypothesis testing. *Psicológica*, 31(2), 357–381.

Speer DC, Greenbaum PE (1995). Five methods for computing significant individual client change and improvement rates: Support for an individual growth curve approach. *Journal of Consulting and Clinical Psychology*, 63(6), 1044–1048.

Spriggs AD, Lane JD, Gast DL (2014). Visual representation of data. In DL Gast and JR Ledford (Eds.), *Single case research methodology: Applications in special education and behavioral sciences* (2nd edn, pp. 154–175). New York: Routledge.

Stewart I, Alderman N (2010). Active versus passive management of post-acquired brain injury challenging behaviour: A case study of multiple operant procedures in the treatment of challenging behaviour maintained by negative reinforcement. *Brain Injury*, 24(13–14), 1616–1627.

Svanberg J, Evans JJ (2014). Impact of SenseCam on memory, identity and mood in Korsakoff's syndrome: A single case experimental design study. *Neuropsychological Rehabilitation*, 24(3–4), 400–418.

Swaminathan H, Rogers HJ, Horner RH, Sugai G, Smolkowski K (2014). Regression models and effect size measures for single case designs. *Neuropsychological Rehabilitation*, *24(3–4)*, 554–571.

Swoboda CM, Kratochwill TR, Levin JR (2010). Conservative dual-criterion method for single-case research: A guide for visual analysis of AB, ABAB, and multiple-baseline designs (WCER Working Paper No. 2010–2013). Accessed 5 November 2017 from: www.wcer.wisc.edu/publications/work ingPapers/papers.php

Tabachnick BG, Fidell LS (2007). *Using multivariate statistics* (5th edn). Boston, MA: Pearson Education.

Tasky KK, Rudrud EH, Schulze KA, Rapp JT (2008). Using choice to increase on-task behaviour in individuals with traumatic brain injury. *Journal of Applied Behavior Analysis*, *41(2)*, 261–265.

Tate RL (1987). Behaviour management techniques for organic psychosocial deficit incurred by severe head injury. *Scandinavian Journal of Rehabilitation Medicine*, *19(1)*, 19–24.

Tate RL, Aird V, Taylor C (2012). Bringing single-case methodology into the clinic to enhance evidence-based practices. *Brain Impairment*, *13(3)*, 347–359.

Tate RL, Douglas JD (2011). Use of reporting guidelines in scientific writing: PRISMA, CONSORT, STROBE, STARD and other resources. *Brain Impairment*, *12(1)*, 1–21.

Tate RL, McDonald S, Perdices M, Togher L, Schultz R, Savage S (2008). Rating the methodological quality of single-subject designs and n-of-1 trials: Introducing the Single-case Experimental Design (SCED) Scale. *Neuropsychological Rehabilitation*, *18(4)*, 385–401.

Tate RL, Perdices M (2017). Avoiding bias in rehabilitation interventions. In BA Wilson, J Winegardner, C van Heugten, T Ownsworth (Eds.), *International handbook of neuropsychological rehabilitation* (pp. 547–558). London: Routledge.

Tate RL, Perdices M, McDonald S, Togher L, Rosenkoetter U (2014). The design, conduct and report of single-case research: Resources to improve the quality of the neurorehabilitation literature. *Neuropsychological Rehabilitation*, *24(3–4)*,315–331.

Tate RL, Perdices M, Rosenkoetter U, Wakim D, Godbee K, Togher L, McDonald S (2013a). Revision of a method quality rating scale for single-case experimental designs and n-of-1 trials: The 15-item Risk of Bias in N-of-1 Trials (RoBiNT) Scale. *Neuropsychological Rehabilitation*, *23(5)*, 619–638.

Tate RL, Perdices M, Rosenkoetter U, Shadish W, Barlow DH, Horner R, ... Wilson B (2016a). The Single-Case Reporting guideline In BEhavioural interventions (SCRIBE) 2016 Statement. *Archives of Scientific Psychology*, *4(1)*, 1–9.

Tate RL, Perdices M, Rosenkoetter U, McDonald S, Togher L, Shadish W, . . . Vohra S, for the SCRIBE Group (2016b). The Single-Case Reporting guideline In BEhavioural interventions (SCRIBE) 2016: Explanation and elaboration. *Archives of Scientific Psychology*, *4(1)*, 10–31.

Tate RL, Rosenkoetter U, Wakim D, Sigmundsdottir L, Doubleday J, Togher L, McDonald S, Perdices M (2015). *The risk of bias in N-of-1 Trials (RoBiNT) Scale: An expanded manual for the critical appraisal of single-case reports*. Sydney: Author.

Tate RL, Sigmundsdottir L, Doubleday J, Rosenkoetter U, Wakim D, Perdices M (2016c). Reporting single-case research in the neurorehabilitation literature: a systematic review indicates there is room for improvement. *Archives of Physical Medicine and Rehabilitation, 97(10)*. Presented at the 93rd conference of the American Congress of Rehabilitation Medicine, November, Chicago, USA.

Tate RL, Taylor C, Aird V (2013b). Applying empirical methods in clinical practice: Introducing the Model for Assessing Treatment Effect (MATE). *Journal of Head Trauma Rehabilitation, 28(2)*, 77–88.

Tate RL, Wakim D, Sigmundsdottir L, Longley W. (2018). Evaluating an intervention to increase meaningful activity after severe traumatic brain injury: A single-case experimental design with direct inter-subject and systematic replications. *Neuropsychological Rehabilitation*. doi: 10.1080/09602011.2018.1488746

Tawney J, Gast DL (1984). *Single subject research in special education*. Columbus, OH: Charles E Merrill.

Toothaker LE, Banz M, Noble C, Camp J, Davis D (1983). N = 1 designs: The failure of ANOVA-based tests. *Journal of Educational Statistics, 8(4)*, 289–309.

Tryon WW (1982). A simplified time series analysis for evaluating treatment interventions. *Journal of Applied Behavior Analysis, 15(3)*, 423–429.

Tunnard C, Wilson BA (2014). Comparison of neuropsychological rehabilitation techniques for unilateral neglect: An ABACADAEAF single-case experimental design. *Neuropsychological Rehabilitation, 24(3–4)*, 382–399.

Valle Padilla D, Daza González MT, Fernández Agis I, Strizzi J, Alarcón Rodríguez R (2013). The effectiveness of control strategies for dementia-driven wandering, preventing scape attempts: A case report. *International Psychogeriatrics, 25(3)*, 500–504.

Van den Noortgate W, Onghena P (2003a). Combining single-case experimental studies using hierarchical linear models. *School Psychology Quarterly, 18(3)*, 325–346.

Van den Noortgate W, Onghena P (2003b). Hierarchical linear models for the quantitative integration of effect sizes in single-case research. *Behavior Research Methods, Instruments, and Computers, 35(1)*, 1–10.

Van den Noortgate W, Onghena P (2008). A multilevel meta-analysis of single-subject experimental design studies. *Evidence-Based Communication Assessment and Intervention, 2(3)*, 142–151.

van Heugten C, Gregório GW, Wade D (2012). Evidence-based cognitive rehabilitation after acquired brain injury: A systematic review of content of treatment. *Neuropsychological Rehabilitation, 22(5)*, 653–673.

Vannest KJ, Ninci J (2015). Evaluating intervention effects in single-case research designs. *Journal of Counseling and Development*, *93*, 403–411.

Vannest KJ, Parker RI, Gonen O, Adiguzel T (2016). Single case research: Web-based calculators for SCR analysis (version 2.0). College Station, TX: Texas A&M University. Accessed 27 October 2017 from: www.sin glecaseresearch.org/calculators

Velicer WF, Molenaar P (2013). Time series analysis: Research methods in psychology. In IB Weiner, J Schinka, WF Velicer (Eds.), *Handbook of psychology, Volume 2, Research methods in psychology*. (2nd edn, pp. 628–660). New York: Wiley.

Vohra S, Shamseer L, Sampson M, Bukutu C, Schmid CH, Tate R., . . . for the CENT group (2015). CONSORT extension for reporting N-of-1 trials (CENT) 2015 statement. *BMJ*, *350*, doi: https://doi.org/10.1136/bmj.h1738.

Waker DP, Berg WK, Harding JW, Cooper-Brown LJ (2011). Functional and structural approaches to behavioural assessment of problem behaviour. In WW Fisher, CC Piazza, and HE Roane (Eds.), *Handbook of applied behavior analysis* (pp. 165–181). New York: Guildford.

Wambaugh JL, Martinez AL (2000). Effects of rate and rhythm control treatment of consonant production accuracy in apraxia of speech. *Aphasiology*, *14(8)*, 851–871.

Wampold BE, Worsham NL (1986). Randomization tests for multiple-baseline designs. *Behavioral Assessment*, *8(2)*, 135–143.

Watson PJ, Workman EA (1981). The non-concurrent multiple baseline across-individuals design: An extension of the traditional multiple baseline design. *Journal of Behavioural Therapy and Experimental Psychiatry*, *12 (3)*, 257–259.

Webster JS, Jones S, Blanton P, Gross R, Beissel GF, Wofford JD (1984). Visual scanning training with stroke patients. *Behavior Therapy*, *15(2)*, 129–143.

Wehman P, West M, Fry R, Sherron P, Groah C, Kreutzer J, Sale P (1989). Effect of supported employment on the vocational outcomes of persons with traumatic brain injury. *Journal of Applied Behavior Analysis*, *22(4)*, 395–405.

Weis L, Hall RV (1971). Modification of cigarette smoking through avoidance of punishment. In RV Hall (Ed.), *Managing behavior: Behavior modification applications in school and home* (pp. 54–55). Lawrence, KS: H & H Enterprises.

Wells KC, Forehand R, Griest DL (1980). Generality of treatment effects from treated to untreated behaviors resulting from a parent training program. *Journal of Clinical Child Psychology*, *9(3)*, 217–219.

Wendt O, Miller B (2012). Quality appraisal of single-subject experimental designs: an overview and comparison of different appraisal tools. *Education and Treatment of Children*, *35(2)*, 235–268.

Wernicke C (1874). *Der aphasische Symptomenkomplex*. Breslau, Poland: Cohn & Weigert.

White DM, Rusch FR, Kazdin AE, Hartmann DP (1989). Applications of meta analysis in individual subject research. *Behavioral Assessment*, *11*(3), 281–296.

White OR (1977). Data-based instruction: Evaluating educational progress. In JD Cone and RP Hawkins (Eds.), *Behavioral assessments: New directions in clinical psychology* (pp. 344–368). New York: Brunner/Maze.

White OR, Haring NG (1980). *Exceptional teaching* (2nd edn). Columbus, OH: Merrill.

Whyte J, Hart T (2003). It's more than a black box; it's a Russian doll. Defining rehabilitation treatments. *American Journal of Physical Medicine and Rehabilitation*, *82*(8), 639–652.

Wine B, Freeman TR, King A (2015). Withdrawal versus reversal: a necessary distinction? *Behavioral Interventions*, *30*(1), 87–93.

Wilson B (1981). Teaching a patient to remember people's names after removal of a left temporal lobe tumour. *Behavioural Psychotherapy*, *9*(4), 338–344.

Wilson B (1982). Success and failure in memory training following a cerebral vascular accident. *Cortex*, *18*(4), 581–594.

Wilson B (1987). Single-case experimental designs in neuropsychological rehabilitation. *Journal of Clinical and Experimental Neuropsychology*, *9*(5), 527–544.

Wilson BA, Winegardner J, van Heugten C, Ownsworth T (Eds.) (2000). *Neuropsychological rehabilitation: The international handbook*. Abingdon: Routledge.

Windelband W (1894/1980). Rectorial address, Strasbourg, 1894. *History and Theory*, *19*(2), 165–168.

Wolery M, Busick M, Reichow B, Barton E (2008). Quantitative synthesis of single subject research. Paper presented at the Conference on Research Innovations in Early Intervention, San Diego, CA. [Cited in Wolery et al., 2010]

Wolery M, Busick M, Reichow B, Barton E (2010). Comparison of overlap methods for quantitatively synthesizing single-subject data. *Journal of Special Education*, *44*(1), 18–28.

Wolery M, Gast DL, Ledford JR (2014). Comparison designs. In DL Gast and JR Ledford (Eds.), *Single case research methodology: Applications in special education and behavioral sciences* (2nd edn, pp. 297–345). New York: Routledge.

Wood RL (1986). Rehabilitation of patients with disorders of attention. *Journal of Head Trauma Rehabilitation*, *1*(3), 43–53.

Wright HH, Marshall RC, Wilson KB, Page JL (2008). Using a written cueing hierarchy to improve verbal naming in aphasia. *Aphasiology*, *22*(5), 522–536.

Yeaton WH, Sechrest L (1981). Critical dimensions in the choice and maintenance of successful treatments: Strength, integrity, and effectiveness. *Journal of Consulting and Clinical Psychology*, *49*(2), 156–167.

Ylvisaker M, Feeney T (2000). Reconstruction of identity after brain injury. *Brain Impairment*, *1* (1), 12–28.

Ylvisaker M, Turkstra L, Coehlo C, Yorkston K, Kennedy M, Sohlberg M, Avery J (2007). Behavioral interventions for individuals with behaviour disorders after TBI: a systematic review of the evidence. *Brain Injury*, *21* (*8*), 769–805.

Zucker DR, Ruthazer R., Schmid CH, Feuer JM, Fischer PA, Kieval RI, . . . Winston E (2006). Lessons learned combining N-of-1 trials to assess fibromyalgia therapies. *Journal of Rheumatology*, *33(10)*, 2069–2077.

INDEX

comparison of interventions 3, 11, 13, 31, 73, 75, 77, 99, 101, 102, 130, 194, 197; comparison of interventions in the neurorehabilitation literature **214, 215, 216, 217, 218, 222, 223, 224, 228**; in N-of-1 trials 105; *see also* alternating-treatment designs

comparison phase: *see* alternating treatment designs

conduction aphasia 76; conduction aphasia as target behaviour area in neurorehabilitation literature **219**; *see also* aphasia

confidence interval 171, 172

Connors' 3 Behavior Rating Inventory 106; as measure of target behaviour in neuroehabilitation literature 224

consent 83, 197, 198, in SCRIBE check list 48; *see also* informed consent

conservative dual criteria (CDC) method 167, 171; *see also* dual criteria method

consistency of experimental effect 155; withdrawal designs 92, 93; A-B-A-B designs 98; ATDs 134; CCDs 147, 148, *149*; MBDs 112, 114, 119, 126; *see also* experimental control; experimental effect

CONSORT (Consolidated Standards of Reporting Trials) 24, 40, 47

construct: confounding **25**; explication **25**, 39; underrepresentation **25**; validity 24, **25**, 39, **42**, 44, 51, 66

consumer advocacy 4

continuous measurement: direct 62–64; of target behaviour 4, 10, 11, 14, 60, 61, 70, 93, 94, 109, 112, 122, 126, 144, 188, 206; of generalisation measures 34

contrast effects 141

Copy and Recall Treatment (CART) 76, 77; measure of target behaviour in neurorehabilitation literature **219**

counterbalancing 101, 132, 137, 140, 141

critical appraisal scales 18, 24, 40–44, 47, 50, 88

cyclicity 14, **21**, 76, 79, 92, 111, 112, 115, 118, 134, 150

d for single-case designs 166

data analysis 43; 154–182; in RoBiNT Scale **46**, in SCRIBE checklist 49; *see also* statistical analysis; visual analysis

data fidelity 51, 199, 200; data integrity 28, 67–69; *see also* interrater reliability

dementia 35, 52, 55, 62, 63, 102, *120*; neurological condition in neurorehabilitation literature **210**, 211, 214, 215, 218, 221; semantic 119

dependence in behaviours: *see* behavioural covariation

dependent variable 1, 10, 14, 17, 19, 20, 21, 23, 24, 34, 35, 41, 51–70, 71, 85, 91, 94, 154, 157, 196; in A-B designs 94; in RoBiNT Scale **46**; in SCRIBE checklist 48; *see also* continuous measurement; direct measurement; event-based measurement; intensity-based measures; target behaviour; time-based measures

depression 53, 57, 62, 76, 188; as target behaviour in neurorehabilitation literature **225, 227**

descriptive analysis 56–57; *see also* applied behaviour analysis; experimental analysis of behaviour; functional analysis/assessment of behaviour

design standards 17–21, 40, 42, 69, 157, 158; *see also* critical appraisal scales; standards of evidence

differential reinforcement of alternative behaviour (DRA) 59, *60*; as intervention in neurorehabilitation literature **212**

differential reinforcement of incompatible behaviour (DRI) 102, 206; as intervention in neurorehabilitation literature **214, 215**

differential reinforcement of low rates of responding (DRL) 206

diffusion of treatment effect 27, 29, 75, 118, 200, 202; across conditions 39; definition **25**; in RoBiNT Scale **45**

direct measurement: *see* continuous measurement; discontinuous direct measurement